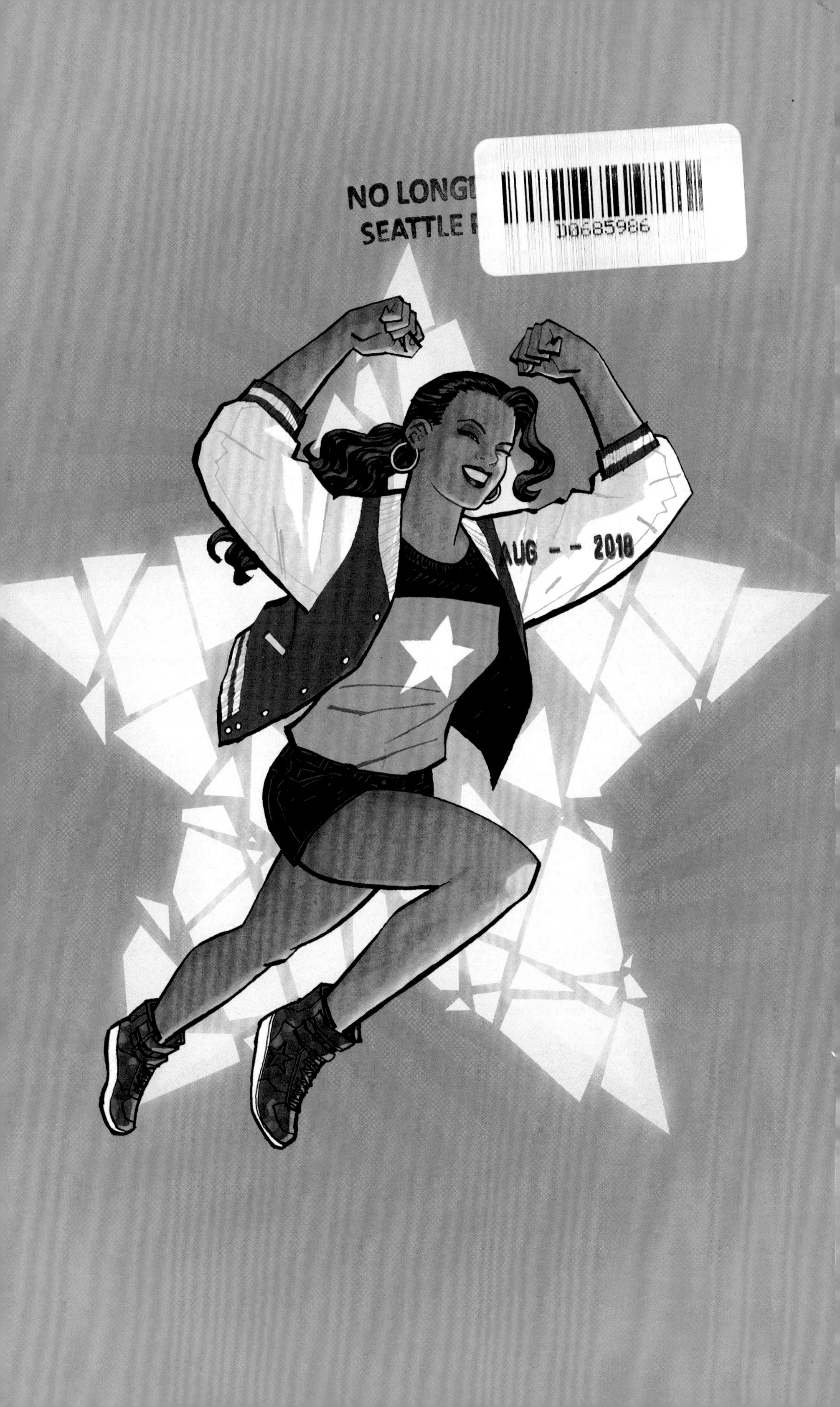

AMERICA VOL. 1: THE LIFE AND TIMES OF AMERICA CHAVEZ. Contains material originally published in magazine form as AMERICA #1-6. Second printing 2018. ISBN 978-1-302-90881-?
Published by MARVEL WORLDWIDE, INC., a subsidiary of MARVEL ENTERTAINMENT, LLC. OFFICE OF PUBLICATION: 135 West 50th Street, New York, NY 10020. Copyright © 2017 MARVEL. N
similarity between any of the names, characters, persons, and/or institutions in this magazine with those of any living or dead person or institution is intended, and any such similarity which ma
exist is purely coincidental. **Printed in Canada.** DAN BUCKLEY, President, Marvel Entertainment; JOE QUESADA, Chief Creative Officer; TOM BREVOORT, SVP of Publishing; DAVID BOGART, SVP o
Business Affairs & Operations, Publishing & Partnership; DAVID GABRIEL, SVP of Sales & Marketing, Publishing; JEFF YOUNGQUIST, VP of Production & Special Projects; DAN CARR, Executive Directo
of Publishing Technology; ALEX MORALES, Director of Publishing Operations; SUSAN CRESPI, Production Manager; STAN LEE, Chairman Emeritus. For information regarding advertising in Marv
Comics or on Marvel.com, please contact Vit DeBellis, Custom Solutions & Integrated Advertising Manager, at vdebellis@marvel.com. For Marvel subscription inquiries, please call 888-511-548
Manufactured between 1/12/2018 and 2/5/2018 by SOLISCO PRINTERS, SCOTT, QC, CANADA.

10 9 8 7 6 5 4 3 2

AMERICA

★ THE LIFE AND TIMES OF AMERICA CHAVEZ ★

GABBY RIVERA
WRITER

★ ISSUES #1-4 ★

JOE QUINONES WITH **MING DOYLE** (#2, #4) & **STACEY LEE** (#3)
PENCILERS

JOE RIVERA WITH **PAOLO RIVERA** (#1), **MING DOYLE** (#2, #4), **STACEY LEE** (#3) & **JOE QUINONES** (#4)
INKERS

JOSÉ VILLARRUBIA WITH **JORDAN GIBSON** (#3, #4) & **JOE QUINONES** (#4)
COLORISTS

JOE QUINONES WITH **JORDAN GIBSON** (#2, #3) & **MATTHEW WILSON** (#4)
COVER ART

★ ISSUES #5-6 ★

KELLY THOMPSON
ARCHERY CONSULTANT

RAMON VILLALOBOS
ARTIST

WALDEN WONG
ADDITIONAL INKS, #6

TAMRA BONVILLAIN WITH **BRITTANY PEER** (#5)
COLOR ARTISTS

JEN BARTEL
COVER ART

VC'S TRAVIS LANHAM
LETTERER

CHARLES BEACHAM
ASSISTANT EDITOR

SARAH BRUNSTAD
ASSOCIATE EDITOR

WIL MOSS
EDITOR

★

JENNIFER GRÜNWALD
COLLECTION EDITOR

CAITLIN O'CONNELL
ASSISTANT EDITOR

KATERI WOODY
ASSOCIATE MANAGING EDITOR

MARK D. BEAZLEY
EDITOR, SPECIAL PROJECTS

JEFF YOUNGQUIST
VP PRODUCTION & SPECIAL PROJECTS

DAVID GABRIEL
SVP PRINT, SALES & MARKETING

ADAM DEL RE
BOOK DESIGNER

C.B. CEBULSKI
EDITOR IN CHIEF

JOE QUESADA
CHIEF CREATIVE OFFICER

DAN BUCKLEY
PRESIDENT

ALAN FINE
EXECUTIVE PRODUCER

INTRODUCTION

Dandelions of the Revolution,

Every day that you push forward in this world is a day to be proud of. Look at you, you vibrant human, with all of your magic and brilliance. Have you taken a moment to honor yourself? Take that moment now if you haven't. It's vital, just like you.

Y'all, thank you so much for coming on this wild beautiful ride with us.

AMERICA, the first solo series of the one and only America Chavez, has made its mark on comic-book history. And just by holding this book in your hands, for taking this leap of faith with us, you're now part of America Chavez's legacy, too.

You're about to dive deep into the world of a star-portal punching babe named America. You'll see her go through a breakup with her girlfriend, Lisa, and watch as she goes on an action-packed road trip with her best friend, Kate Bishop (A.K.A. Hawkeye). And I know you'll have America's back as she captures Entities, prays to Selena and TKO's a bunch of Mindless Ones.

Because this is how a chosen family fights.

We stick together through the mess and the muck, through the triumphs and victories. There's room for all of us at the table — well, except for the Nazis. At the end of the first issue, America reminds us of how important it is to have a mean left hook at the ready for *that type* of evil.

America Chavez, a powerful and confident strong brown girl, has every right to be front and center in her own comics series. And all of you know this. Even with all the haters shouting and doubting, you believe in her.

And so please allow me, Gabby Rivera, writer of AMERICA, and the wildly talented Joe Quinones, illustrator of AMERICA, along with the rest of our amazing team, to thank you all from the bottom of our hearts.

We made it to this first collection, and we're still pushing to bring you more America Chavez.

Pa'lante. Siempre pa'lante.

Anyway, enough out of me. For now, keep daydreaming about star portals and designing your America Chavez cosplay looks.

Much respect,

G. Rivera

Gabby Rivera is a queer Latinx writer living in Brooklyn, NY. Gabby's critically acclaimed debut novel Juliet Takes A Breath was listed by Mic.com as one of the 25 essential books to read for women's history month, and it was called the "dopest LGBTQA YA book ever" by Latina.com.

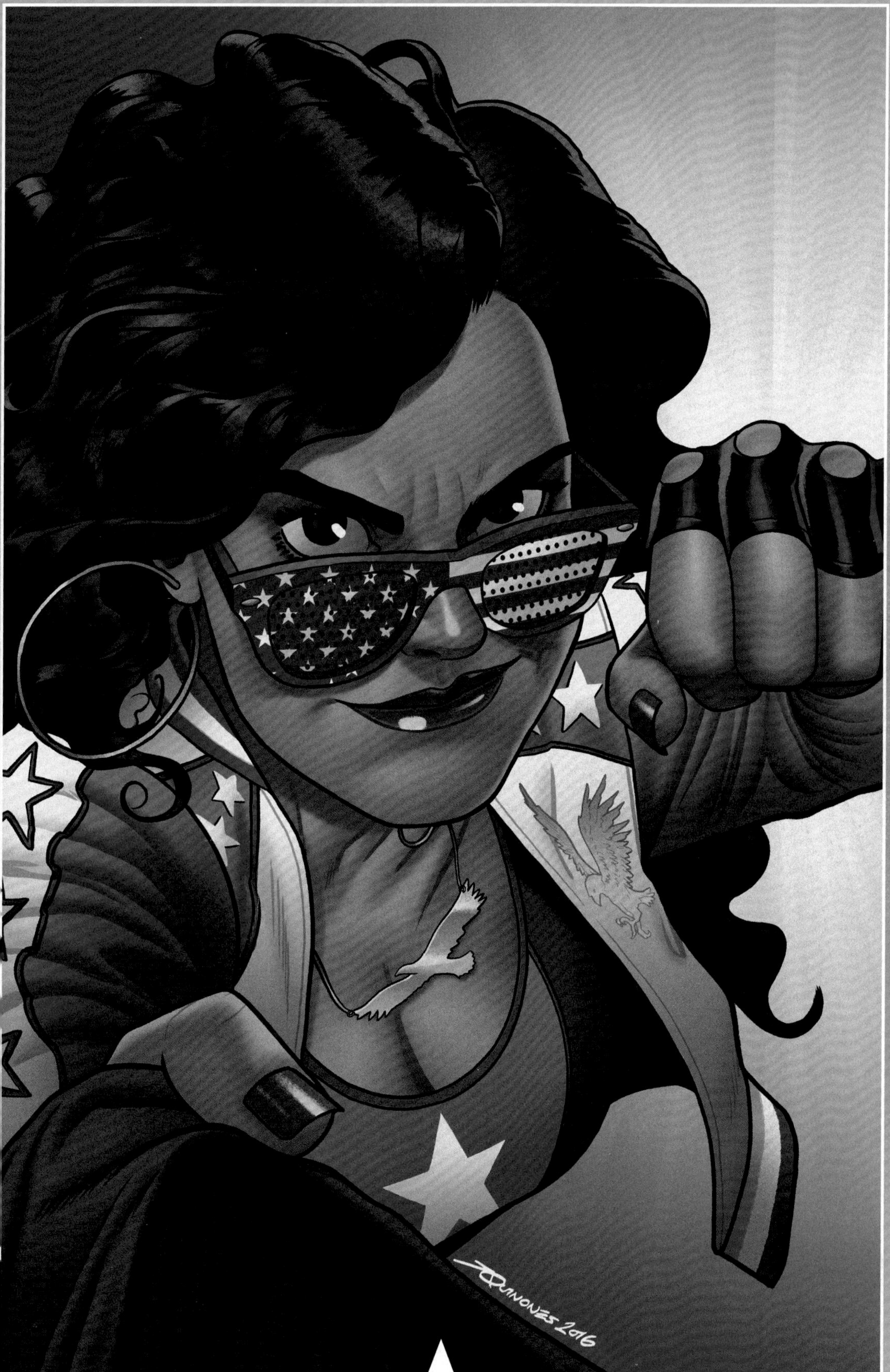
QUINONES 2016

1

WE ASKED 100 PEOPLE
"WHO IS AMERICA TO YOU?"

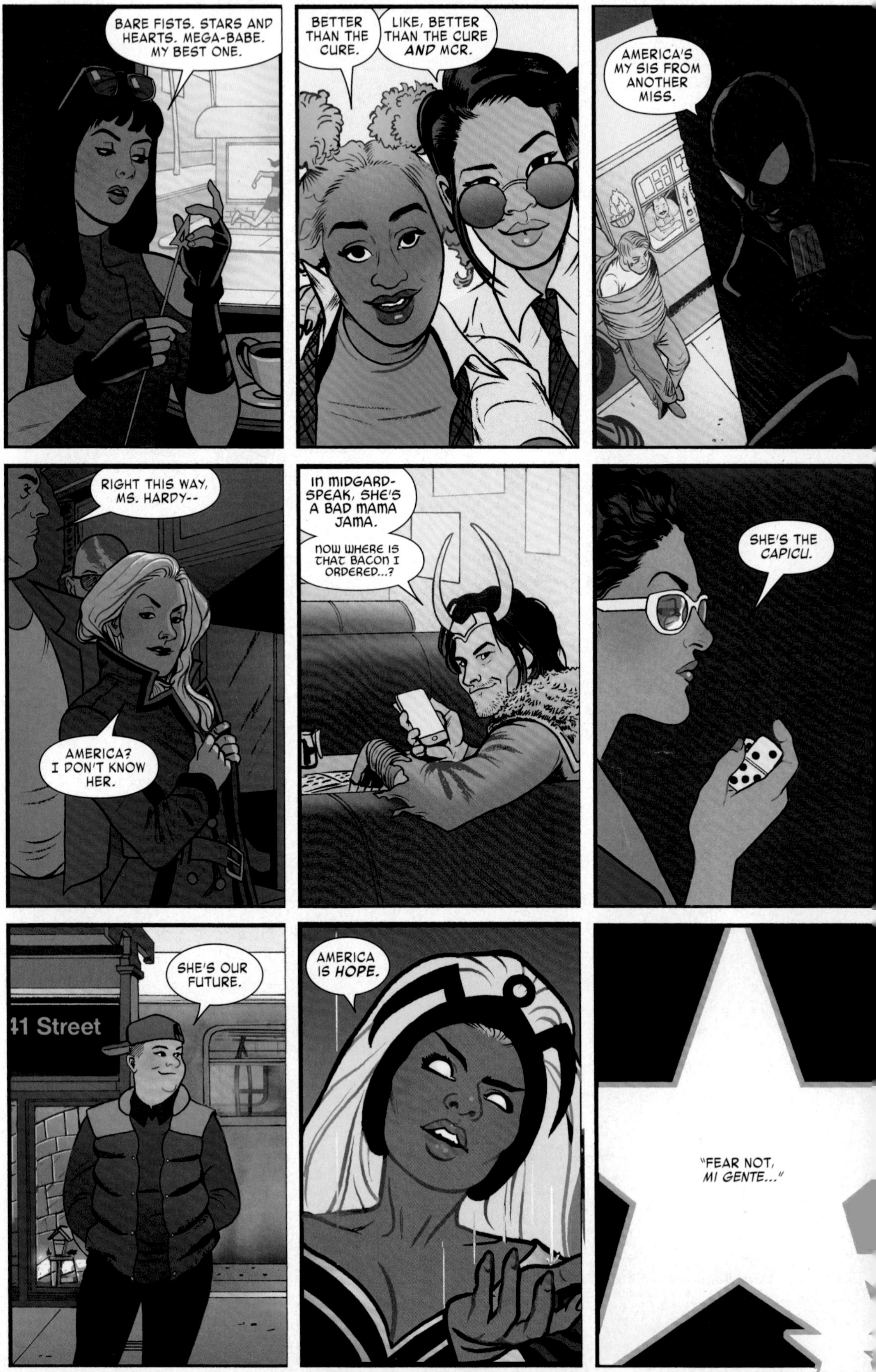

BARE FISTS. STARS AND HEARTS. MEGA-BABE. MY BEST ONE.
BETTER THAN THE CURE.
LIKE, BETTER THAN THE CURE *AND* MCR.
AMERICA'S MY SIS FROM ANOTHER MISS.
RIGHT THIS WAY, MS. HARDY--
AMERICA? I DON'T KNOW HER.
IN MIDGARD-SPEAK, SHE'S A BAD MAMA JAMA.
NOW WHERE IS THAT BACON I ORDERED...?
SHE'S THE *CAPICU.*
41 Street
SHE'S OUR FUTURE.
AMERICA IS *HOPE.*
"FEAR NOT, *MI GENTE...*"

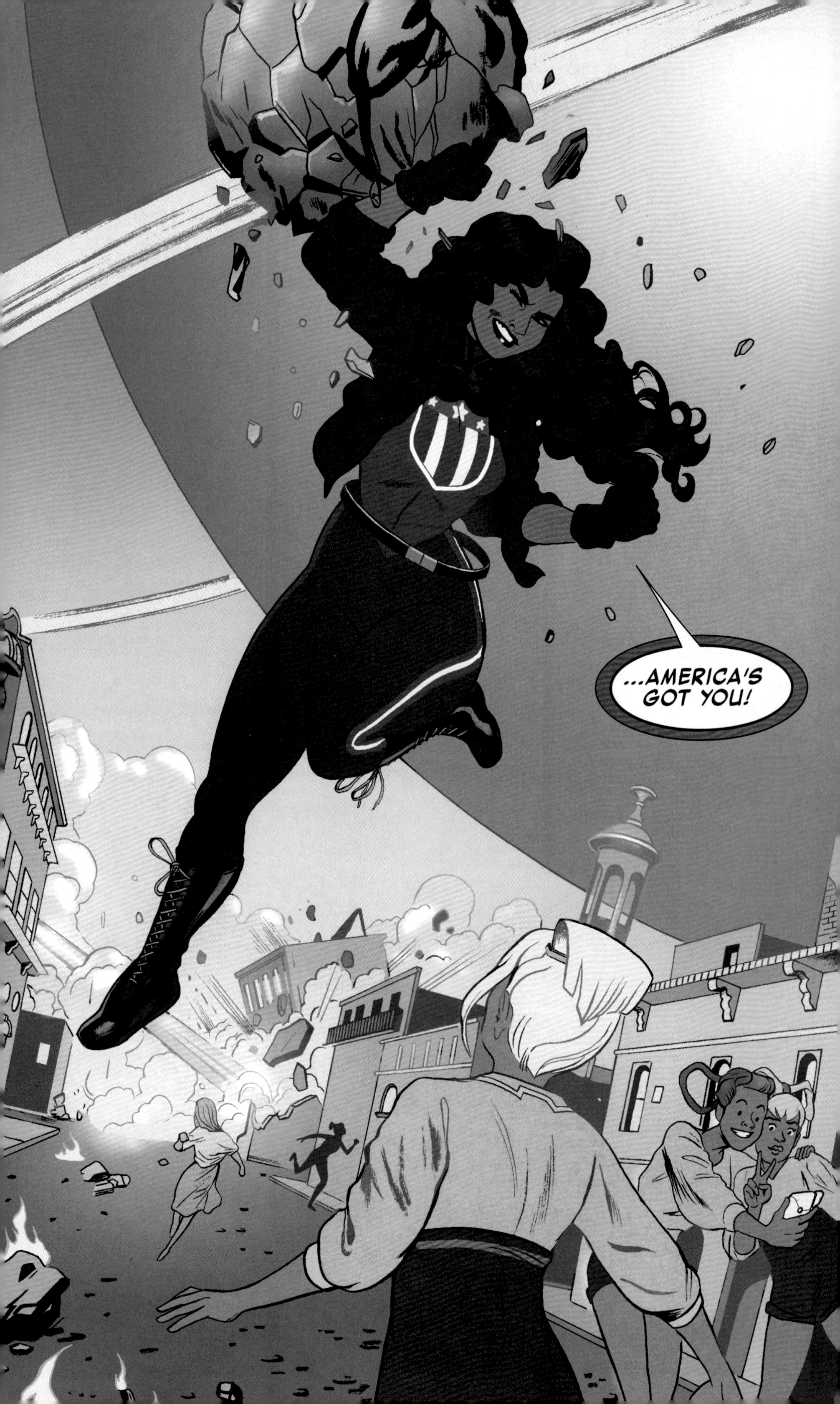
...AMERICA'S GOT YOU!

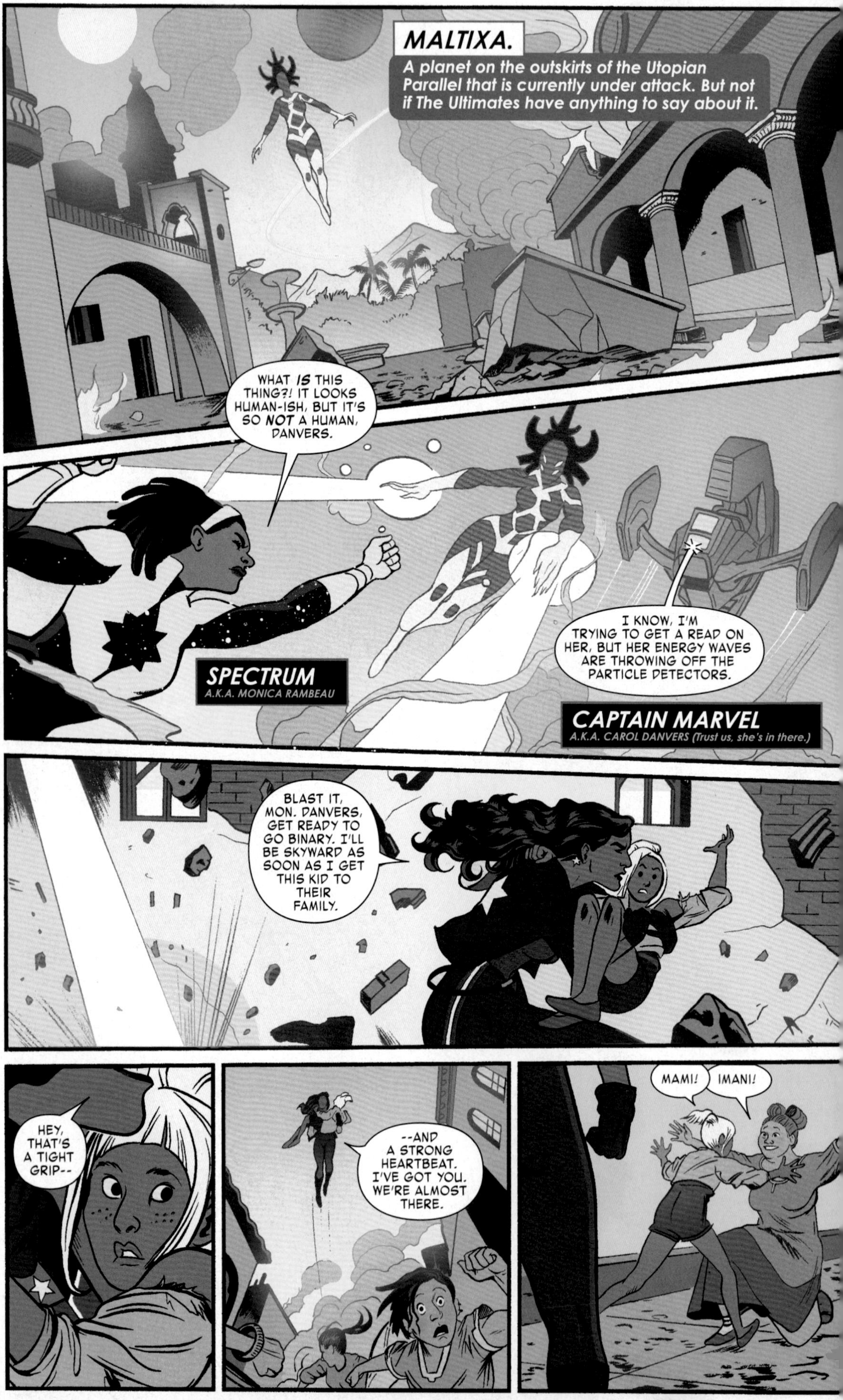
MALTIXA.
A planet on the outskirts of the Utopian Parallel that is currently under attack. But not if The Ultimates have anything to say about it.
WHAT IS THIS THING?! IT LOOKS HUMAN-ISH, BUT IT'S SO NOT A HUMAN, DANVERS.
SPECTRUM
A.K.A. MONICA RAMBEAU
I KNOW, I'M TRYING TO GET A READ ON HER, BUT HER ENERGY WAVES ARE THROWING OFF THE PARTICLE DETECTORS.
CAPTAIN MARVEL
A.K.A. CAROL DANVERS (Trust us, she's in there.)
BLAST IT, MON. DANVERS, GET READY TO GO BINARY. I'LL BE SKYWARD AS SOON AS I GET THIS KID TO THEIR FAMILY.
HEY, THAT'S A TIGHT GRIP--
--AND A STRONG HEARTBEAT. I'VE GOT YOU. WE'RE ALMOST THERE.
MAMI!
IMANI!

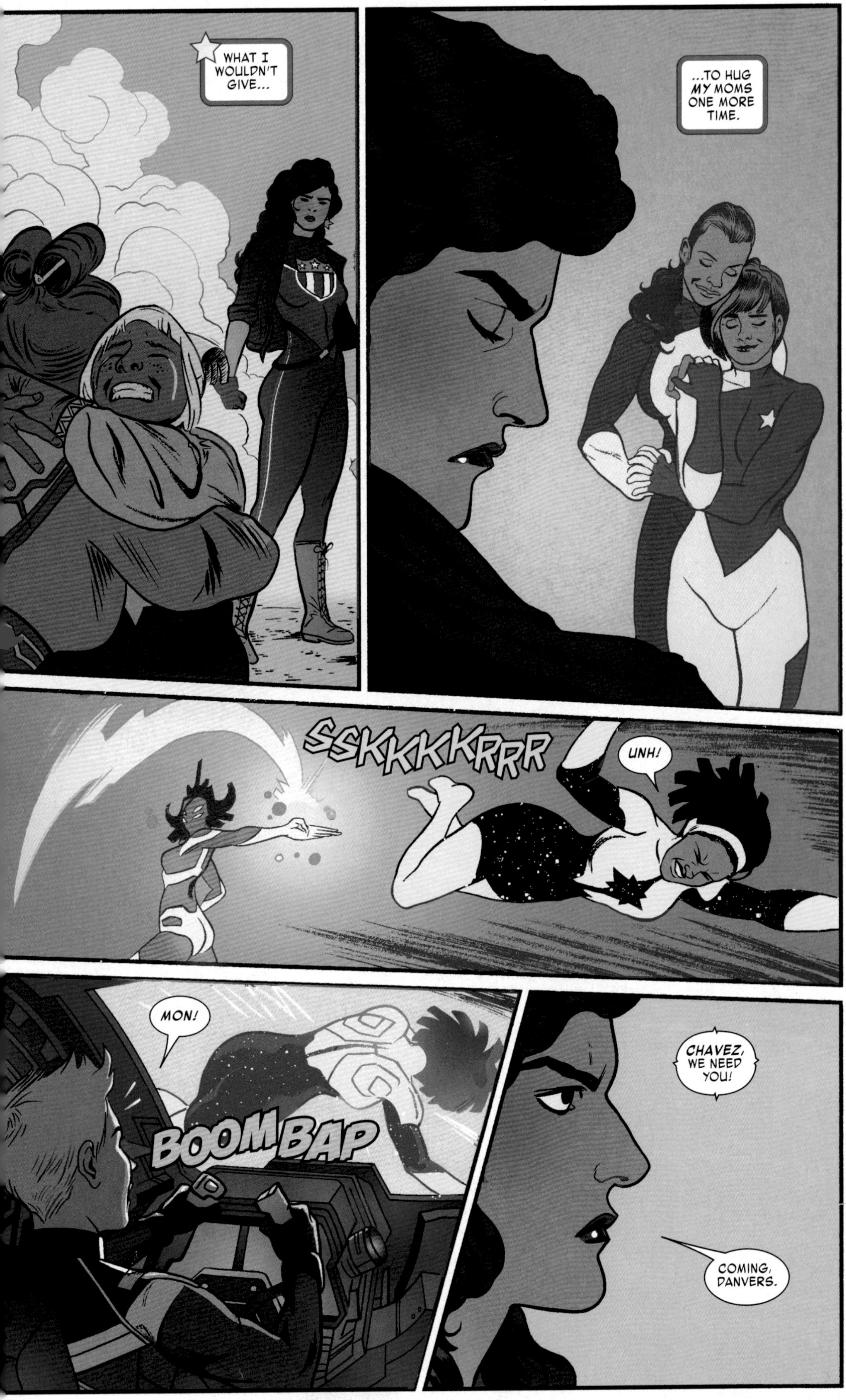
WHAT I WOULDN'T GIVE...
...TO HUG MY MOMS ONE MORE TIME.
SSKKKKRRR
UNH!
MON!
BOOM BAP
CHAVEZ, WE NEED YOU!
COMING, DANVERS.

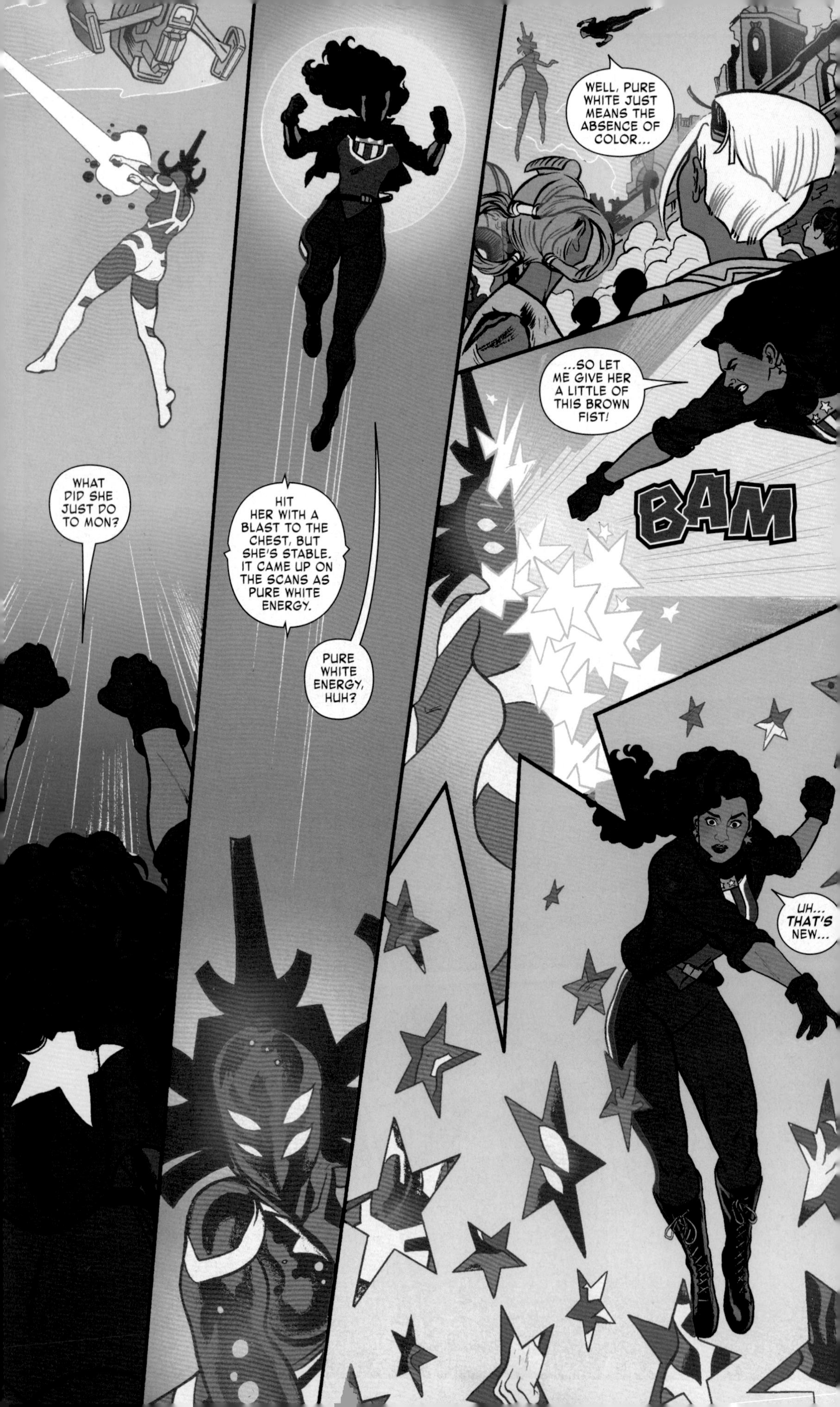
WHAT DID SHE JUST DO TO MON?
HIT HER WITH A BLAST TO THE CHEST, BUT SHE'S STABLE. IT CAME UP ON THE SCANS AS PURE WHITE ENERGY.
PURE WHITE ENERGY, HUH?
WELL, PURE WHITE JUST MEANS THE ABSENCE OF COLOR...
...SO LET ME GIVE HER A LITTLE OF THIS BROWN FIST!
BAM
UH... THAT'S NEW...

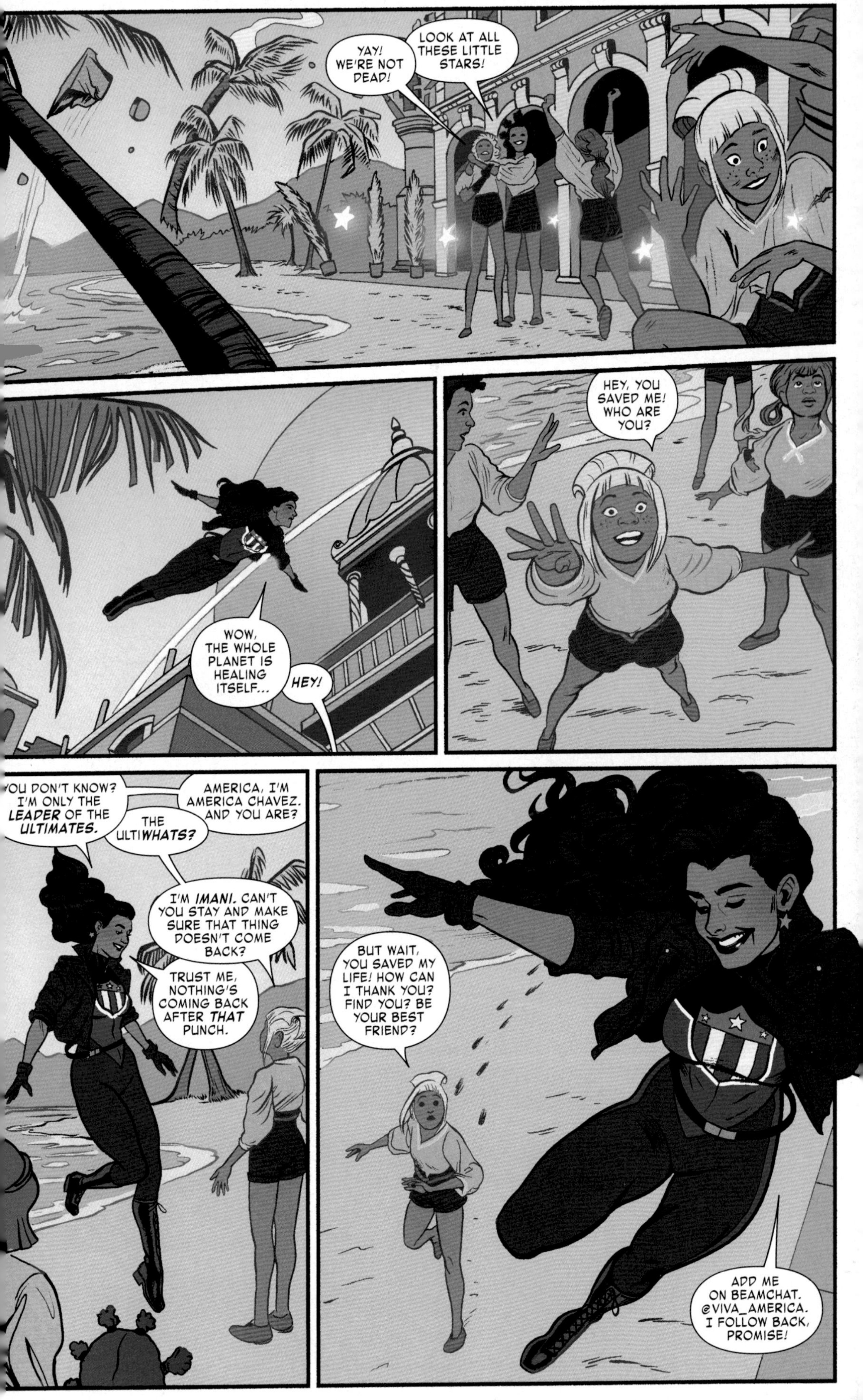
YAY! WE'RE NOT DEAD!
LOOK AT ALL THESE LITTLE STARS!
WOW, THE WHOLE PLANET IS HEALING ITSELF...
HEY!
HEY, YOU SAVED ME! WHO ARE YOU?
AMERICA, I'M AMERICA CHAVEZ. AND YOU ARE?
YOU DON'T KNOW? I'M ONLY THE LEADER OF THE ULTIMATES.
THE ULTIWHATS?
I'M IMANI. CAN'T YOU STAY AND MAKE SURE THAT THING DOESN'T COME BACK?
TRUST ME, NOTHING'S COMING BACK AFTER THAT PUNCH.
BUT WAIT, YOU SAVED MY LIFE! HOW CAN I THANK YOU? FIND YOU? BE YOUR BEST FRIEND?
ADD ME ON BEAMCHAT. @VIVA_AMERICA. I FOLLOW BACK, PROMISE!

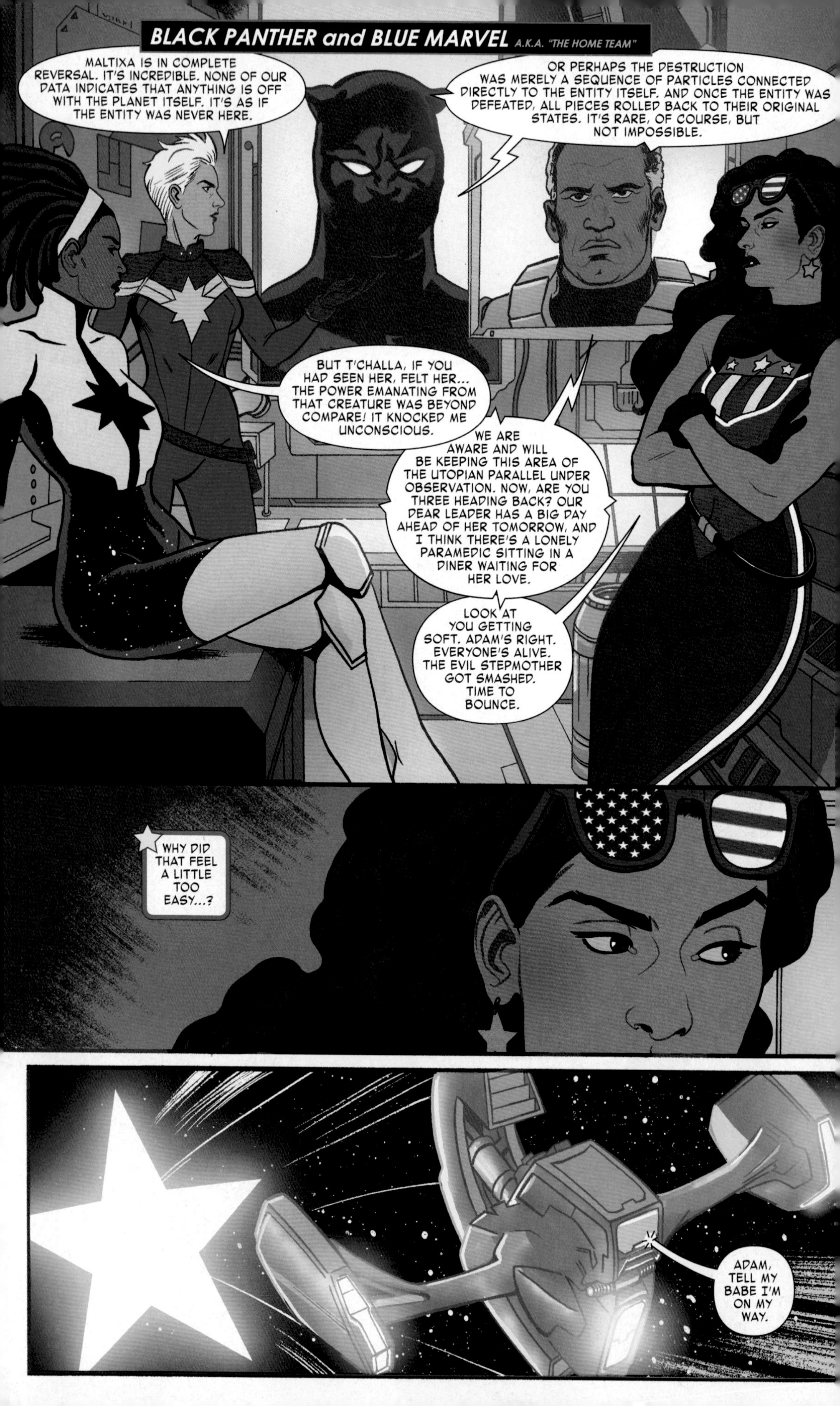
BLACK PANTHER and BLUE MARVEL A.K.A. "THE HOME TEAM"
MALTIXA IS IN COMPLETE REVERSAL. IT'S INCREDIBLE. NONE OF OUR DATA INDICATES THAT ANYTHING IS OFF WITH THE PLANET ITSELF. IT'S AS IF THE ENTITY WAS NEVER HERE.
OR PERHAPS THE DESTRUCTION WAS MERELY A SEQUENCE OF PARTICLES CONNECTED DIRECTLY TO THE ENTITY ITSELF. AND ONCE THE ENTITY WAS DEFEATED, ALL PIECES ROLLED BACK TO THEIR ORIGINAL STATES. IT'S RARE, OF COURSE, BUT NOT IMPOSSIBLE.
BUT T'CHALLA, IF YOU HAD SEEN HER, FELT HER... THE POWER EMANATING FROM THAT CREATURE WAS BEYOND COMPARE! IT KNOCKED ME UNCONSCIOUS.
WE ARE AWARE AND WILL BE KEEPING THIS AREA OF THE UTOPIAN PARALLEL UNDER OBSERVATION. NOW, ARE YOU THREE HEADING BACK? OUR DEAR LEADER HAS A BIG DAY AHEAD OF HER TOMORROW, AND I THINK THERE'S A LONELY PARAMEDIC SITTING IN A DINER WAITING FOR HER LOVE.
LOOK AT YOU GETTING SOFT. ADAM'S RIGHT. EVERYONE'S ALIVE. THE EVIL STEPMOTHER GOT SMASHED. TIME TO BOUNCE.
WHY DID THAT FEEL A LITTLE TOO EASY...?
ADAM, TELL MY BABE I'M ON MY WAY.

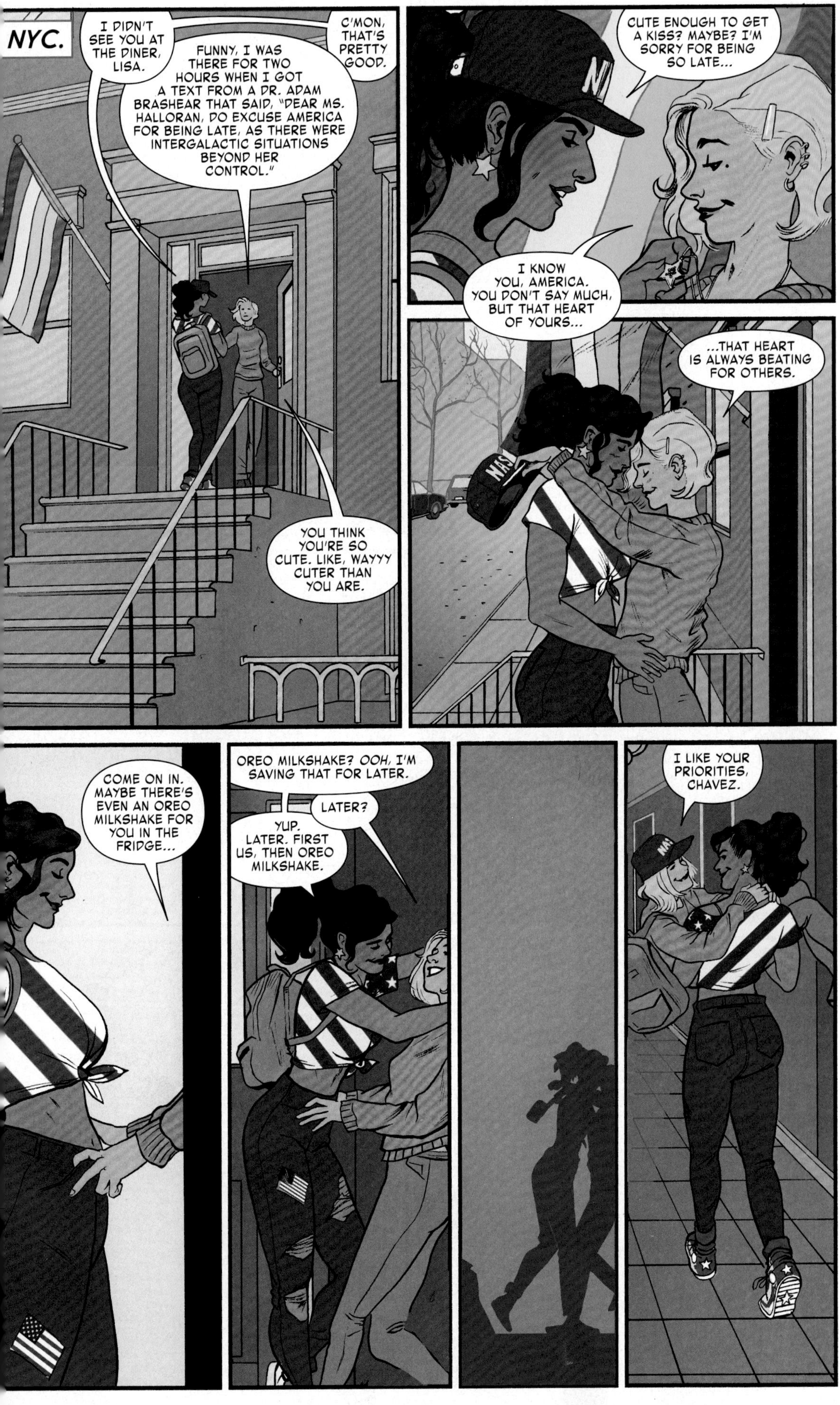
NYC.
I DIDN'T SEE YOU AT THE DINER, LISA.
FUNNY, I WAS THERE FOR TWO HOURS WHEN I GOT A TEXT FROM A DR. ADAM BRASHEAR THAT SAID, "DEAR MS. HALLORAN, DO EXCUSE AMERICA FOR BEING LATE, AS THERE WERE INTERGALACTIC SITUATIONS BEYOND HER CONTROL."
C'MON, THAT'S PRETTY GOOD.
YOU THINK YOU'RE SO CUTE. LIKE, WAYYY CUTER THAN YOU ARE.
CUTE ENOUGH TO GET A KISS? MAYBE? I'M SORRY FOR BEING SO LATE...
I KNOW YOU, AMERICA. YOU DON'T SAY MUCH, BUT THAT HEART OF YOURS...
...THAT HEART IS ALWAYS BEATING FOR OTHERS.
COME ON IN. MAYBE THERE'S EVEN AN OREO MILKSHAKE FOR YOU IN THE FRIDGE...
OREO MILKSHAKE? *OOH,* I'M SAVING THAT FOR LATER.
LATER?
YUP. LATER. FIRST US, THEN OREO MILKSHAKE.
I LIKE YOUR PRIORITIES, CHAVEZ.

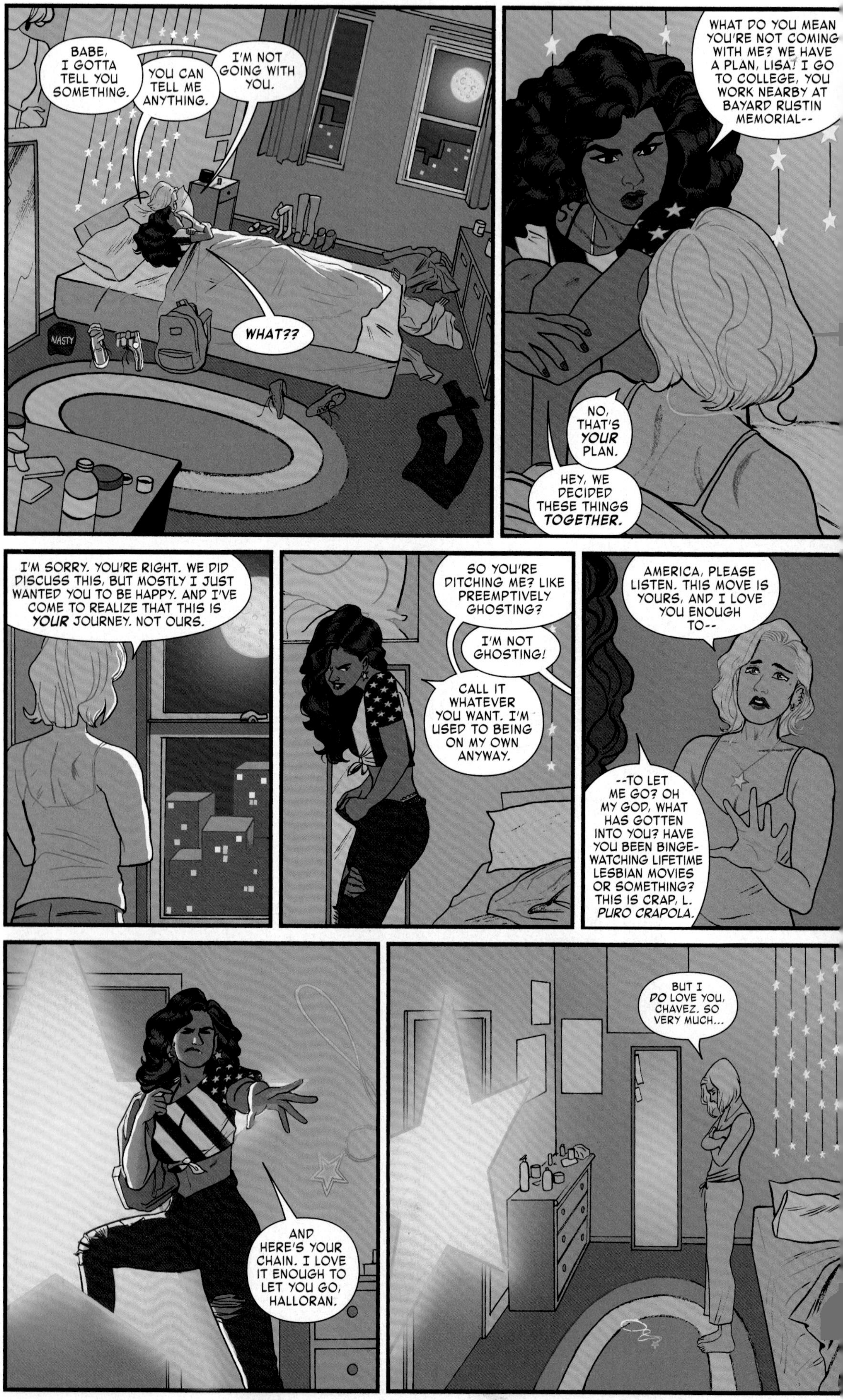
BABE, I GOTTA TELL YOU SOMETHING.
YOU CAN TELL ME ANYTHING.
I'M NOT GOING WITH YOU.
WHAT??
WHAT DO YOU MEAN YOU'RE NOT COMING WITH ME? WE HAVE A PLAN, LISA! I GO TO COLLEGE, YOU WORK NEARBY AT BAYARD RUSTIN MEMORIAL--
NO, THAT'S *YOUR* PLAN.
HEY, WE DECIDED THESE THINGS *TOGETHER.*
I'M SORRY. YOU'RE RIGHT. WE DID DISCUSS THIS, BUT MOSTLY I JUST WANTED YOU TO BE HAPPY. AND I'VE COME TO REALIZE THAT THIS IS *YOUR* JOURNEY. NOT OURS.
SO YOU'RE DITCHING ME? LIKE PREEMPTIVELY GHOSTING?
I'M NOT GHOSTING!
CALL IT WHATEVER YOU WANT. I'M USED TO BEING ON MY OWN ANYWAY.
AMERICA, PLEASE LISTEN. THIS MOVE IS YOURS, AND I LOVE YOU ENOUGH TO--
--TO LET ME GO? OH MY GOD, WHAT HAS GOTTEN INTO YOU? HAVE YOU BEEN BINGE-WATCHING LIFETIME LESBIAN MOVIES OR SOMETHING? THIS IS CRAP, L. *PURO CRAPOLA.*
AND HERE'S YOUR CHAIN. I LOVE IT ENOUGH TO LET YOU GO, HALLORAN.
BUT I *DO* LOVE YOU, CHAVEZ. SO VERY MUCH...

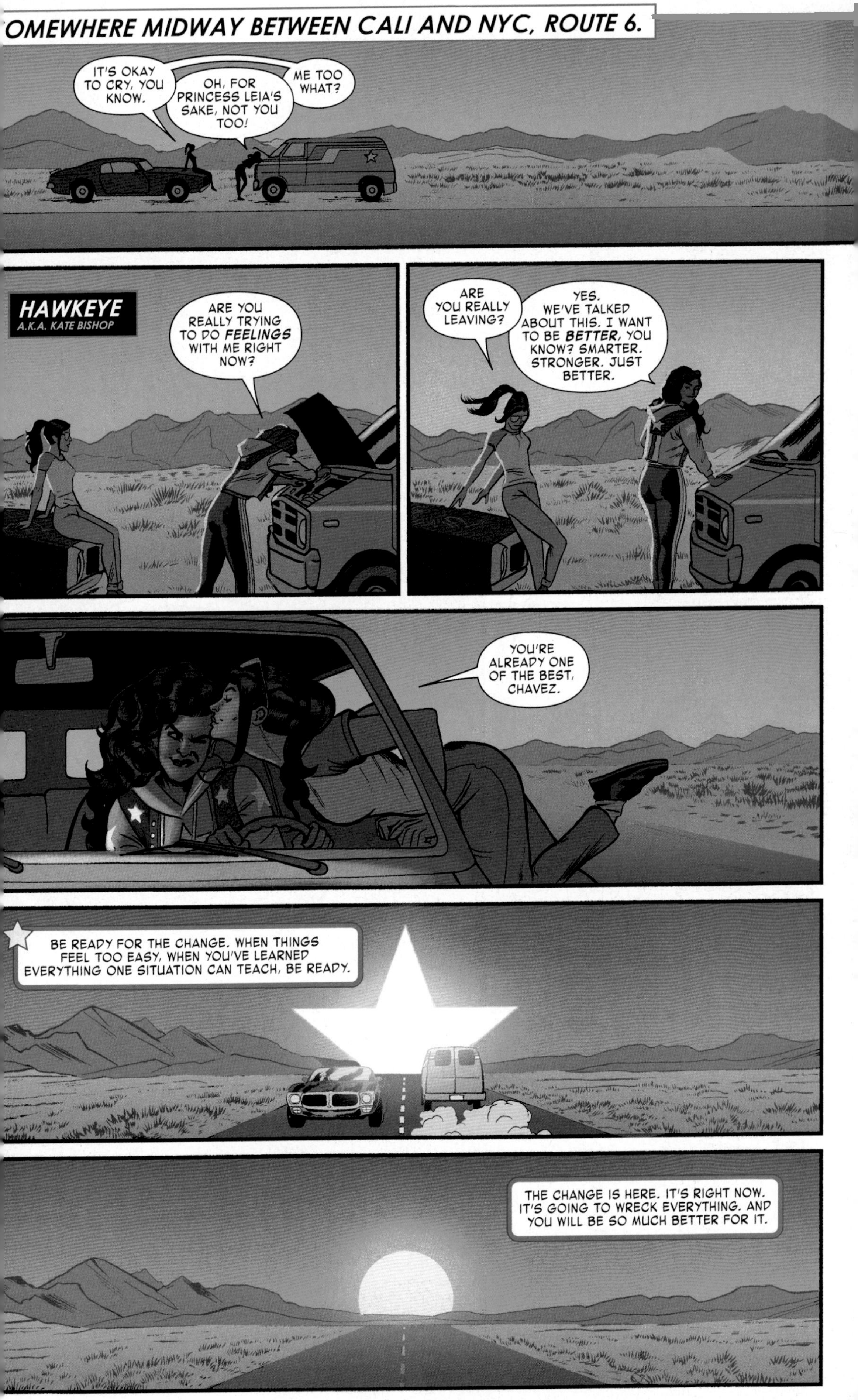
OMEWHERE MIDWAY BETWEEN CALI AND NYC, ROUTE 6.
IT'S OKAY TO CRY, YOU KNOW.
OH, FOR PRINCESS LEIA'S SAKE, NOT YOU TOO!
ME TOO WHAT?
HAWKEYE A.K.A. KATE BISHOP
ARE YOU REALLY TRYING TO DO FEELINGS WITH ME RIGHT NOW?
ARE YOU REALLY LEAVING?
YES. WE'VE TALKED ABOUT THIS. I WANT TO BE BETTER, YOU KNOW? SMARTER. STRONGER. JUST BETTER.
YOU'RE ALREADY ONE OF THE BEST, CHAVEZ.
BE READY FOR THE CHANGE. WHEN THINGS FEEL TOO EASY, WHEN YOU'VE LEARNED EVERYTHING ONE SITUATION CAN TEACH, BE READY.
THE CHANGE IS HERE. IT'S RIGHT NOW. IT'S GOING TO WRECK EVERYTHING. AND YOU WILL BE SO MUCH BETTER FOR IT.

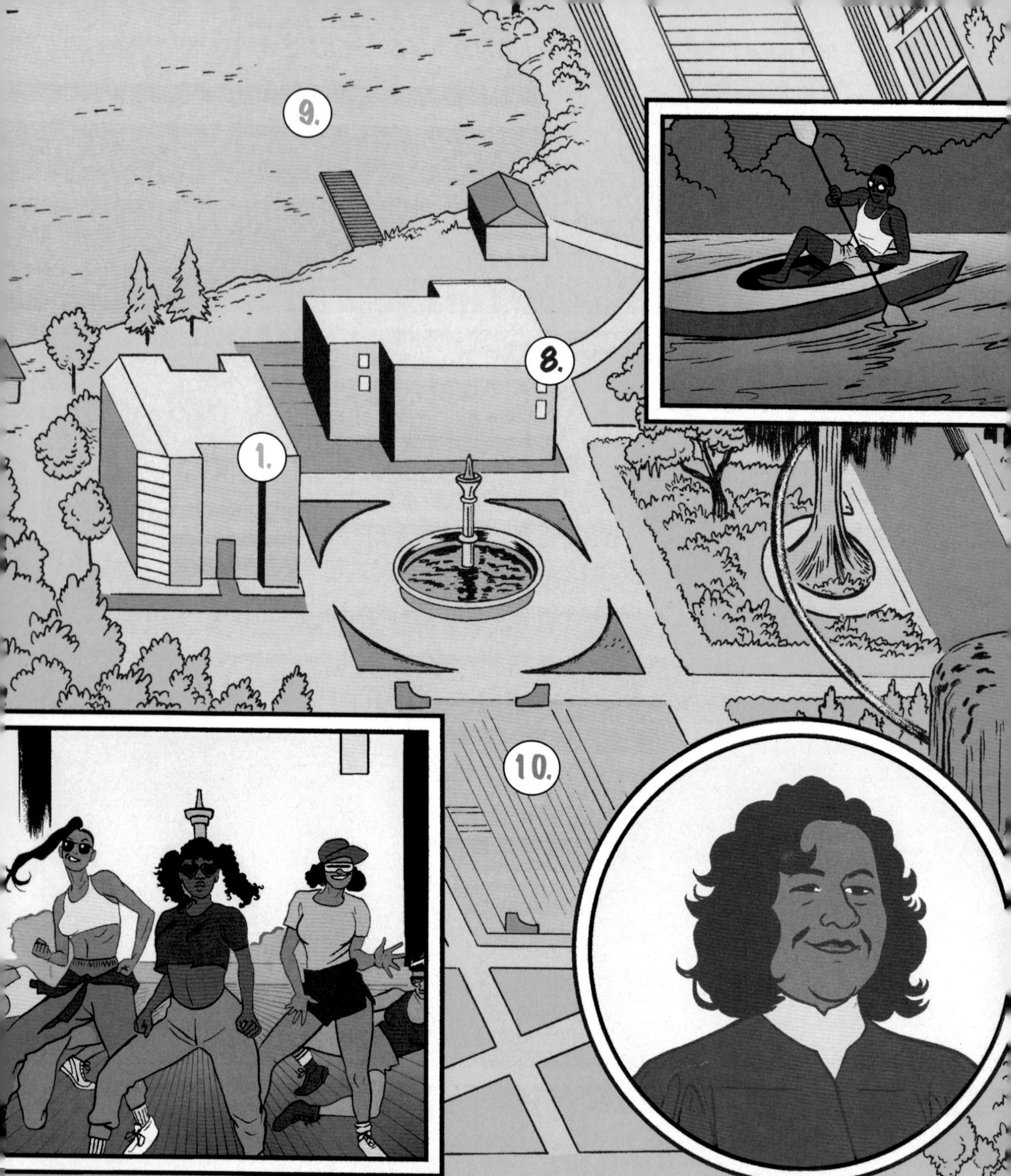
9.
8.
1.
10.

SOTOMAYOR UNIVERSITY

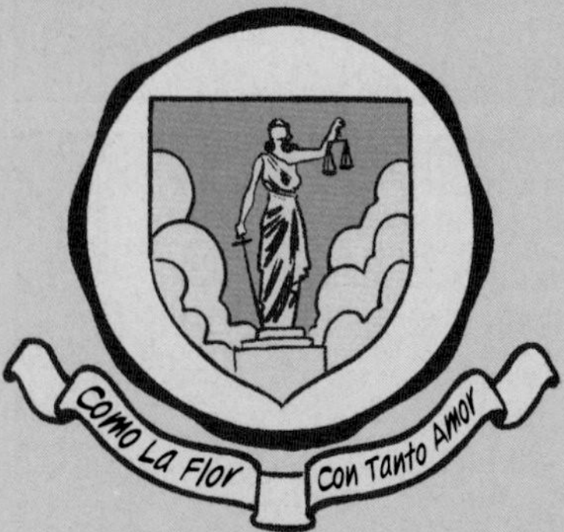
Como La Flor
Con Tanto Amor

MAP KEY

1. HOUSING
2. ACADEMIC AFFAIRS
3. LABS
4. SPORTS/REC
5. FOOD COURT
6. PERFORMING ARTS
7. MAGIC/MUTANT POWER TEST ZONES
8. THE DEPARTMENT OF RADICAL WOMEN & INTERGALACTIC INDIGENOUS PEOPLES
9. ROWING LAKE
10. OUTDOOR DANCE FIELD
11. SONIA SOTOMAYOR HOLOGRAM GREETER
12. THE MAJESTIC GARDENS

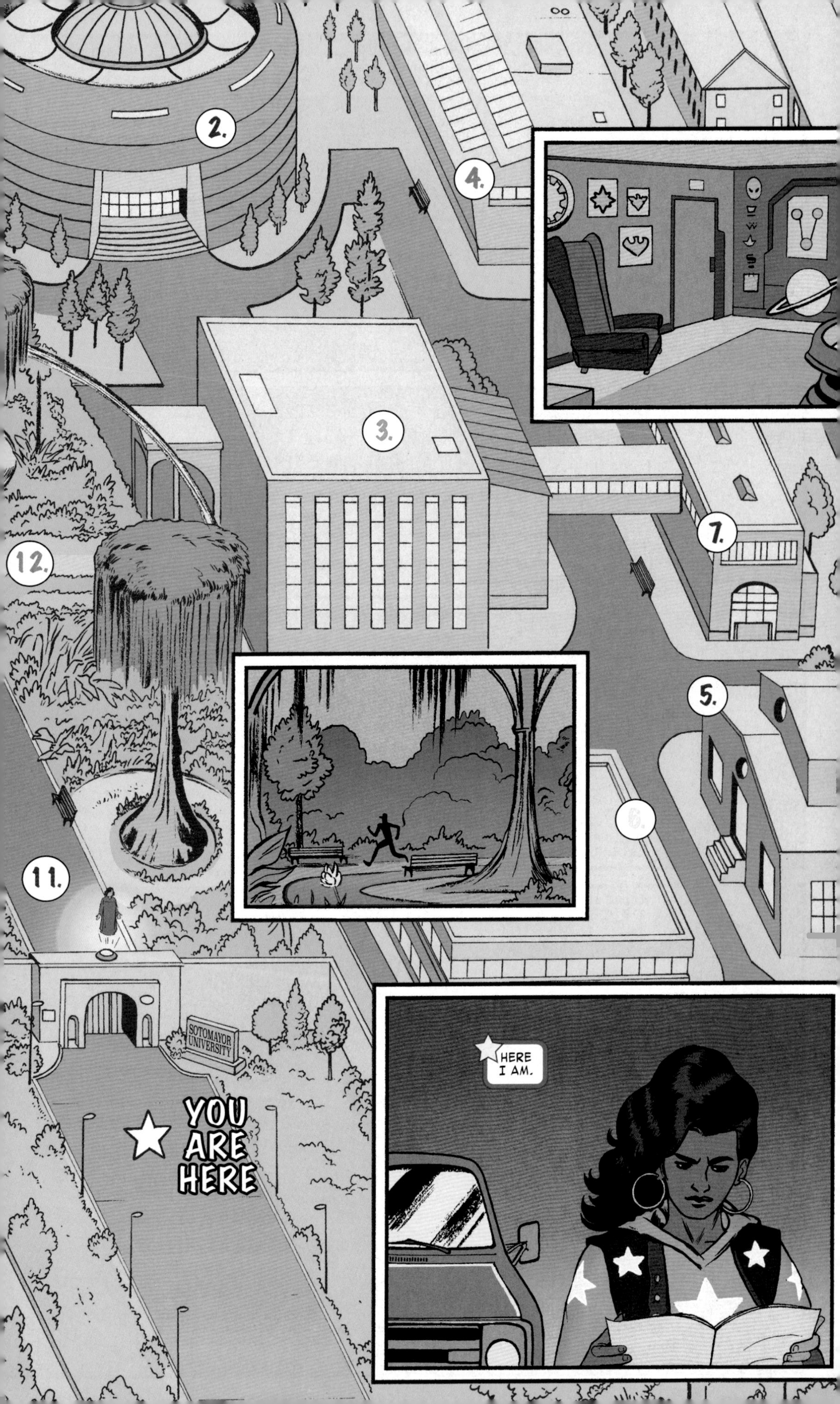
2.
4.
3.
7.
12.
5.
6.
11.
SOTOMAYOR UNIVERSITY
YOU ARE HERE
HERE I AM.

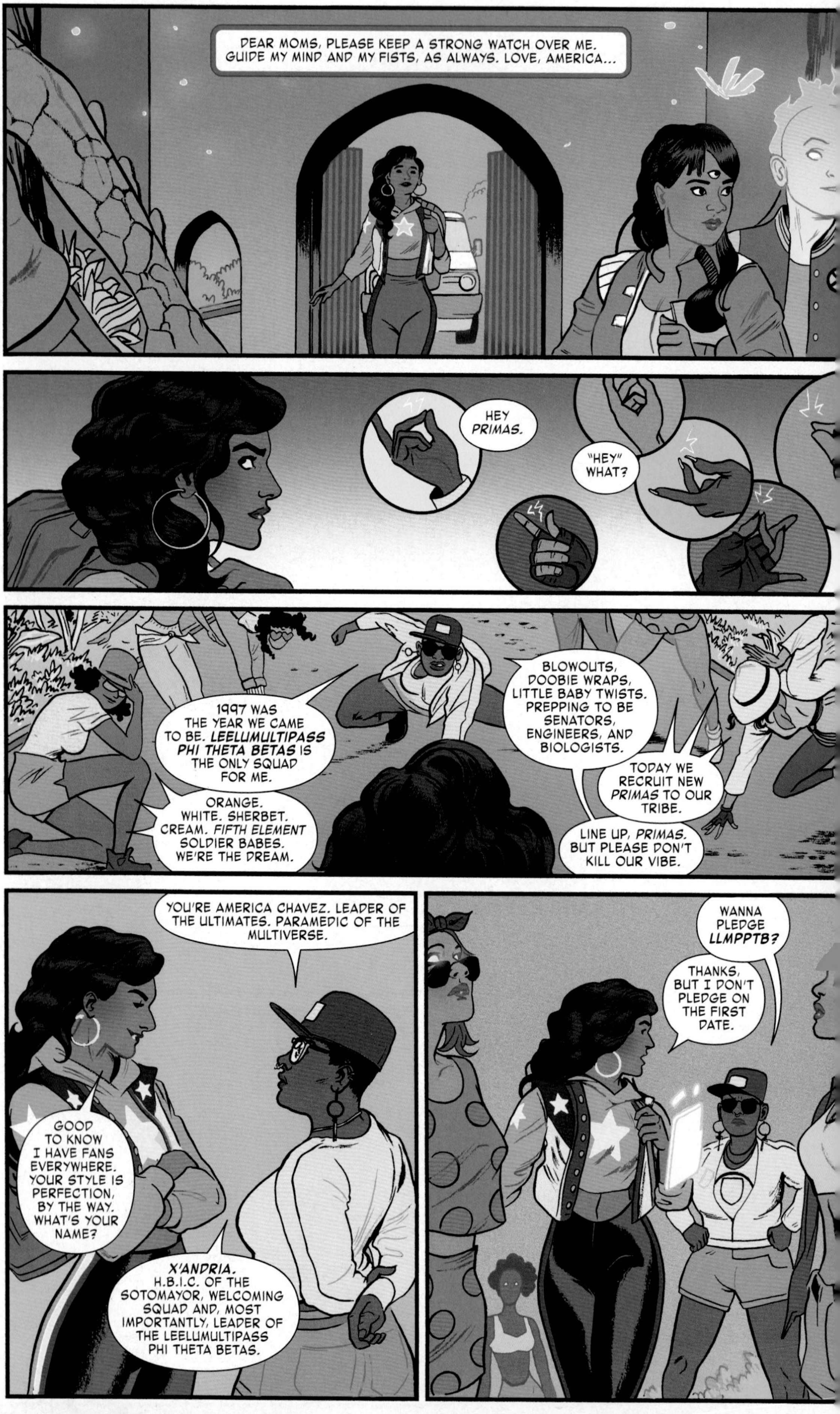
DEAR MOMS, PLEASE KEEP A STRONG WATCH OVER ME. GUIDE MY MIND AND MY FISTS, AS ALWAYS. LOVE, AMERICA...
HEY PRIMAS.
"HEY" WHAT?
1997 WAS THE YEAR WE CAME TO BE. LEELUMULTIPASS PHI THETA BETAS IS THE ONLY SQUAD FOR ME.
ORANGE. WHITE. SHERBET. CREAM. FIFTH ELEMENT SOLDIER BABES. WE'RE THE DREAM.
BLOWOUTS, DOOBIE WRAPS, LITTLE BABY TWISTS. PREPPING TO BE SENATORS, ENGINEERS, AND BIOLOGISTS.
TODAY WE RECRUIT NEW PRIMAS TO OUR TRIBE.
LINE UP, PRIMAS. BUT PLEASE DON'T KILL OUR VIBE.
YOU'RE AMERICA CHAVEZ. LEADER OF THE ULTIMATES. PARAMEDIC OF THE MULTIVERSE.
GOOD TO KNOW I HAVE FANS EVERYWHERE. YOUR STYLE IS PERFECTION, BY THE WAY. WHAT'S YOUR NAME?
X'ANDRIA. H.B.I.C. OF THE SOTOMAYOR, WELCOMING SQUAD AND, MOST IMPORTANTLY, LEADER OF THE LEELUMULTIPASS PHI THETA BETAS.
WANNA PLEDGE LLMPPTB?
THANKS, BUT I DON'T PLEDGE ON THE FIRST DATE.

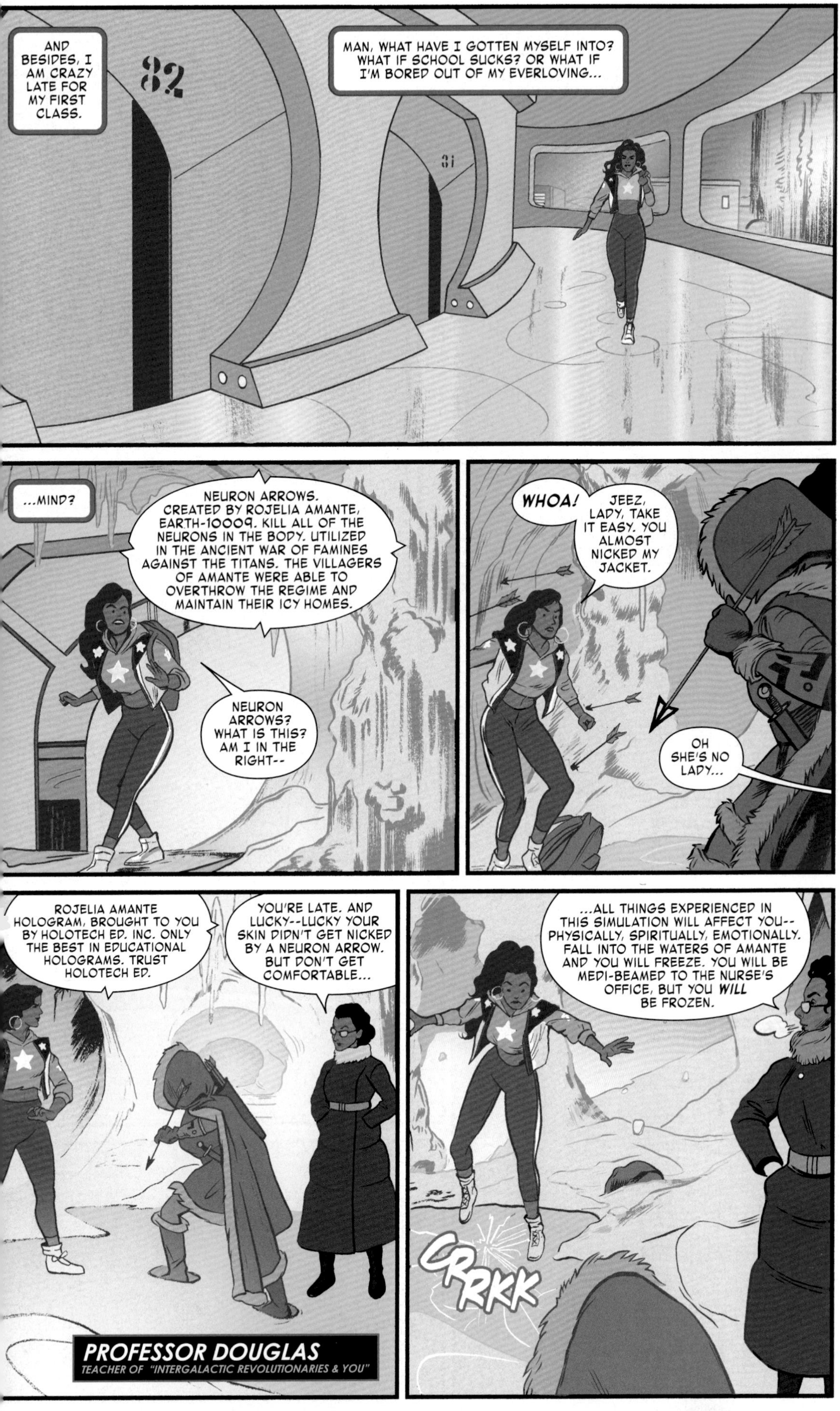

AND BESIDES, I AM CRAZY LATE FOR MY FIRST CLASS.
MAN, WHAT HAVE I GOTTEN MYSELF INTO? WHAT IF SCHOOL SUCKS? OR WHAT IF I'M BORED OUT OF MY EVERLOVING...
82
...MIND?
NEURON ARROWS. CREATED BY ROJELIA AMANTE, EARTH-10009. KILL ALL OF THE NEURONS IN THE BODY. UTILIZED IN THE ANCIENT WAR OF FAMINES AGAINST THE TITANS. THE VILLAGERS OF AMANTE WERE ABLE TO OVERTHROW THE REGIME AND MAINTAIN THEIR ICY HOMES.
NEURON ARROWS? WHAT IS THIS? AM I IN THE RIGHT--
WHOA!
JEEZ, LADY, TAKE IT EASY. YOU ALMOST NICKED MY JACKET.
OH SHE'S NO LADY...
ROJELIA AMANTE HOLOGRAM, BROUGHT TO YOU BY HOLOTECH ED. INC. ONLY THE BEST IN EDUCATIONAL HOLOGRAMS. TRUST HOLOTECH ED.
YOU'RE LATE. AND LUCKY--LUCKY YOUR SKIN DIDN'T GET NICKED BY A NEURON ARROW. BUT DON'T GET COMFORTABLE...
PROFESSOR DOUGLAS
TEACHER OF "INTERGALACTIC REVOLUTIONARIES & YOU"
...ALL THINGS EXPERIENCED IN THIS SIMULATION WILL AFFECT YOU--PHYSICALLY, SPIRITUALLY, EMOTIONALLY. FALL INTO THE WATERS OF AMANTE AND YOU WILL FREEZE. YOU WILL BE MEDI-BEAMED TO THE NURSE'S OFFICE, BUT YOU *WILL* BE FROZEN.
CRRKK

ROJELIA AMANTE BROUGHT HER PEOPLE TO GLORY AS THE ICE BENEATH THEM TREMBLED AND BROKE. WHAT DID SHE DO TO DEFEAT THE TITANS WHOSE GREED AND MEDDLING INTO THEIR NATURAL RESOURCES THREATENED THE HARMONY OF THEIR ENVIRONMENT?

MS. CHAVEZ, YOU HAVE *THREE MINUTES* BEFORE THIS ENTIRE SIMULATION SENDS YOU AND YOUR FELLOW CLASSMATES CRASHING INTO THE WATERS OF AMANTE.

HEY, WHAT GIVES? WHY CAN'T I USE MY POWERS?

HAD YOU BEEN ON *TIME*, YOU'D KNOW THAT I NEUTRALIZE POWERS AND MAGIC IN THESE SIMULATIONS. THE TEST IS TO RELY ON ANCESTRAL KNOWLEDGE AND NOT JUST BRUTE FORCE.

NO STAR PORTALS EITHER? *UGH*, FINE. TOTALLY NOT FAIR, BUT OKAY.

FIFTY SECONDS.

PROFESSOR, IF I MAY?

YOU MAY, DAVID.

PRODIGY
A.K.A. DAVID ALLEYNE, FORMER MUTANT, FORMER YOUNG AVENGER, STILL A GENIUS

ROJELIA AMANTE SACRIFICED HER POWERS TO THE GODDESSES OF THE ICE, VIEJAS HELADAS.

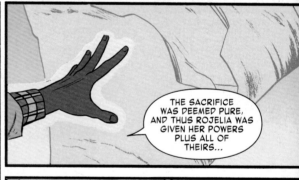

THE SACRIFICE WAS DEEMED PURE, AND THUS ROJELIA WAS GIVEN HER POWERS PLUS ALL OF THEIRS...

...INCLUDING THE ABILITY TO MANIPULATE WATER MOLECULES, AND THE ELEMENTS THEMSELVES.

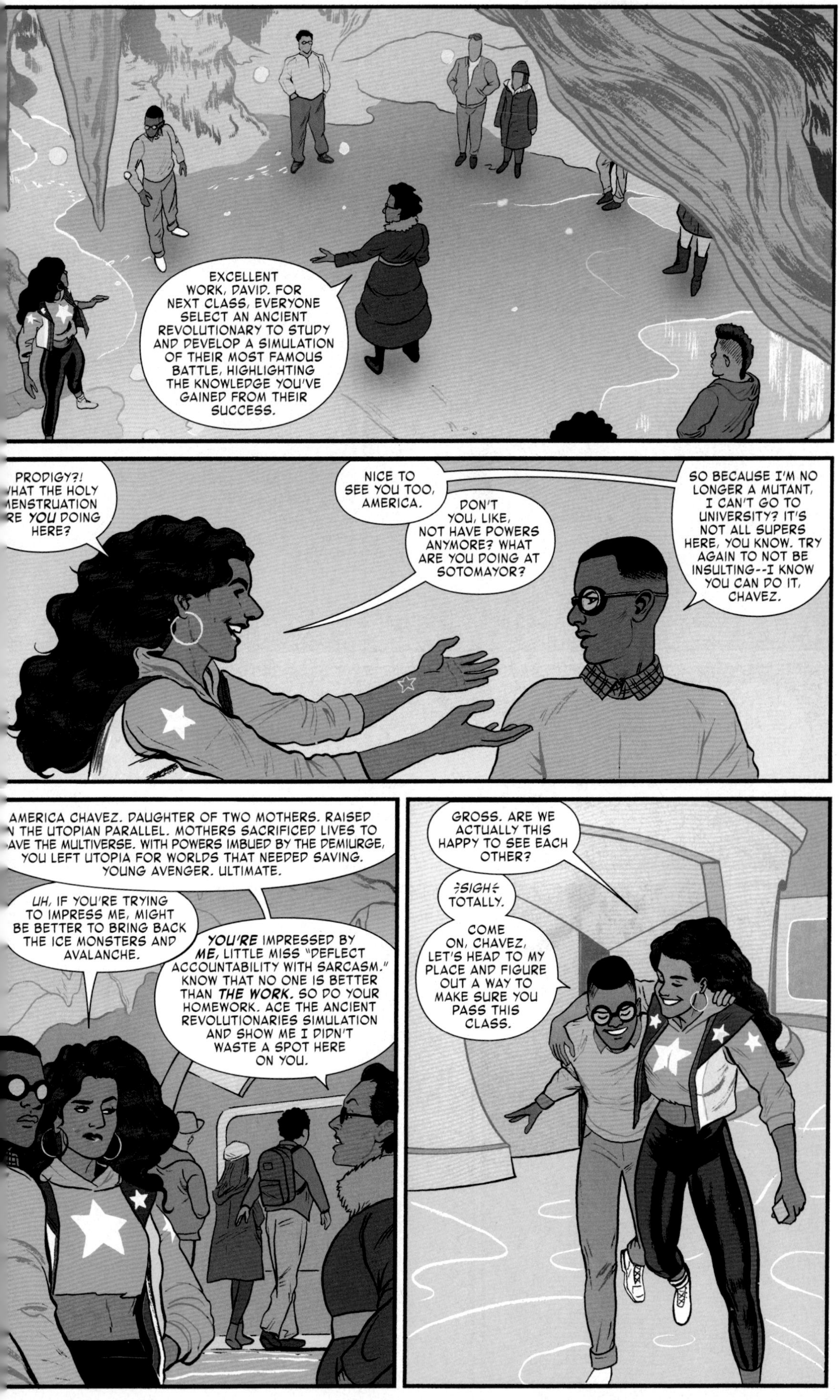
EXCELLENT WORK, DAVID. FOR NEXT CLASS, EVERYONE SELECT AN ANCIENT REVOLUTIONARY TO STUDY AND DEVELOP A SIMULATION OF THEIR MOST FAMOUS BATTLE, HIGHLIGHTING THE KNOWLEDGE YOU'VE GAINED FROM THEIR SUCCESS.
PRODIGY?! WHAT THE HOLY MENSTRUATION ARE *YOU* DOING HERE?
NICE TO SEE YOU TOO, AMERICA.
DON'T YOU, LIKE, NOT HAVE POWERS ANYMORE? WHAT ARE YOU DOING AT SOTOMAYOR?
SO BECAUSE I'M NO LONGER A MUTANT, I CAN'T GO TO UNIVERSITY? IT'S NOT ALL SUPERS HERE, YOU KNOW. TRY AGAIN TO NOT BE INSULTING--I KNOW YOU CAN DO IT, CHAVEZ.
AMERICA CHAVEZ. DAUGHTER OF TWO MOTHERS. RAISED IN THE UTOPIAN PARALLEL. MOTHERS SACRIFICED LIVES TO SAVE THE MULTIVERSE. WITH POWERS IMBUED BY THE DEMIURGE, YOU LEFT UTOPIA FOR WORLDS THAT NEEDED SAVING. YOUNG AVENGER. ULTIMATE.
UH, IF YOU'RE TRYING TO IMPRESS ME, MIGHT BE BETTER TO BRING BACK THE ICE MONSTERS AND AVALANCHE.
YOU'RE IMPRESSED BY *ME*, LITTLE MISS "DEFLECT ACCOUNTABILITY WITH SARCASM." KNOW THAT NO ONE IS BETTER THAN *THE WORK*. SO DO YOUR HOMEWORK. ACE THE ANCIENT REVOLUTIONARIES SIMULATION AND SHOW ME I DIDN'T WASTE A SPOT HERE ON YOU.
GROSS. ARE WE ACTUALLY THIS HAPPY TO SEE EACH OTHER?
SIGH TOTALLY.
COME ON, CHAVEZ, LET'S HEAD TO MY PLACE AND FIGURE OUT A WAY TO MAKE SURE YOU PASS THIS CLASS.

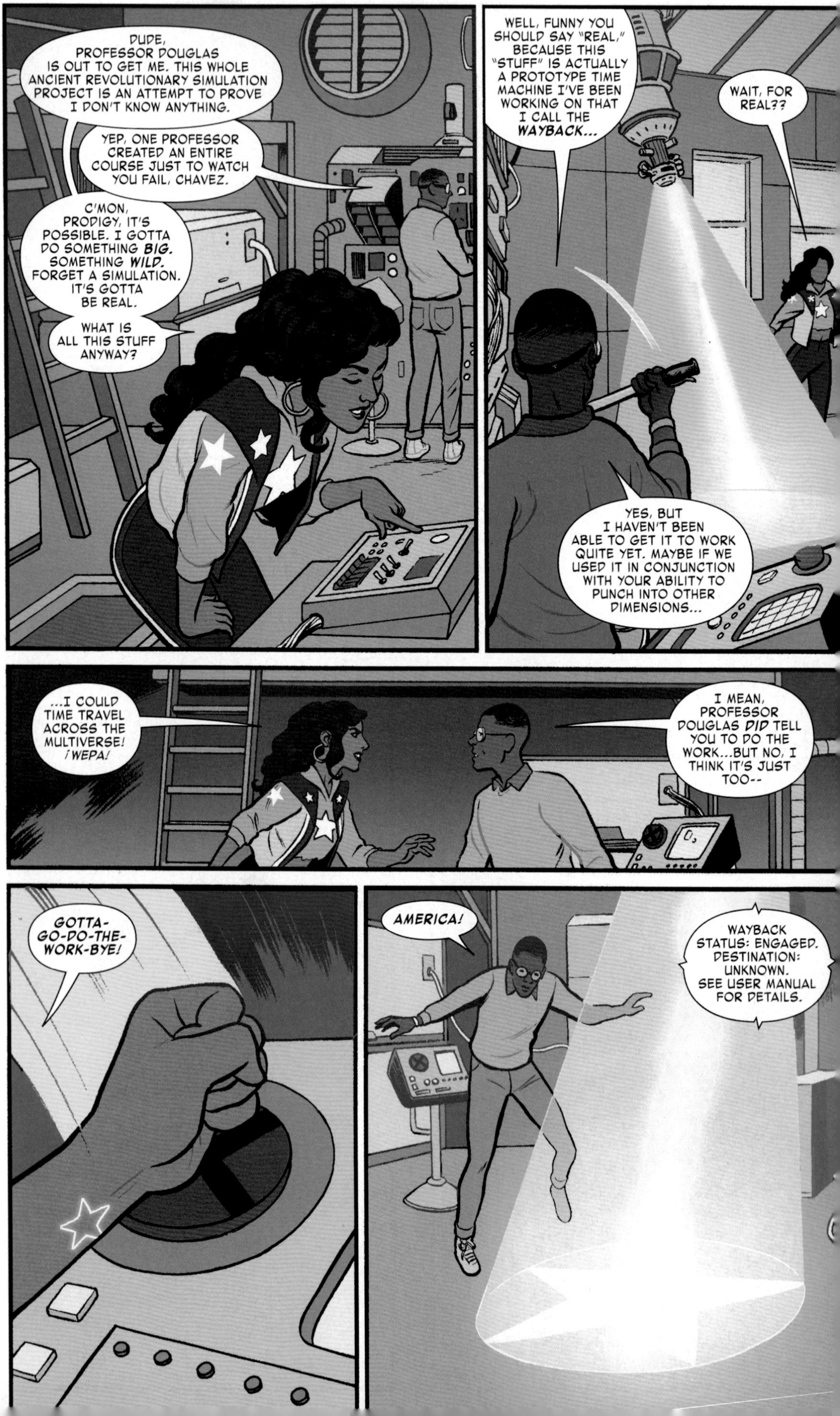
DUDE, PROFESSOR DOUGLAS IS OUT TO GET ME. THIS WHOLE ANCIENT REVOLUTIONARY SIMULATION PROJECT IS AN ATTEMPT TO PROVE I DON'T KNOW ANYTHING.
YEP, ONE PROFESSOR CREATED AN ENTIRE COURSE JUST TO WATCH YOU FAIL, CHAVEZ.
C'MON, PRODIGY, IT'S POSSIBLE. I GOTTA DO SOMETHING BIG. SOMETHING WILD. FORGET A SIMULATION. IT'S GOTTA BE REAL.
WHAT IS ALL THIS STUFF ANYWAY?
WELL, FUNNY YOU SHOULD SAY "REAL," BECAUSE THIS "STUFF" IS ACTUALLY A PROTOTYPE TIME MACHINE I'VE BEEN WORKING ON THAT I CALL THE WAYBACK...
WAIT, FOR REAL??
YES, BUT I HAVEN'T BEEN ABLE TO GET IT TO WORK QUITE YET. MAYBE IF WE USED IT IN CONJUNCTION WITH YOUR ABILITY TO PUNCH INTO OTHER DIMENSIONS...
...I COULD TIME TRAVEL ACROSS THE MULTIVERSE! ¡WEPA!
I MEAN, PROFESSOR DOUGLAS DID TELL YOU TO DO THE WORK...BUT NO, I THINK IT'S JUST TOO--
GOTTA-GO-DO-THE-WORK-BYE!
AMERICA!
WAYBACK STATUS: ENGAGED. DESTINATION: UNKNOWN. SEE USER MANUAL FOR DETAILS.

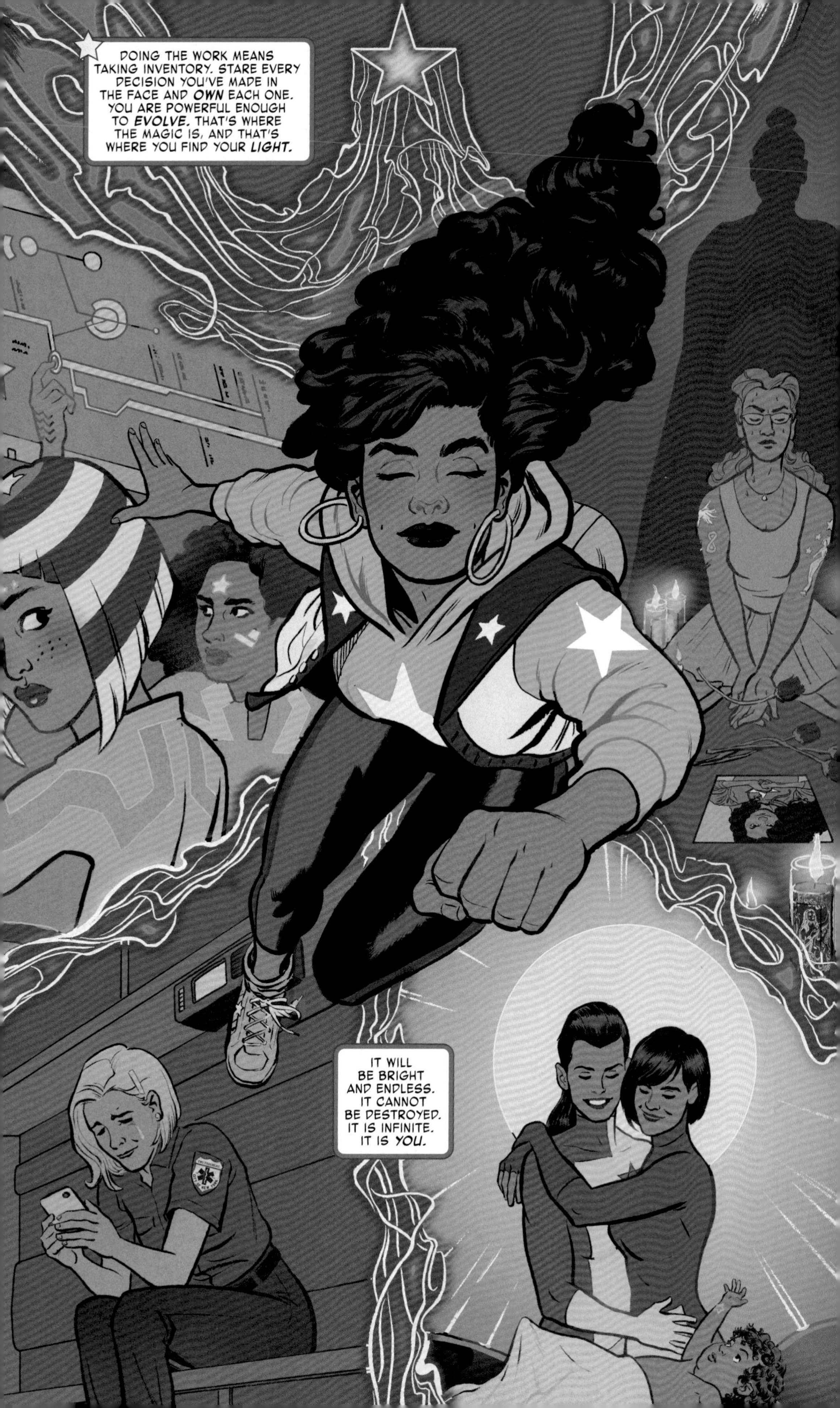
DOING THE WORK MEANS TAKING INVENTORY. STARE EVERY DECISION YOU'VE MADE IN THE FACE AND *OWN* EACH ONE. YOU ARE POWERFUL ENOUGH TO *EVOLVE.* THAT'S WHERE THE MAGIC IS, AND THAT'S WHERE YOU FIND YOUR *LIGHT.*
IT WILL BE BRIGHT AND ENDLESS. IT CANNOT BE DESTROYED. IT IS INFINITE. IT IS *YOU.*

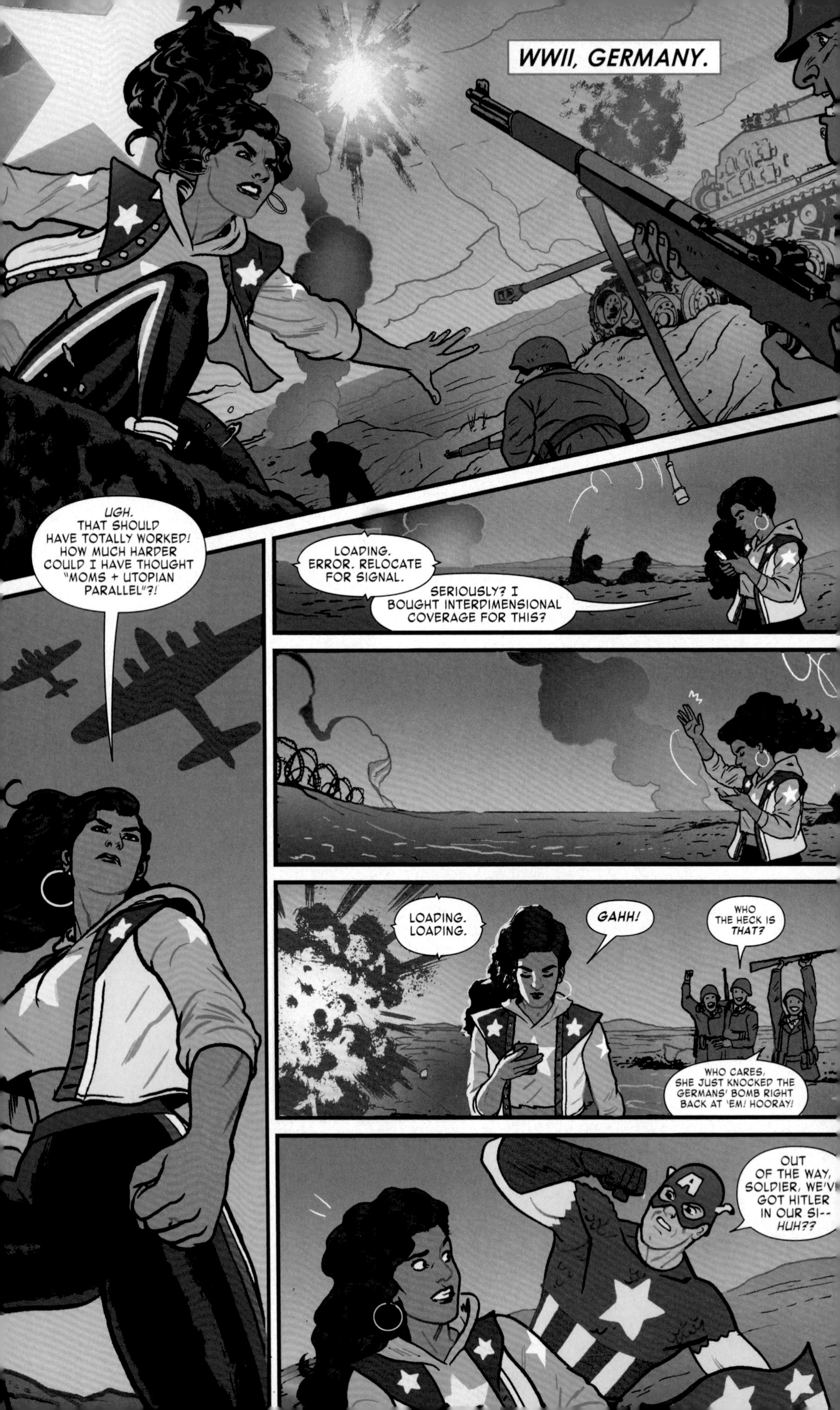
WWII, GERMANY.
UGH. THAT SHOULD HAVE TOTALLY WORKED! HOW MUCH HARDER COULD I HAVE THOUGHT "MOMS + UTOPIAN PARALLEL"?!
LOADING. ERROR. RELOCATE FOR SIGNAL.
SERIOUSLY? I BOUGHT INTERDIMENSIONAL COVERAGE FOR THIS?
LOADING. LOADING.
GAHH!
WHO THE HECK IS THAT?
WHO CARES, SHE JUST KNOCKED THE GERMANS' BOMB RIGHT BACK AT 'EM! HOORAY!
OUT OF THE WAY, SOLDIER, WE'V GOT HITLER IN OUR SI-- HUH??

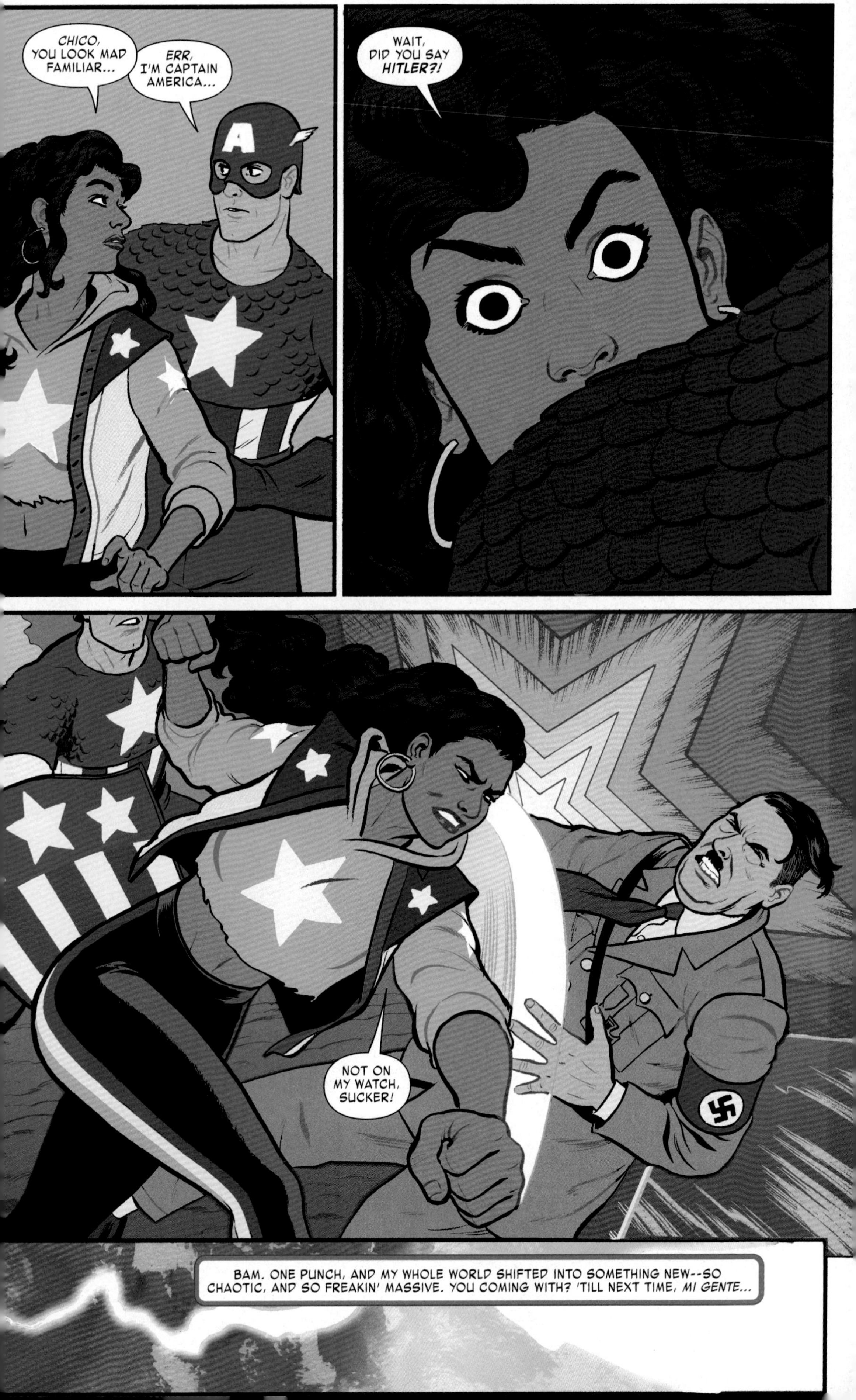
CHICO, YOU LOOK MAD FAMILIAR...
ERR, I'M CAPTAIN AMERICA...
WAIT, DID YOU SAY HITLER?!
NOT ON MY WATCH, SUCKER!
BAM. ONE PUNCH, AND MY WHOLE WORLD SHIFTED INTO SOMETHING NEW--SO CHAOTIC, AND SO FREAKIN' MASSIVE. YOU COMING WITH? 'TILL NEXT TIME, MI GENTE...

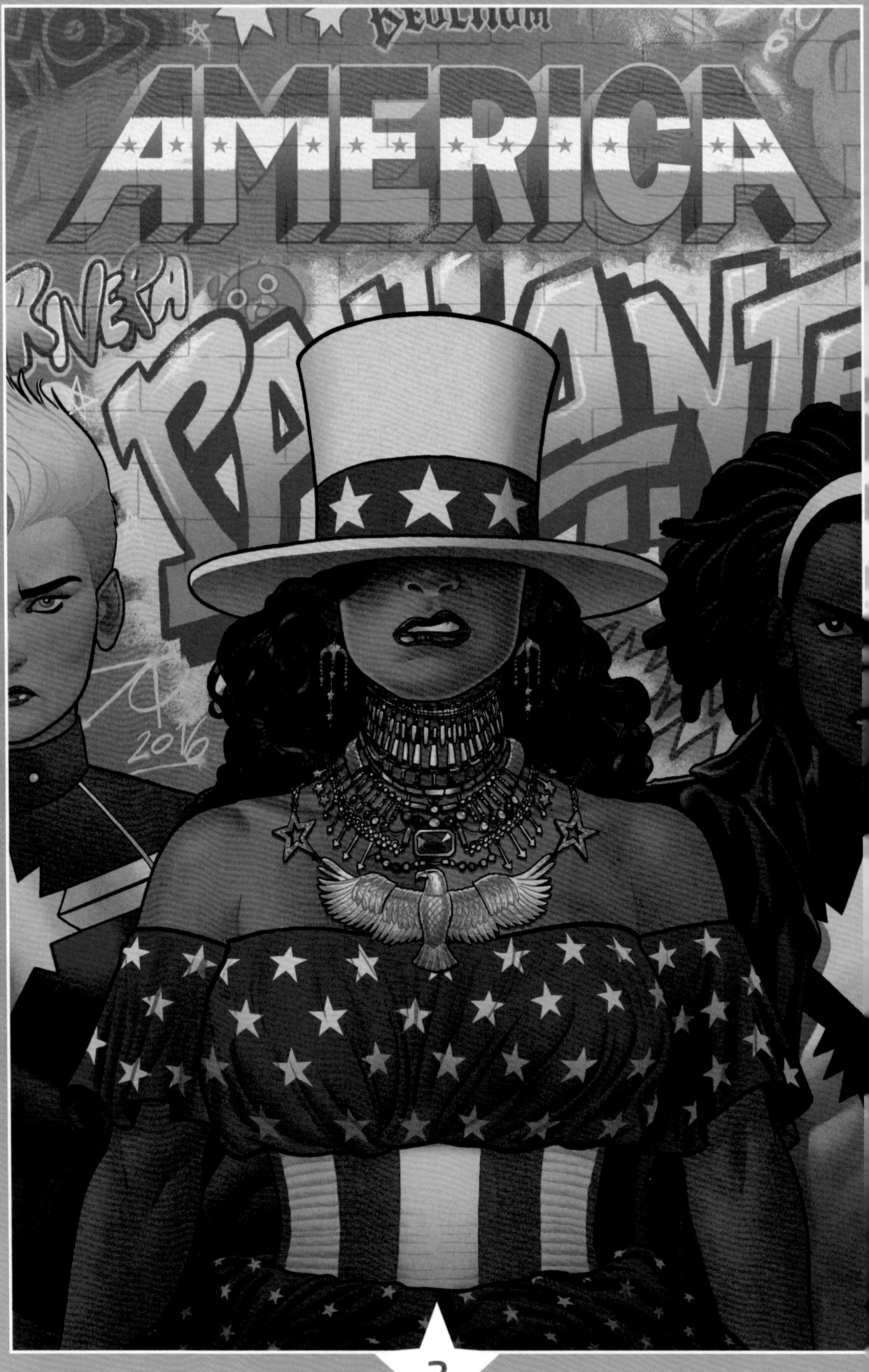
AMERICA

2

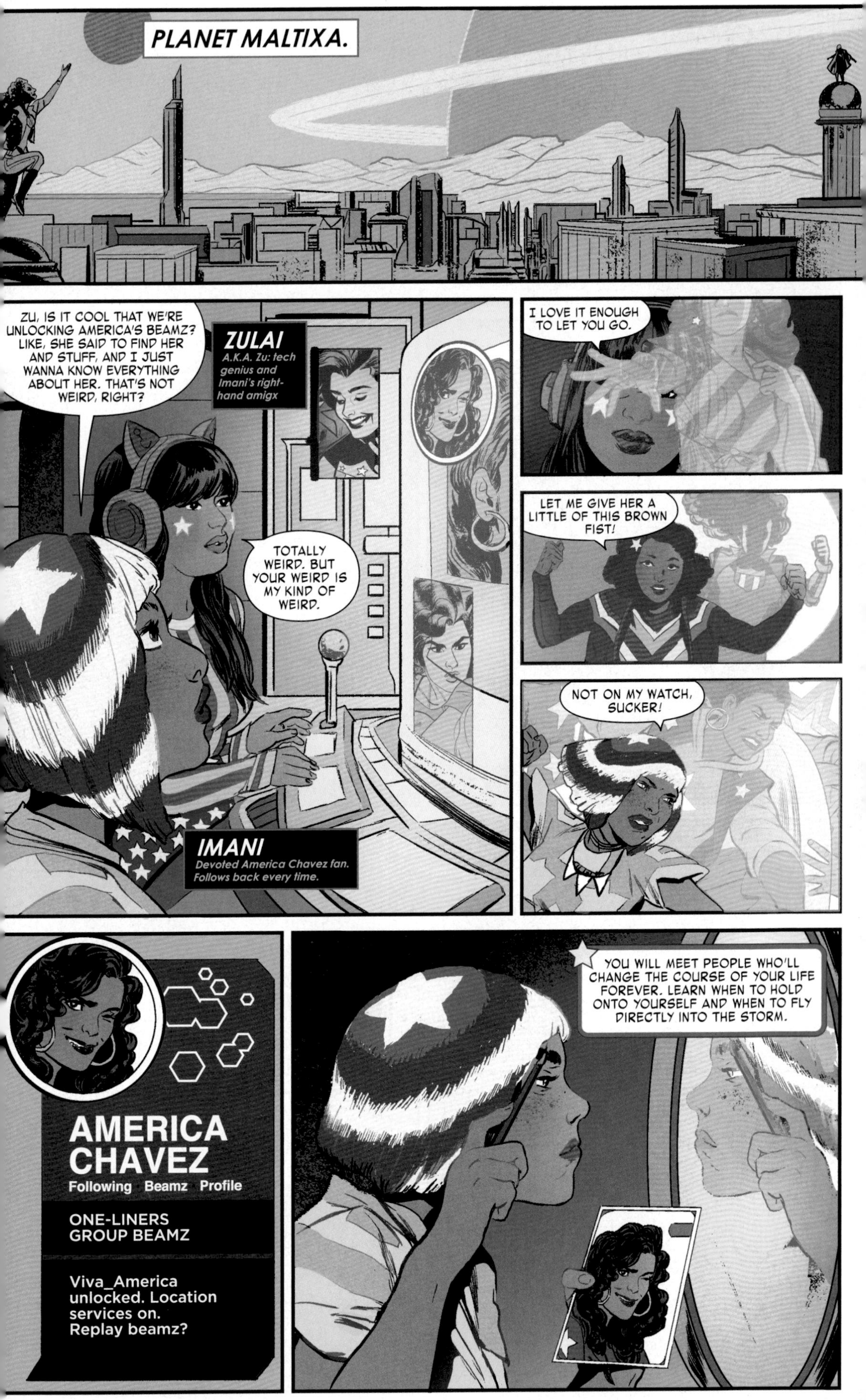
PLANET MALTIXA.
ZU, IS IT COOL THAT WE'RE UNLOCKING AMERICA'S BEAMZ? LIKE, SHE SAID TO FIND HER AND STUFF, AND I JUST WANNA KNOW EVERYTHING ABOUT HER. THAT'S NOT WEIRD, RIGHT?
ZULAI
A.K.A. Zu: tech genius and Imani's right-hand amigx
TOTALLY WEIRD. BUT YOUR WEIRD IS MY KIND OF WEIRD.
IMANI
Devoted America Chavez fan. Follows back every time.
I LOVE IT ENOUGH TO LET YOU GO.
LET ME GIVE HER A LITTLE OF THIS BROWN FIST!
NOT ON MY WATCH, SUCKER!
AMERICA CHAVEZ
Following Beamz Profile
ONE-LINERS
GROUP BEAMZ
Viva_America unlocked. Location services on. Replay beamz?
YOU WILL MEET PEOPLE WHO'LL CHANGE THE COURSE OF YOUR LIFE FOREVER. LEARN WHEN TO HOLD ONTO YOURSELF AND WHEN TO FLY DIRECTLY INTO THE STORM.

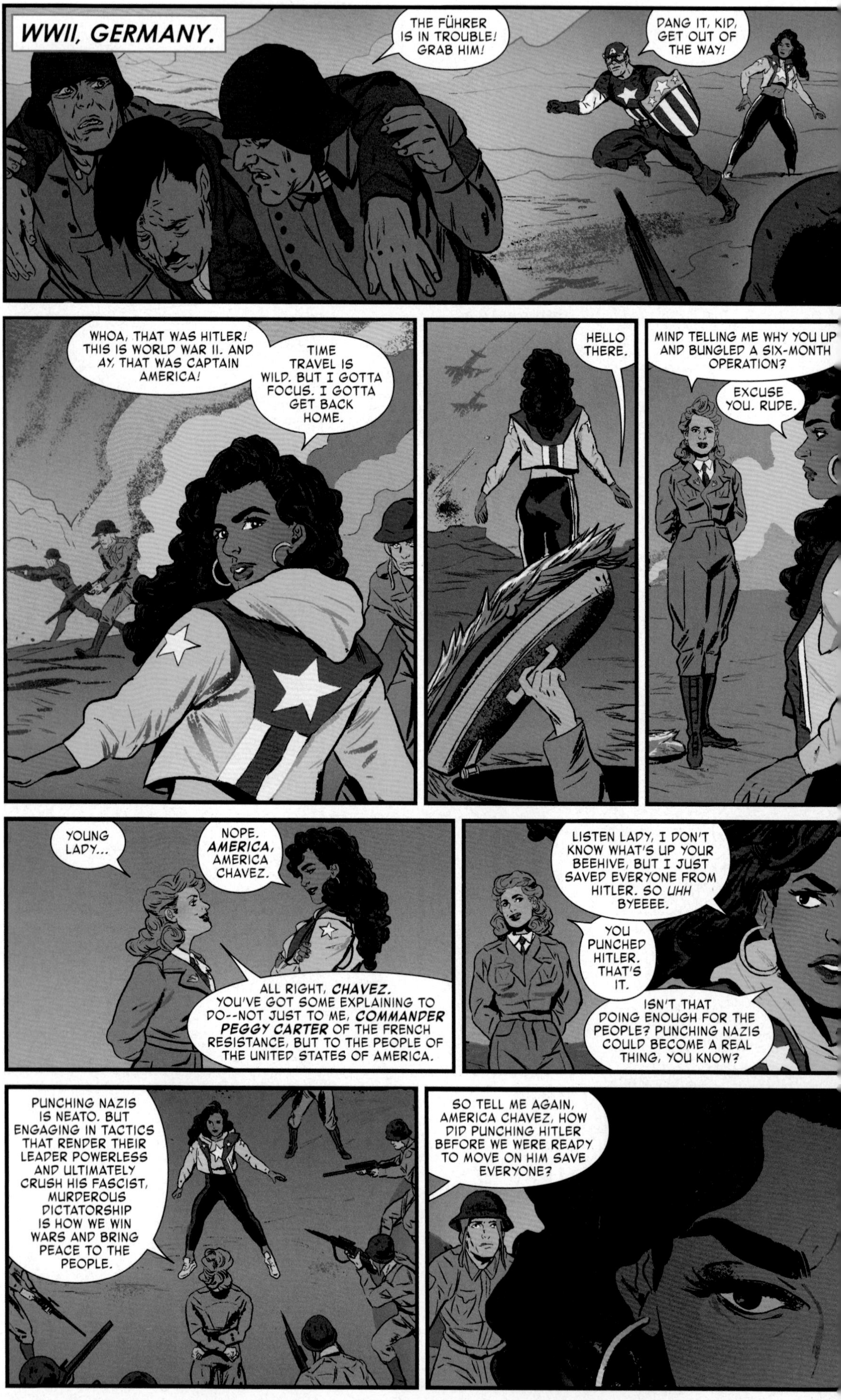
WWII, GERMANY.
THE FÜHRER IS IN TROUBLE! GRAB HIM!
DANG IT, KID, GET OUT OF THE WAY!
WHOA, THAT WAS HITLER! THIS IS WORLD WAR II. AND AY, THAT WAS CAPTAIN AMERICA!
TIME TRAVEL IS WILD. BUT I GOTTA FOCUS. I GOTTA GET BACK HOME.
HELLO THERE.
MIND TELLING ME WHY YOU UP AND BUNGLED A SIX-MONTH OPERATION?
EXCUSE YOU. RUDE.
YOUNG LADY...
NOPE. AMERICA, AMERICA CHAVEZ.
ALL RIGHT, CHAVEZ. YOU'VE GOT SOME EXPLAINING TO DO--NOT JUST TO ME, COMMANDER PEGGY CARTER OF THE FRENCH RESISTANCE, BUT TO THE PEOPLE OF THE UNITED STATES OF AMERICA.
LISTEN LADY, I DON'T KNOW WHAT'S UP YOUR BEEHIVE, BUT I JUST SAVED EVERYONE FROM HITLER. SO UHH BYEEEE.
YOU PUNCHED HITLER. THAT'S IT.
ISN'T THAT DOING ENOUGH FOR THE PEOPLE? PUNCHING NAZIS COULD BECOME A REAL THING, YOU KNOW?
PUNCHING NAZIS IS NEATO. BUT ENGAGING IN TACTICS THAT RENDER THEIR LEADER POWERLESS AND ULTIMATELY CRUSH HIS FASCIST, MURDEROUS DICTATORSHIP IS HOW WE WIN WARS AND BRING PEACE TO THE PEOPLE.
SO TELL ME AGAIN, AMERICA CHAVEZ, HOW DID PUNCHING HITLER BEFORE WE WERE READY TO MOVE ON HIM SAVE EVERYONE?

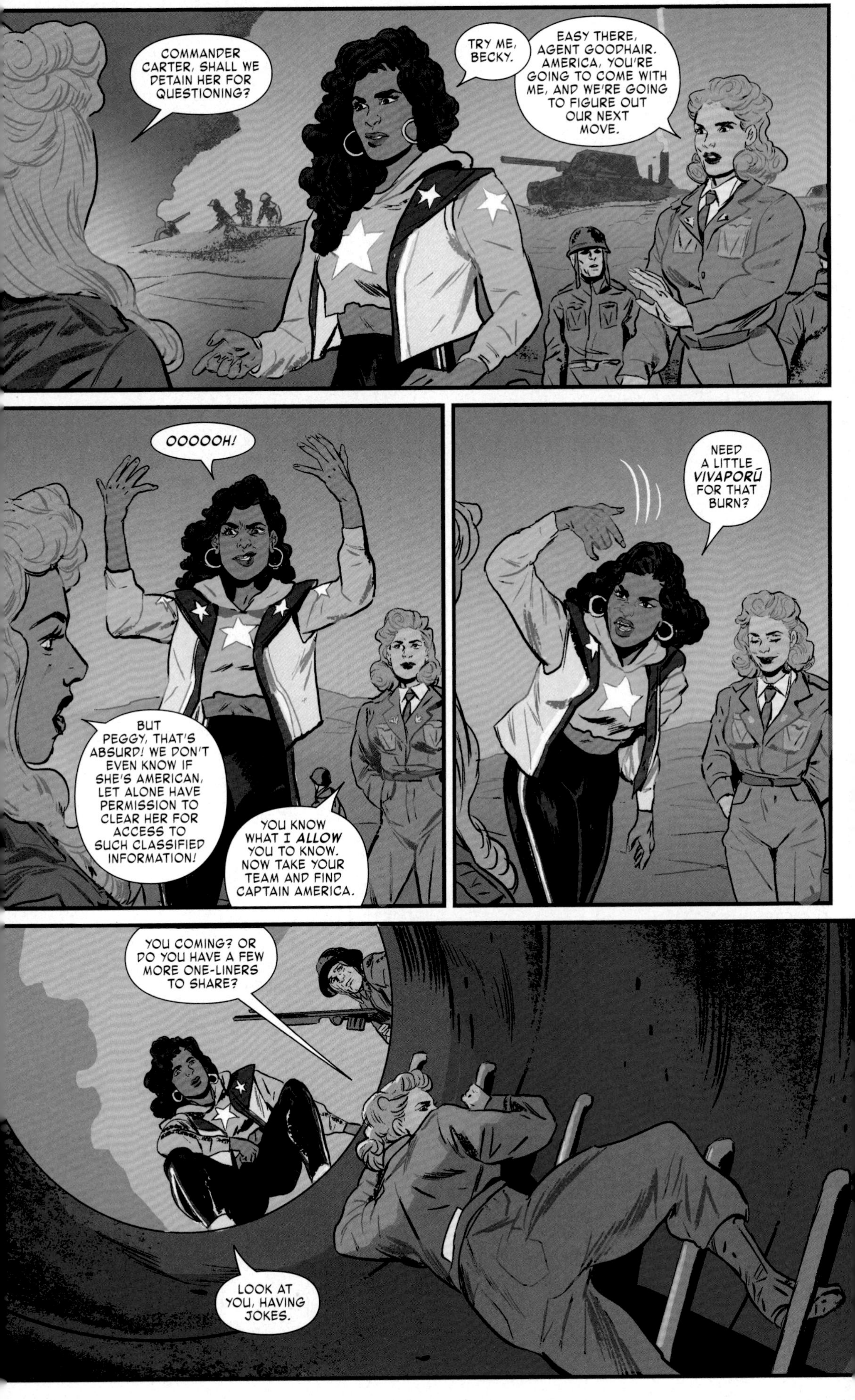

COMMANDER CARTER, SHALL WE DETAIN HER FOR QUESTIONING?
TRY ME, BECKY.
EASY THERE, AGENT GOODHAIR. AMERICA, YOU'RE GOING TO COME WITH ME, AND WE'RE GOING TO FIGURE OUT OUR NEXT MOVE.
OOOOOH!
BUT PEGGY, THAT'S ABSURD! WE DON'T EVEN KNOW IF SHE'S AMERICAN, LET ALONE HAVE PERMISSION TO CLEAR HER FOR ACCESS TO SUCH CLASSIFIED INFORMATION!
YOU KNOW WHAT I *ALLOW* YOU TO KNOW. NOW TAKE YOUR TEAM AND FIND CAPTAIN AMERICA.
NEED A LITTLE *VIVAPORŪ* FOR THAT BURN?
YOU COMING? OR DO YOU HAVE A FEW MORE ONE-LINERS TO SHARE?
LOOK AT YOU, HAVING JOKES.

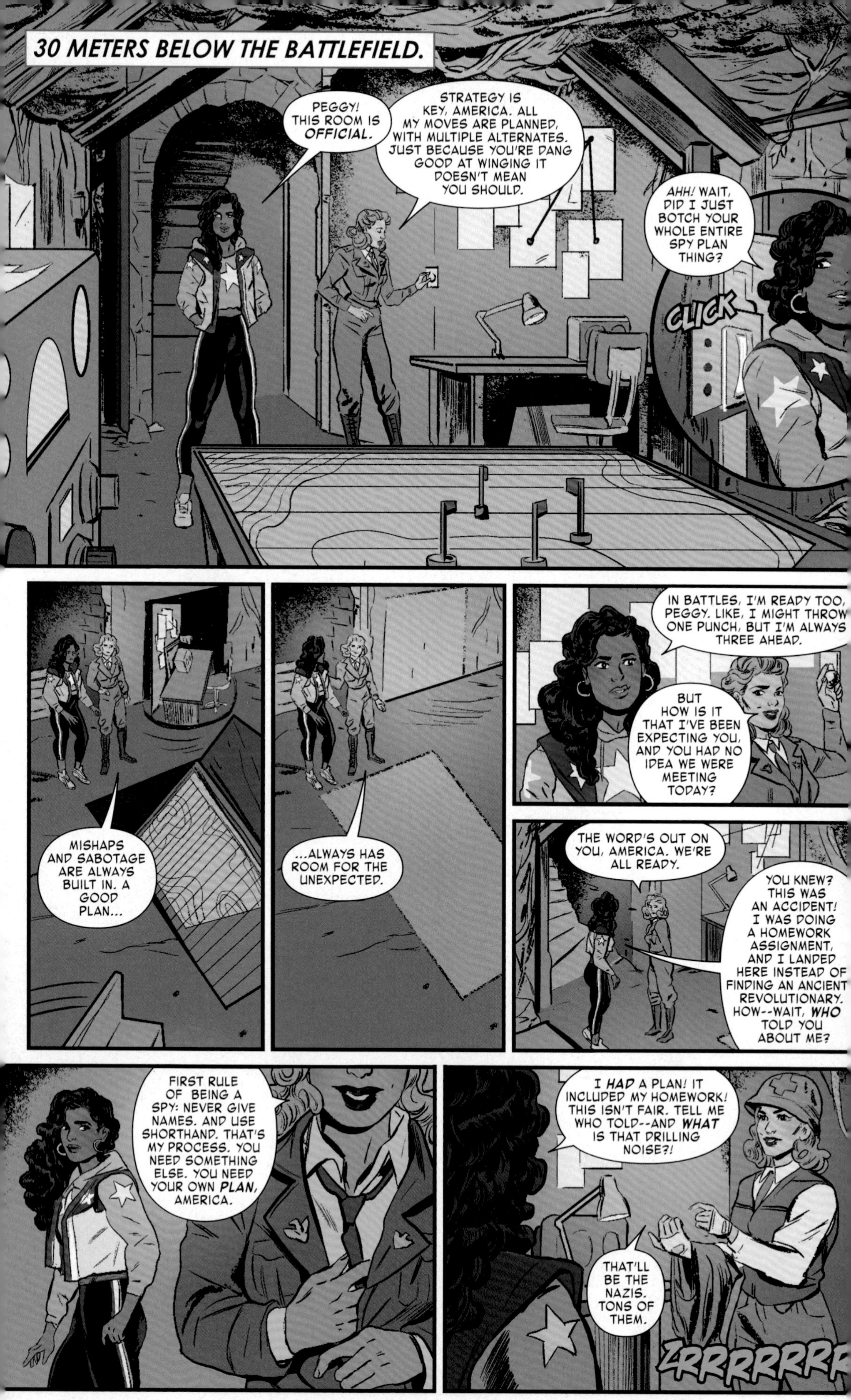

30 METERS BELOW THE BATTLEFIELD.
PEGGY! THIS ROOM IS OFFICIAL.
STRATEGY IS KEY, AMERICA. ALL MY MOVES ARE PLANNED, WITH MULTIPLE ALTERNATES. JUST BECAUSE YOU'RE DANG GOOD AT WINGING IT DOESN'T MEAN YOU SHOULD.
CLICK
AHH! WAIT, DID I JUST BOTCH YOUR WHOLE ENTIRE SPY PLAN THING?
MISHAPS AND SABOTAGE ARE ALWAYS BUILT IN. A GOOD PLAN...
...ALWAYS HAS ROOM FOR THE UNEXPECTED.
IN BATTLES, I'M READY TOO, PEGGY. LIKE, I MIGHT THROW ONE PUNCH, BUT I'M ALWAYS THREE AHEAD.
BUT HOW IS IT THAT I'VE BEEN EXPECTING YOU, AND YOU HAD NO IDEA WE WERE MEETING TODAY?
THE WORD'S OUT ON YOU, AMERICA. WE'RE ALL READY.
YOU KNEW? THIS WAS AN ACCIDENT! I WAS DOING A HOMEWORK ASSIGNMENT, AND I LANDED HERE INSTEAD OF FINDING AN ANCIENT REVOLUTIONARY. HOW--WAIT, WHO TOLD YOU ABOUT ME?
FIRST RULE OF BEING A SPY: NEVER GIVE NAMES. AND USE SHORTHAND. THAT'S MY PROCESS. YOU NEED SOMETHING ELSE. YOU NEED YOUR OWN PLAN, AMERICA.
I HAD A PLAN! IT INCLUDED MY HOMEWORK! THIS ISN'T FAIR. TELL ME WHO TOLD--AND WHAT IS THAT DRILLING NOISE?!
THAT'LL BE THE NAZIS. TONS OF THEM.
ZRRRRRRR

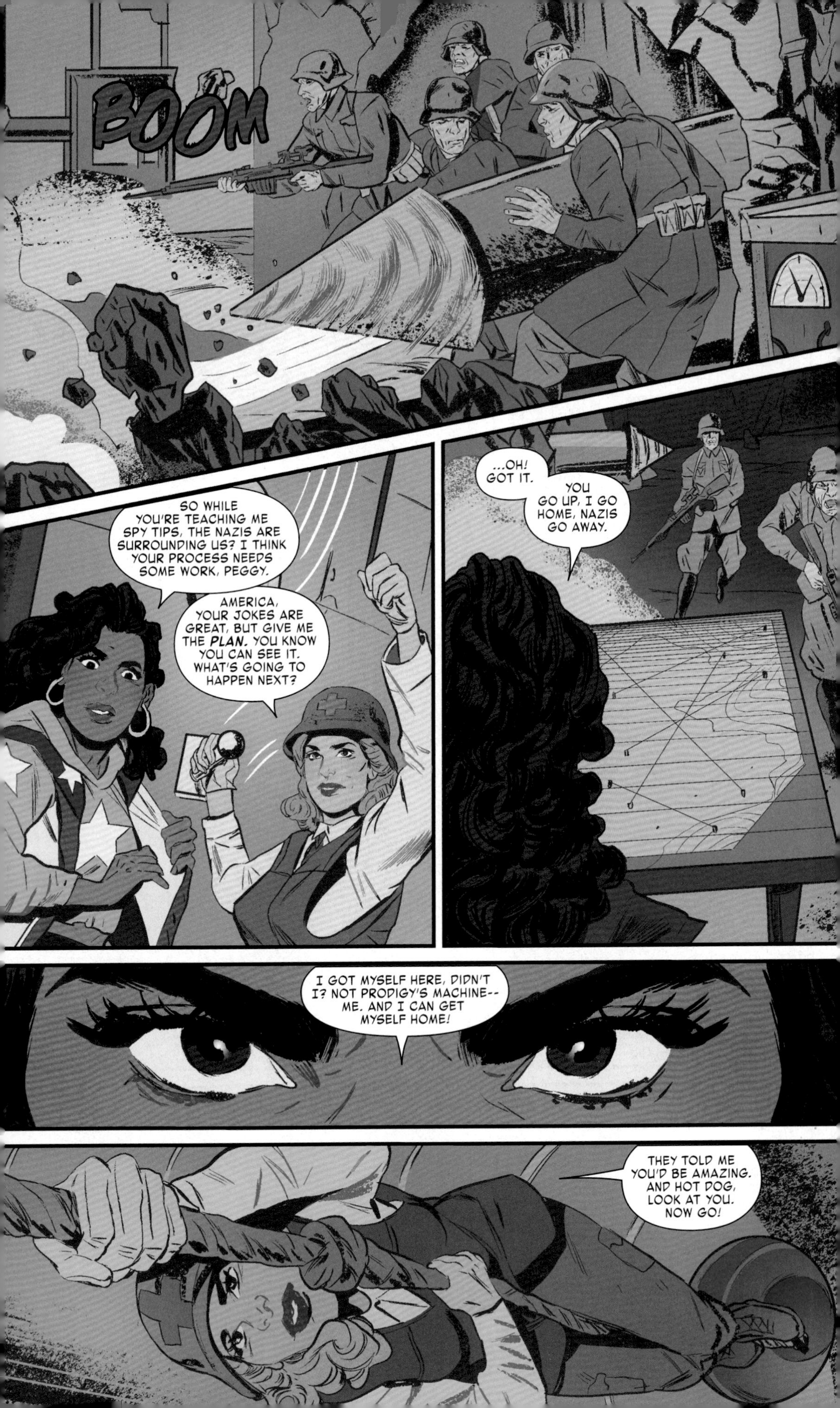
BOOM
SO WHILE YOU'RE TEACHING ME SPY TIPS, THE NAZIS ARE SURROUNDING US? I THINK YOUR PROCESS NEEDS SOME WORK, PEGGY.
AMERICA, YOUR JOKES ARE GREAT, BUT GIVE ME THE PLAN. YOU KNOW YOU CAN SEE IT. WHAT'S GOING TO HAPPEN NEXT?
...OH! GOT IT.
YOU GO UP, I GO HOME, NAZIS GO AWAY.
I GOT MYSELF HERE, DIDN'T I? NOT PRODIGY'S MACHINE-- ME. AND I CAN GET MYSELF HOME!
THEY TOLD ME YOU'D BE AMAZING. AND HOT DOG, LOOK AT YOU. NOW GO!

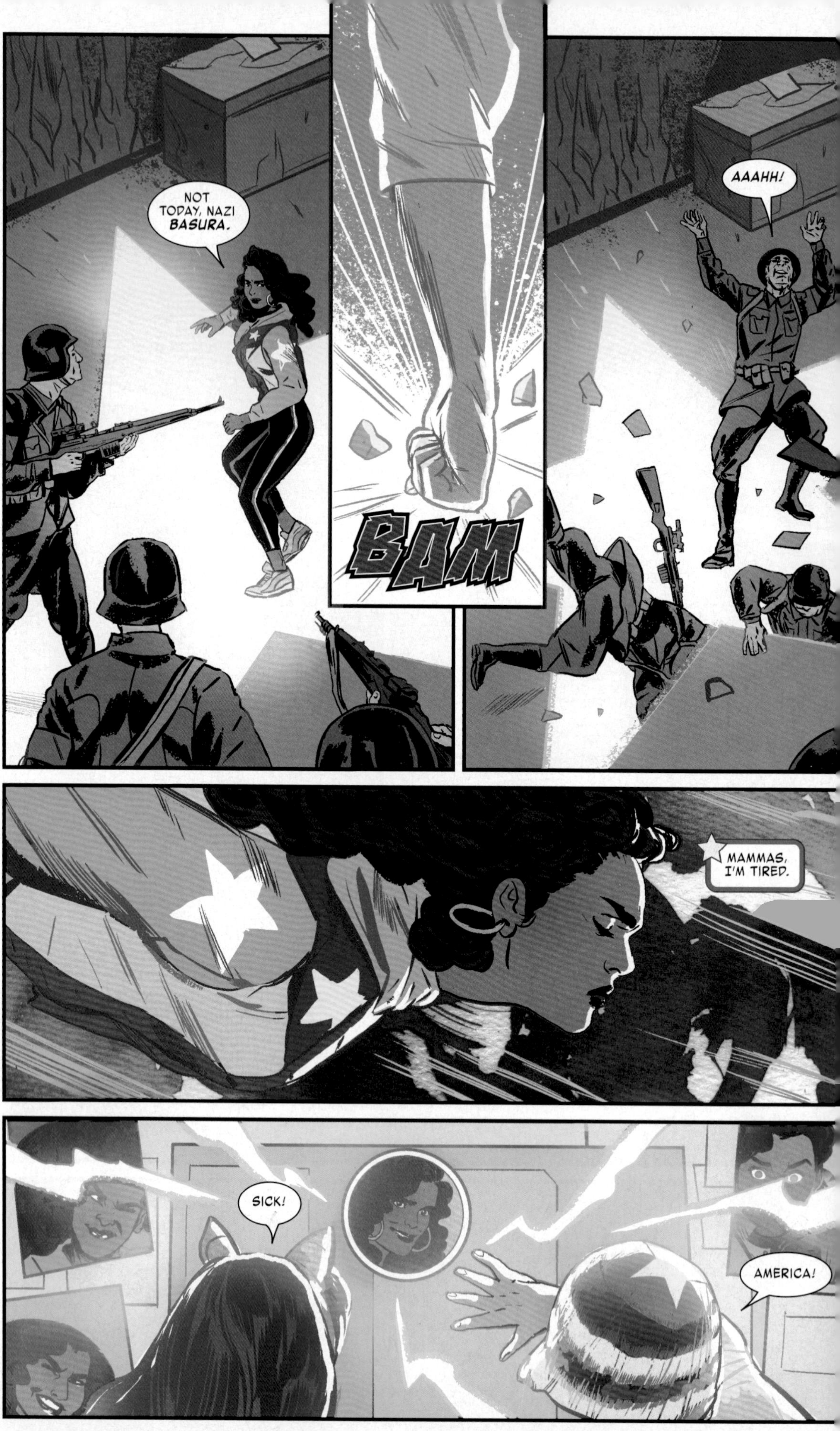
NOT TODAY, NAZI BASURA.
BAM
AAAHH!
MAMMAS, I'M TIRED.
SICK!
AMERICA!

UNIVERSE, CAN I GET A BREAK? YOU'VE GOT ME FIGHTING NAZIS AND FLUNKING ANCIENT REVOLUTIONARIES. DO I NEED A CONCUSSION TOO?

OOF!

I GUESS I SHOULDN'T COMPLAIN TOO MUCH. LEAST I MADE IT HOME...A.K.A. THE VAN I BOUGHT FOR FIFTY BUCKS AFTER ME AND LISA BROKE UP 'CUZ I WAS TOO SCARED TO GET A ROOMMATE.

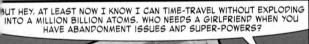

BUT HEY, AT LEAST NOW I KNOW I CAN TIME-TRAVEL WITHOUT EXPLODING INTO A MILLION BILLION ATOMS. WHO NEEDS A GIRLFRIEND WHEN YOU HAVE ABANDONMENT ISSUES AND SUPER-POWERS?

AND WHOEVER'S OUT THERE ANNOUNCING ME TO THE WORLD AND FOLLOWING MY MOVES, JUST QUIT IT, OKAY? QUIT IT. *I'M DONE.*

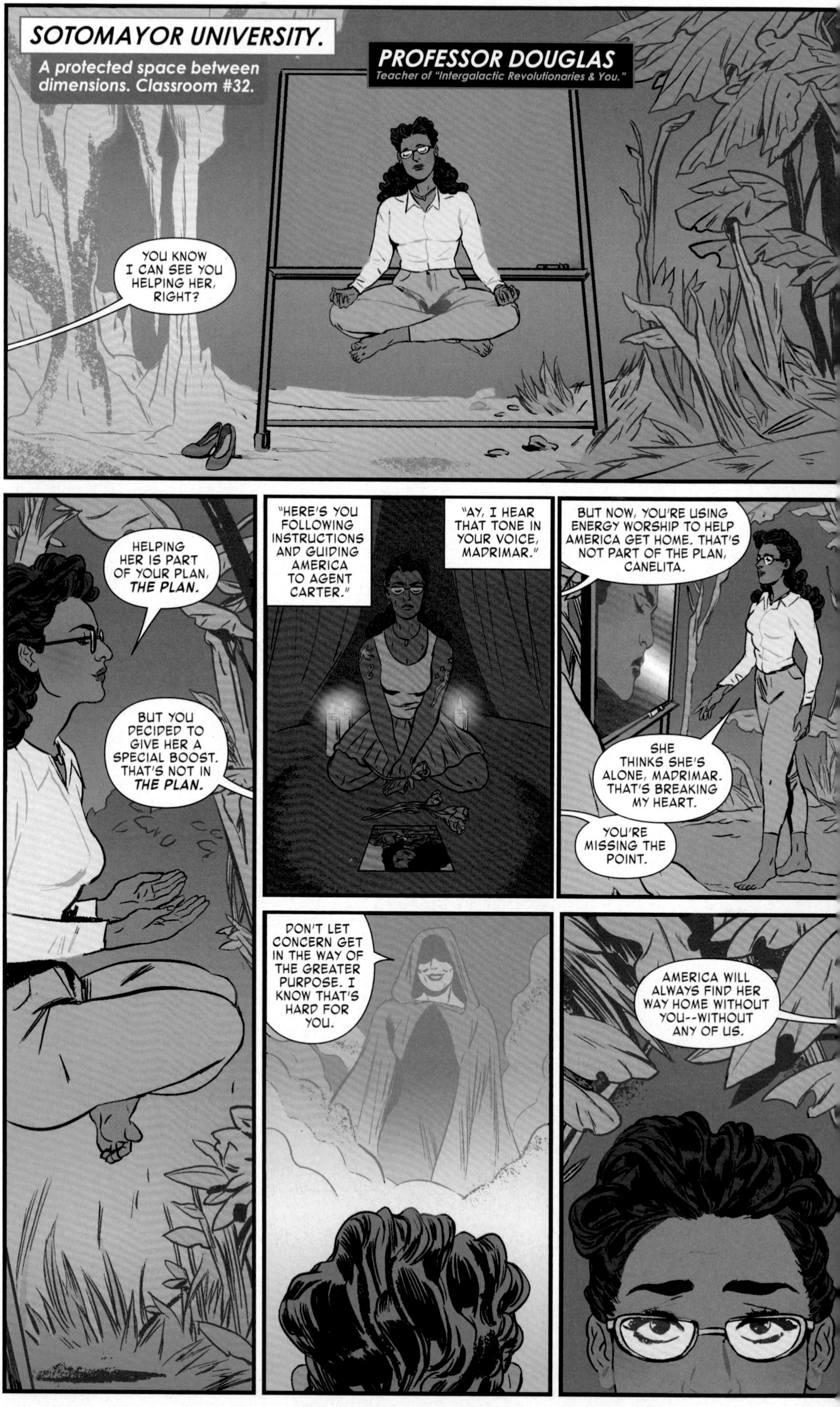

SOTOMAYOR UNIVERSITY.
A protected space between dimensions. Classroom #32.
PROFESSOR DOUGLAS
Teacher of "Intergalactic Revolutionaries & You."
YOU KNOW I CAN SEE YOU HELPING HER, RIGHT?
HELPING HER IS PART OF YOUR PLAN, THE PLAN.
BUT YOU DECIDED TO GIVE HER A SPECIAL BOOST. THAT'S NOT IN THE PLAN.
"HERE'S YOU FOLLOWING INSTRUCTIONS AND GUIDING AMERICA TO AGENT CARTER."
"AY, I HEAR THAT TONE IN YOUR VOICE, MADRIMAR."
BUT NOW, YOU'RE USING ENERGY WORSHIP TO HELP AMERICA GET HOME. THAT'S NOT PART OF THE PLAN, CANELITA.
SHE THINKS SHE'S ALONE, MADRIMAR. THAT'S BREAKING MY HEART.
YOU'RE MISSING THE POINT.
DON'T LET CONCERN GET IN THE WAY OF THE GREATER PURPOSE. I KNOW THAT'S HARD FOR YOU.
AMERICA WILL ALWAYS FIND HER WAY HOME WITHOUT YOU--WITHOUT ANY OF US.

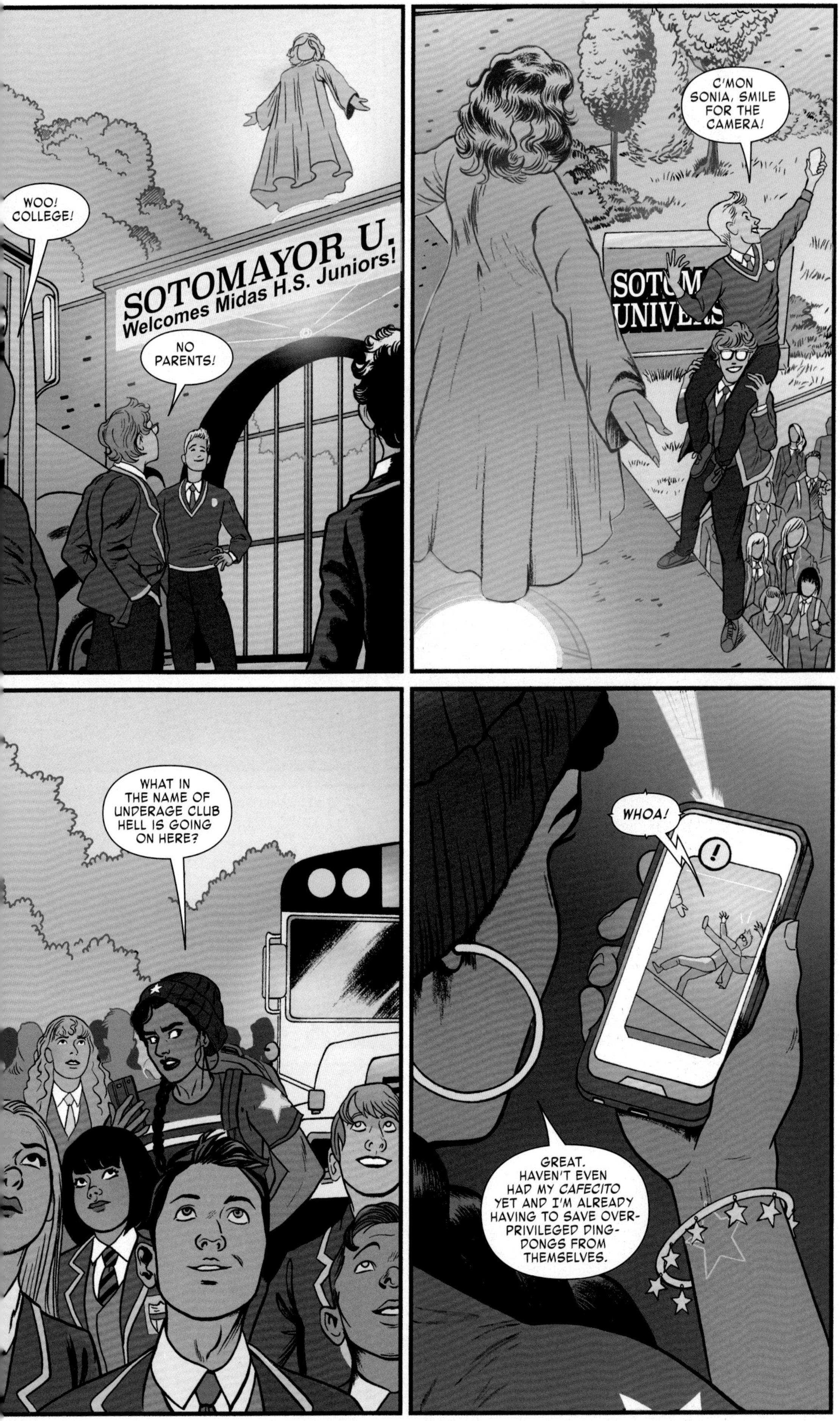
SOTOMAYOR U.
Welcomes Midas H.S. Juniors!
WOO! COLLEGE!
NO PARENTS!
C'MON SONIA, SMILE FOR THE CAMERA!
WHAT IN THE NAME OF UNDERAGE CLUB HELL IS GOING ON HERE?
WHOA!
!
GREAT. HAVEN'T EVEN HAD MY *CAFECITO* YET AND I'M ALREADY HAVING TO SAVE OVER-PRIVILEGED DING-DONGS FROM THEMSELVES.

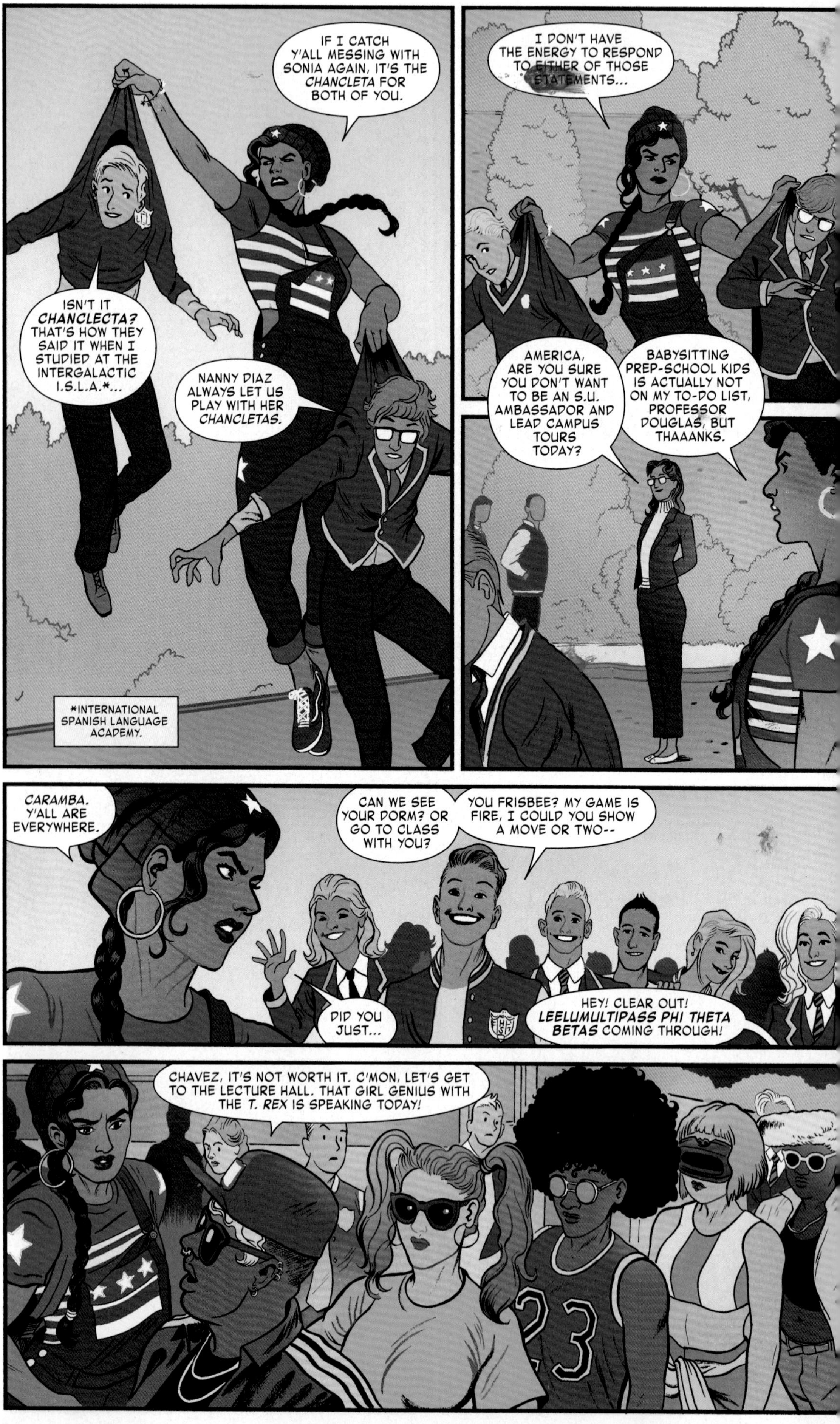
IF I CATCH Y'ALL MESSING WITH SONIA AGAIN, IT'S THE *CHANCLETA* FOR BOTH OF YOU.
ISN'T IT ***CHANCLECTA?*** THAT'S HOW THEY SAID IT WHEN I STUDIED AT THE INTERGALACTIC I.S.L.A.*...
NANNY DIAZ ALWAYS LET US PLAY WITH HER *CHANCLETAS.*
*INTERNATIONAL SPANISH LANGUAGE ACADEMY.
I DON'T HAVE THE ENERGY TO RESPOND TO EITHER OF THOSE STATEMENTS...
AMERICA, ARE YOU SURE YOU DON'T WANT TO BE AN S.U. AMBASSADOR AND LEAD CAMPUS TOURS TODAY?
BABYSITTING PREP-SCHOOL KIDS IS ACTUALLY NOT ON MY TO-DO LIST, PROFESSOR DOUGLAS, BUT THAAANKS.
CARAMBA. Y'ALL ARE EVERYWHERE.
CAN WE SEE YOUR DORM? OR GO TO CLASS WITH YOU?
YOU FRISBEE? MY GAME IS FIRE, I COULD YOU SHOW A MOVE OR TWO--
DID YOU JUST...
HEY! CLEAR OUT! ***LEELUMULTIPASS PHI THETA BETAS*** COMING THROUGH!
CHAVEZ, IT'S NOT WORTH IT. C'MON, LET'S GET TO THE LECTURE HALL. THAT GIRL GENIUS WITH THE *T. REX* IS SPEAKING TODAY!

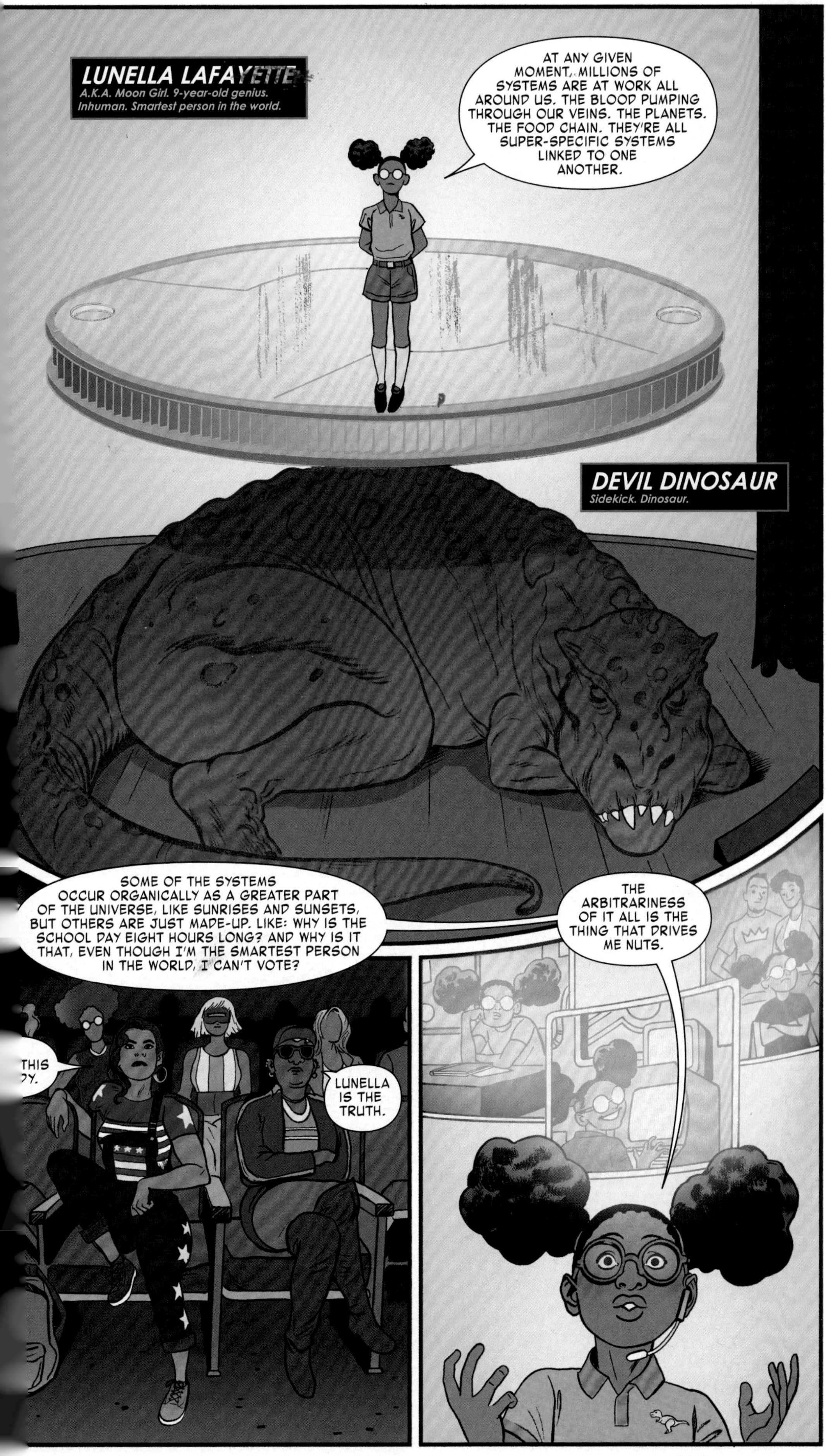
LUNELLA LAFAYETTE
A.K.A. Moon Girl. 9-year-old genius. Inhuman. Smartest person in the world.
AT ANY GIVEN MOMENT, MILLIONS OF SYSTEMS ARE AT WORK ALL AROUND US. THE BLOOD PUMPING THROUGH OUR VEINS. THE PLANETS. THE FOOD CHAIN. THEY'RE ALL SUPER-SPECIFIC SYSTEMS LINKED TO ONE ANOTHER.
DEVIL DINOSAUR
Sidekick. Dinosaur.
SOME OF THE SYSTEMS OCCUR ORGANICALLY AS A GREATER PART OF THE UNIVERSE, LIKE SUNRISES AND SUNSETS, BUT OTHERS ARE JUST MADE-UP. LIKE: WHY IS THE SCHOOL DAY EIGHT HOURS LONG? AND WHY IS IT THAT, EVEN THOUGH I'M THE SMARTEST PERSON IN THE WORLD, I CAN'T VOTE?
THIS
LUNELLA IS THE TRUTH.
THE ARBITRARINESS OF IT ALL IS THE THING THAT DRIVES ME NUTS.

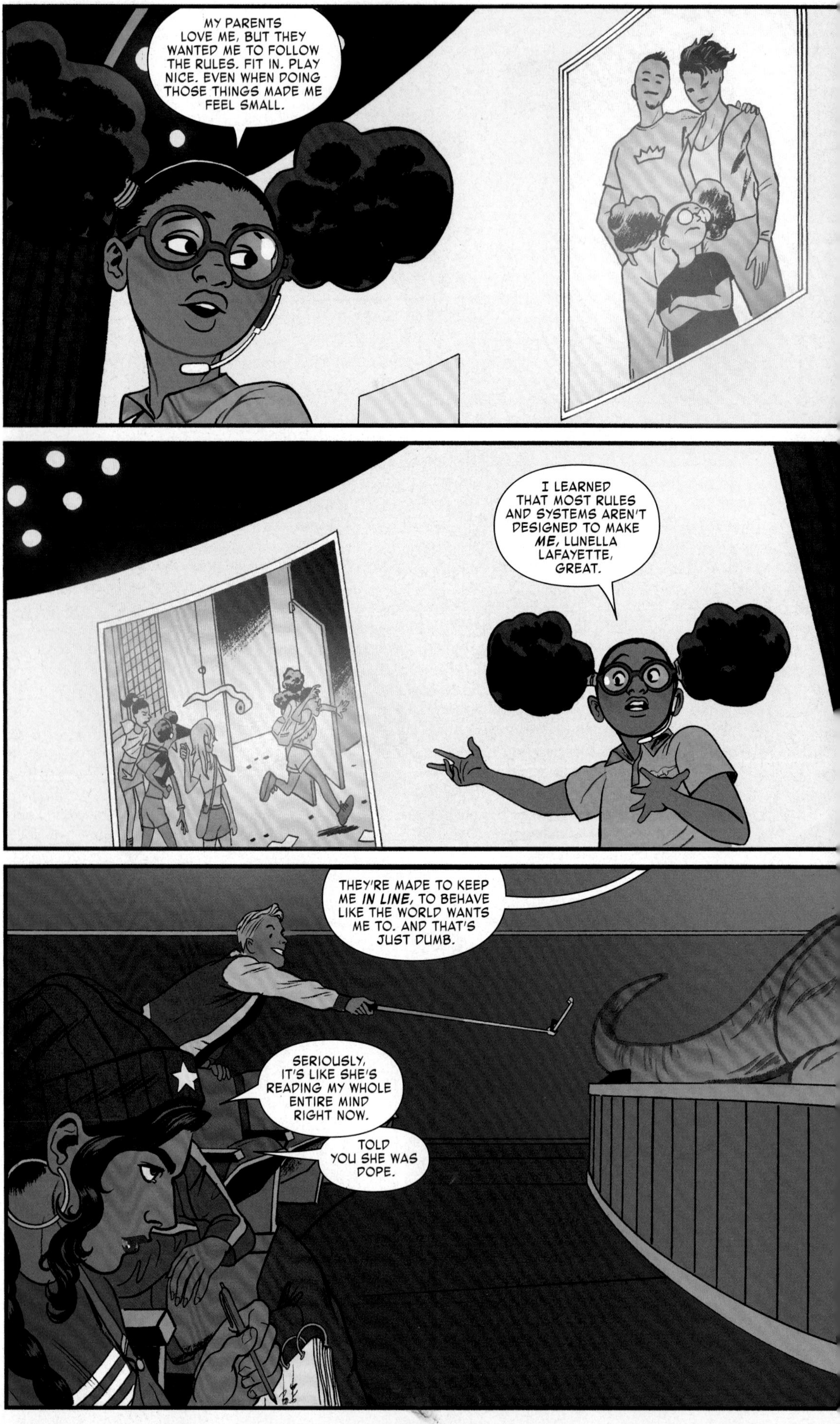
MY PARENTS LOVE ME, BUT THEY WANTED ME TO FOLLOW THE RULES. FIT IN. PLAY NICE. EVEN WHEN DOING THOSE THINGS MADE ME FEEL SMALL.
I LEARNED THAT MOST RULES AND SYSTEMS AREN'T DESIGNED TO MAKE *ME*, LUNELLA LAFAYETTE, GREAT.
THEY'RE MADE TO KEEP ME *IN LINE*, TO BEHAVE LIKE THE WORLD WANTS ME TO. AND THAT'S JUST DUMB.
SERIOUSLY, IT'S LIKE SHE'S READING MY WHOLE ENTIRE MIND RIGHT NOW.
TOLD YOU SHE WAS DOPE.

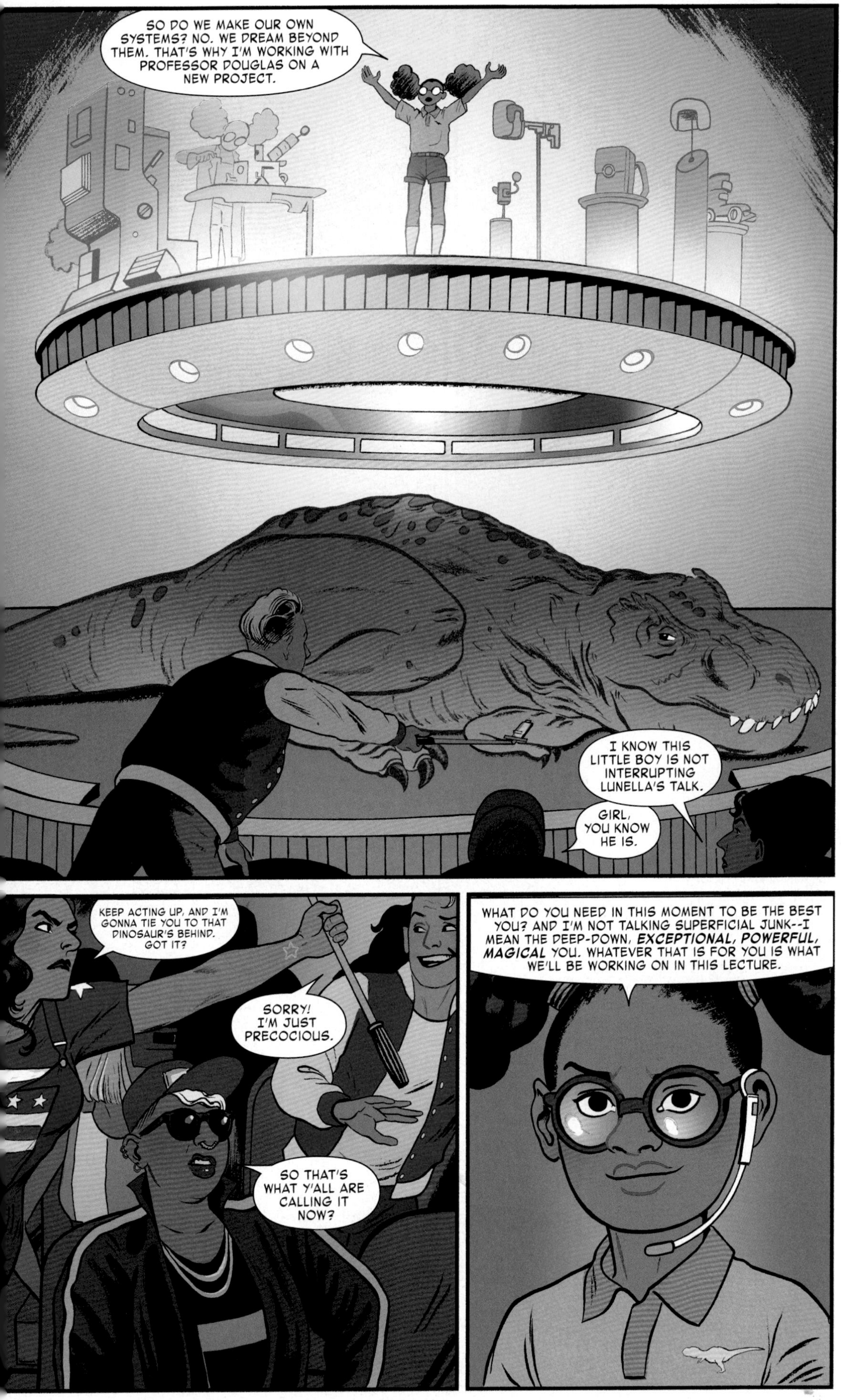
SO DO WE MAKE OUR OWN SYSTEMS? NO. WE DREAM BEYOND THEM. THAT'S WHY I'M WORKING WITH PROFESSOR DOUGLAS ON A NEW PROJECT.
I KNOW THIS LITTLE BOY IS NOT INTERRUPTING LUNELLA'S TALK.
GIRL, YOU KNOW HE IS.
KEEP ACTING UP, AND I'M GONNA TIE YOU TO THAT DINOSAUR'S BEHIND. GOT IT?
SORRY! I'M JUST PRECOCIOUS.
SO THAT'S WHAT Y'ALL ARE CALLING IT NOW?
WHAT DO YOU NEED IN THIS MOMENT TO BE THE BEST YOU? AND I'M NOT TALKING SUPERFICIAL JUNK--I MEAN THE DEEP-DOWN, ***EXCEPTIONAL, POWERFUL, MAGICAL*** YOU. WHATEVER THAT IS FOR YOU IS WHAT WE'LL BE WORKING ON IN THIS LECTURE.

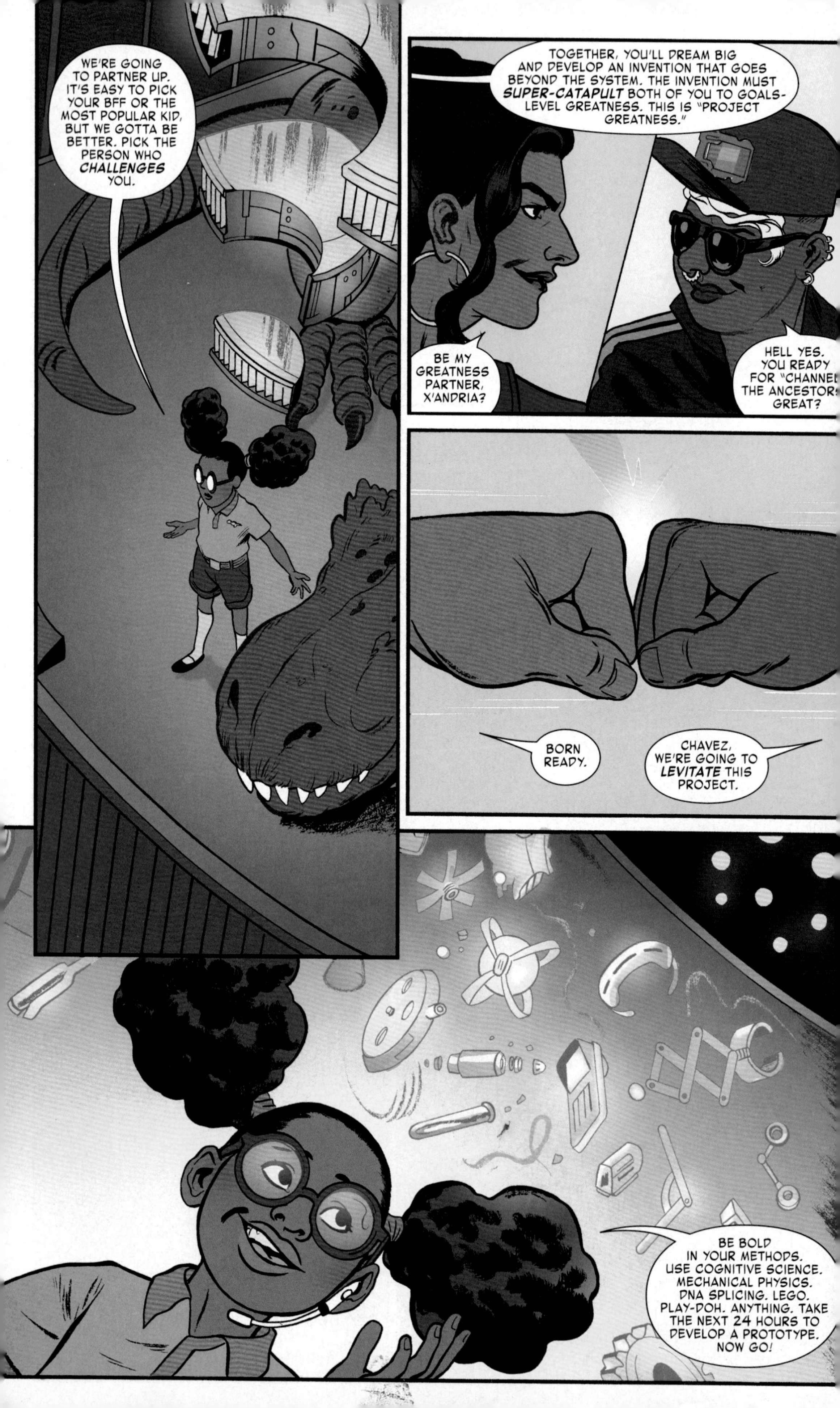

WE'RE GOING TO PARTNER UP. IT'S EASY TO PICK YOUR BFF OR THE MOST POPULAR KID, BUT WE GOTTA BE BETTER. PICK THE PERSON WHO *CHALLENGES* YOU.
TOGETHER, YOU'LL DREAM BIG AND DEVELOP AN INVENTION THAT GOES BEYOND THE SYSTEM. THE INVENTION MUST *SUPER-CATAPULT* BOTH OF YOU TO GOALS-LEVEL GREATNESS. THIS IS "PROJECT GREATNESS."
BE MY GREATNESS PARTNER, X'ANDRIA?
HELL YES. YOU READY FOR "CHANNEL THE ANCESTORS GREAT?
BORN READY.
CHAVEZ, WE'RE GOING TO *LEVITATE* THIS PROJECT.
BE BOLD IN YOUR METHODS. USE COGNITIVE SCIENCE. MECHANICAL PHYSICS. DNA SPLICING. LEGO. PLAY-DOH. ANYTHING. TAKE THE NEXT 24 HOURS TO DEVELOP A PROTOTYPE. NOW GO!

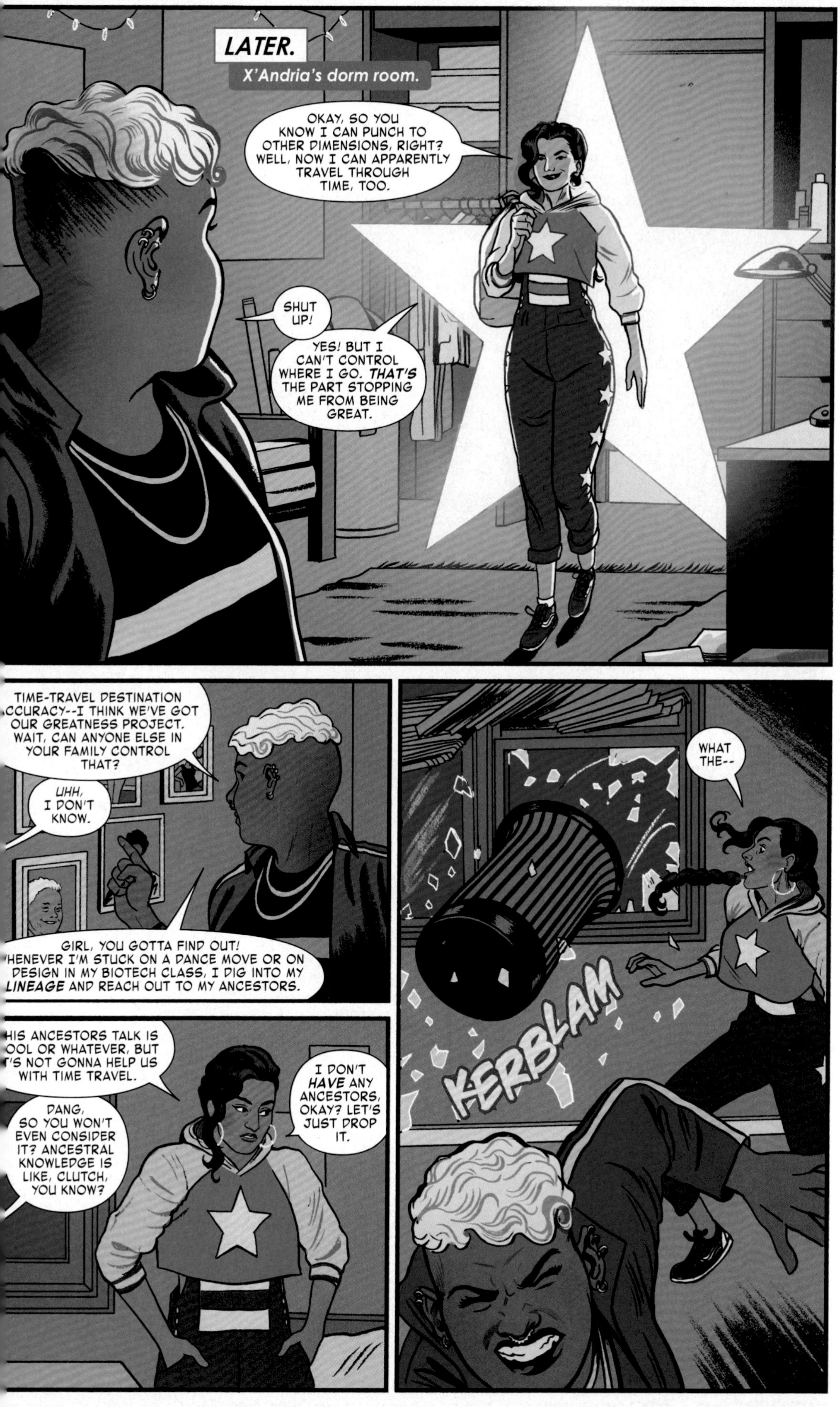

LATER.
X'Andria's dorm room.
OKAY, SO YOU KNOW I CAN PUNCH TO OTHER DIMENSIONS, RIGHT? WELL, NOW I CAN APPARENTLY TRAVEL THROUGH TIME, TOO.
SHUT UP!
YES! BUT I CAN'T CONTROL WHERE I GO. THAT'S THE PART STOPPING ME FROM BEING GREAT.
TIME-TRAVEL DESTINATION ACCURACY--I THINK WE'VE GOT OUR GREATNESS PROJECT. WAIT, CAN ANYONE ELSE IN YOUR FAMILY CONTROL THAT?
UHH, I DON'T KNOW.
GIRL, YOU GOTTA FIND OUT! WHENEVER I'M STUCK ON A DANCE MOVE OR ON DESIGN IN MY BIOTECH CLASS, I DIG INTO MY LINEAGE AND REACH OUT TO MY ANCESTORS.
THIS ANCESTORS TALK IS COOL OR WHATEVER, BUT IT'S NOT GONNA HELP US WITH TIME TRAVEL.
DANG, SO YOU WON'T EVEN CONSIDER IT? ANCESTRAL KNOWLEDGE IS LIKE, CLUTCH, YOU KNOW?
I DON'T HAVE ANY ANCESTORS, OKAY? LET'S JUST DROP IT.
WHAT THE--
KERBLAM

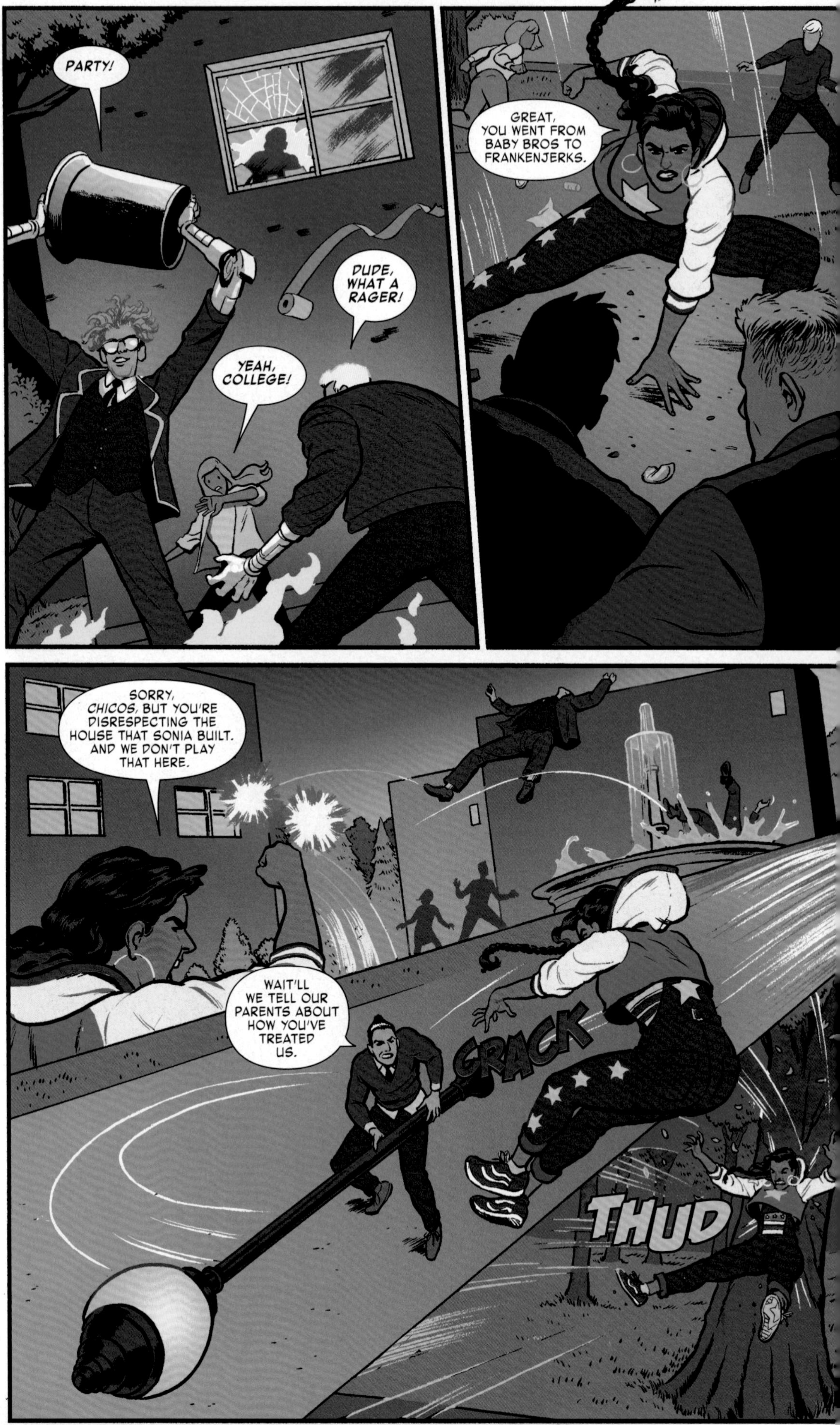
PARTY!
DUDE, WHAT A RAGER!
YEAH, COLLEGE!
GREAT, YOU WENT FROM BABY BROS TO FRANKENJERKS.
SORRY, CHICOS, BUT YOU'RE DISRESPECTING THE HOUSE THAT SONIA BUILT. AND WE DON'T PLAY THAT HERE.
WAIT'LL WE TELL OUR PARENTS ABOUT HOW YOU'VE TREATED US.
CRACK
THUD

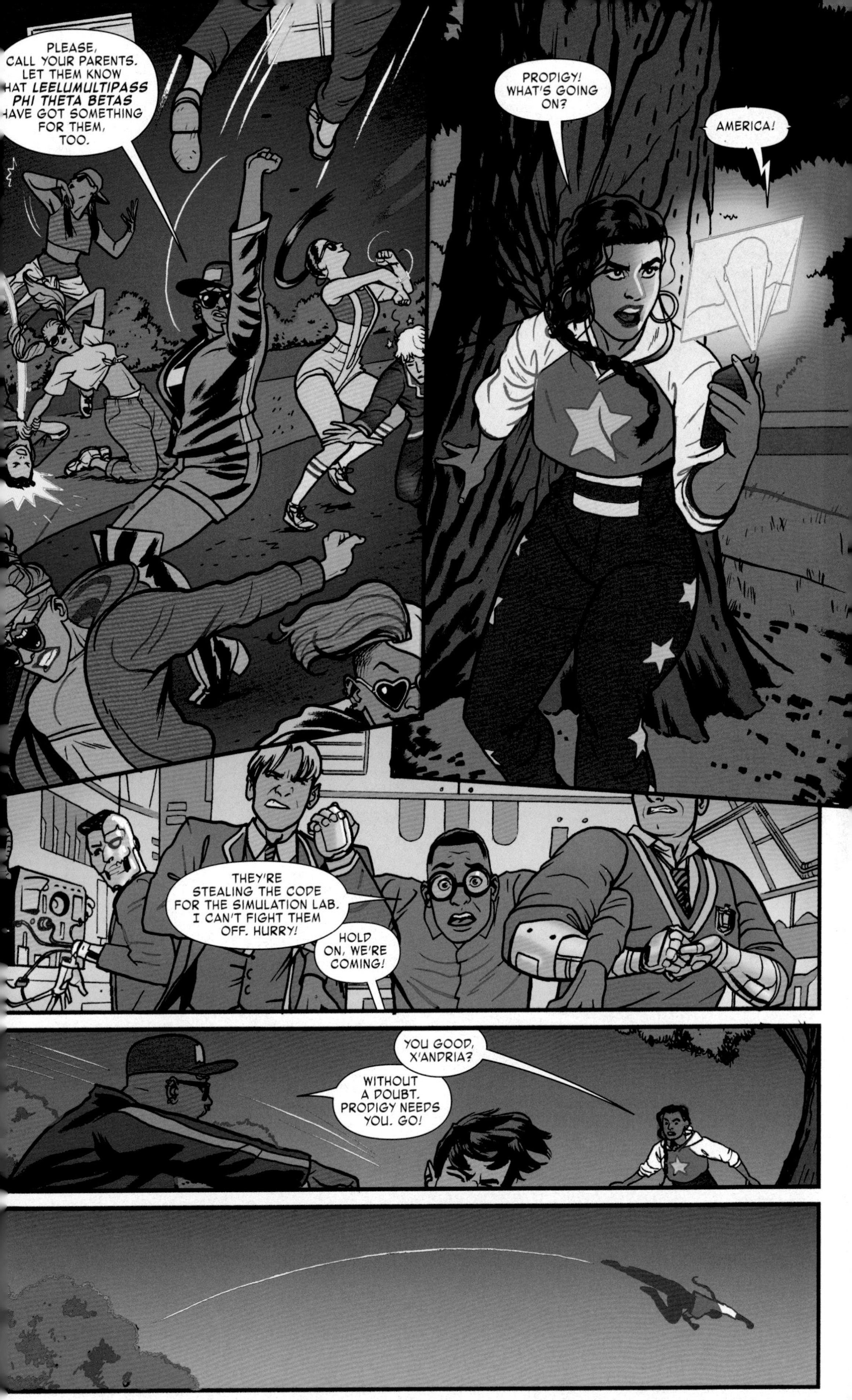
PLEASE, CALL YOUR PARENTS. LET THEM KNOW HAT LEELUMULTIPASS PHI THETA BETAS HAVE GOT SOMETHING FOR THEM, TOO.
PRODIGY! WHAT'S GOING ON?
AMERICA!
THEY'RE STEALING THE CODE FOR THE SIMULATION LAB. I CAN'T FIGHT THEM OFF. HURRY!
HOLD ON, WE'RE COMING!
YOU GOOD, X'ANDRIA?
WITHOUT A DOUBT. PRODIGY NEEDS YOU. GO!

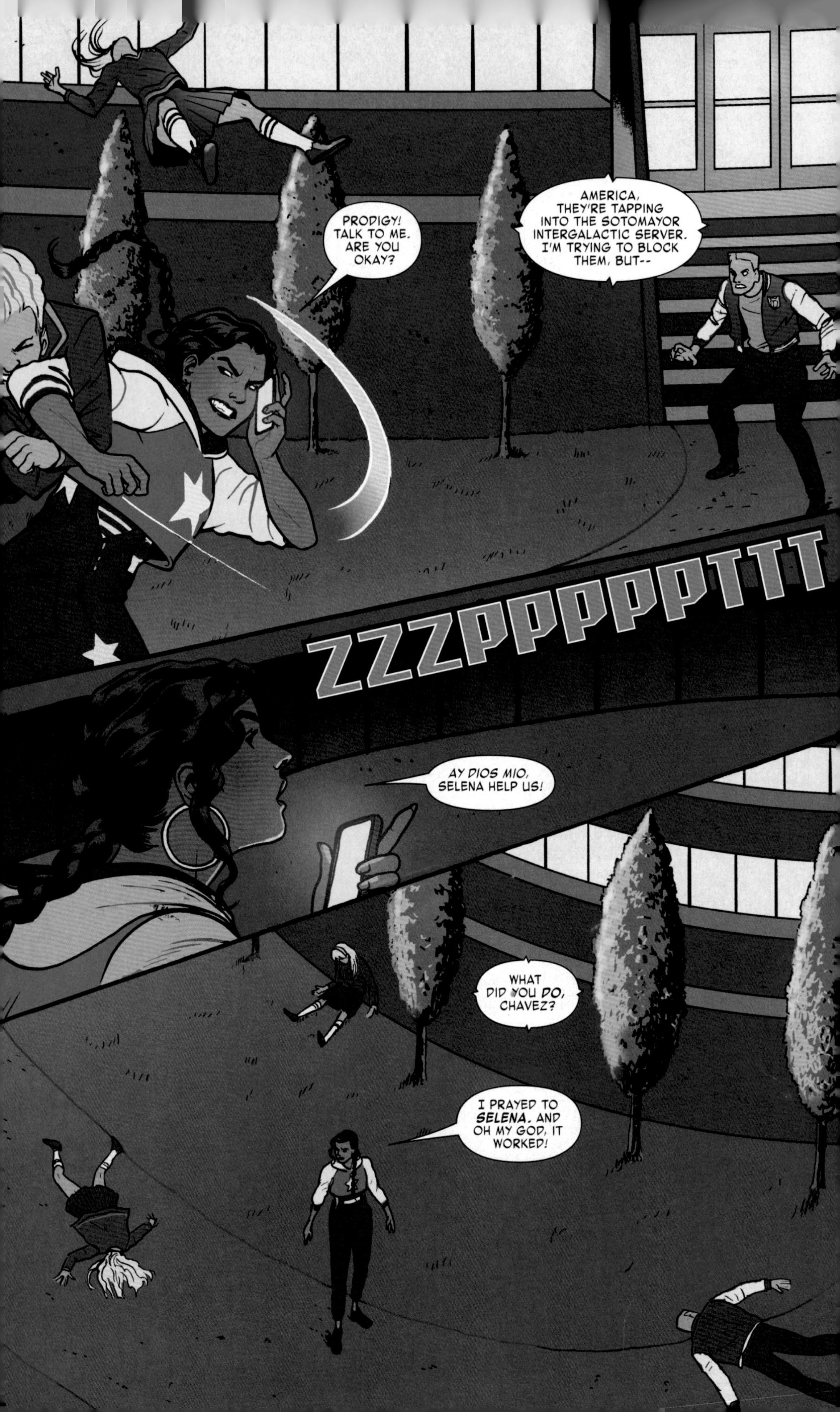
PRODIGY! TALK TO ME. ARE YOU OKAY?
AMERICA, THEY'RE TAPPING INTO THE SOTOMAYOR INTERGALACTIC SERVER. I'M TRYING TO BLOCK THEM, BUT--
ZZZPPPPPTTT
AY DIOS MIO, SELENA HELP US!
WHAT DID YOU DO, CHAVEZ?
I PRAYED TO SELENA. AND OH MY GOD, IT WORKED!

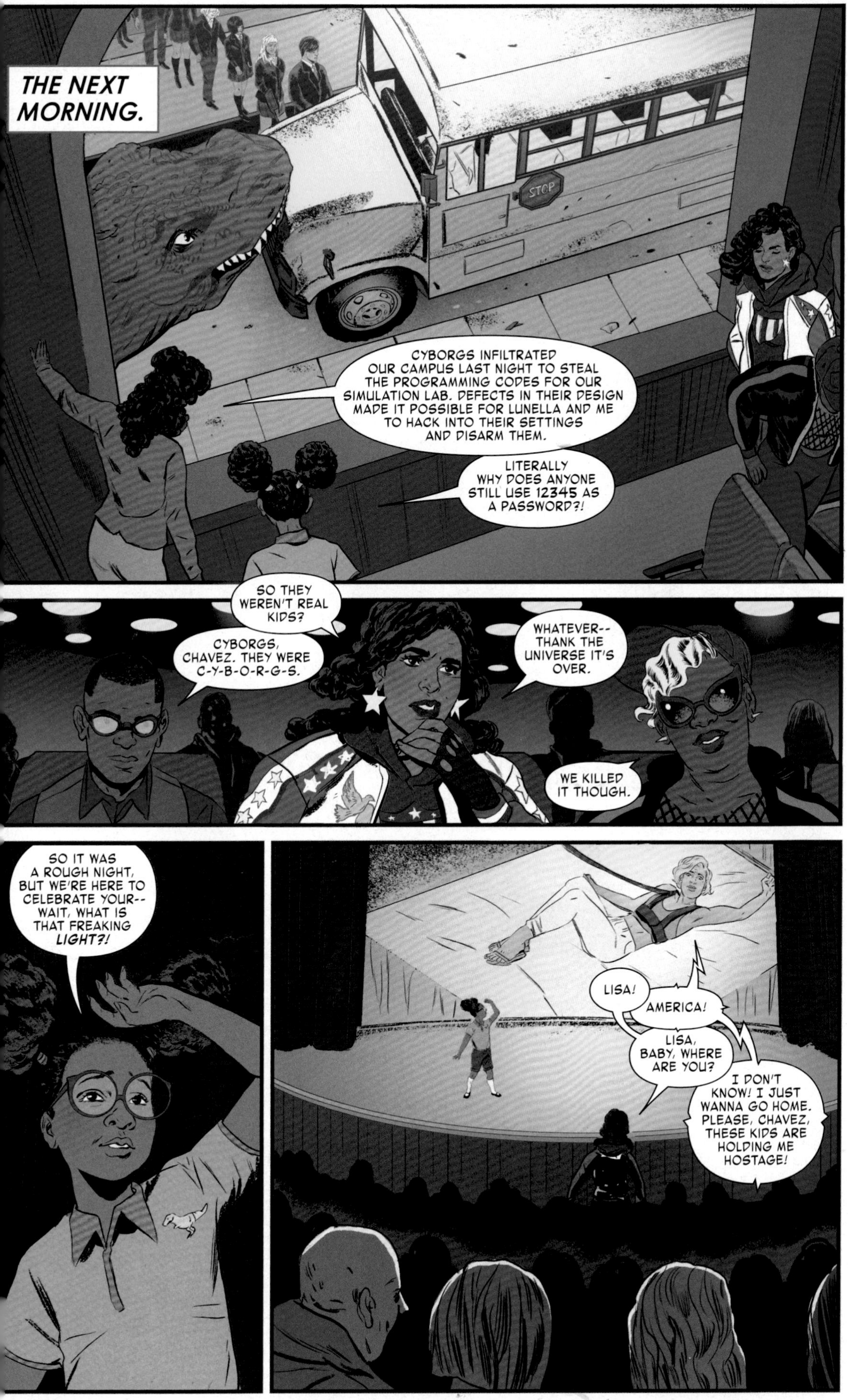
THE NEXT MORNING.
CYBORGS INFILTRATED OUR CAMPUS LAST NIGHT TO STEAL THE PROGRAMMING CODES FOR OUR SIMULATION LAB. DEFECTS IN THEIR DESIGN MADE IT POSSIBLE FOR LUNELLA AND ME TO HACK INTO THEIR SETTINGS AND DISARM THEM.
LITERALLY WHY DOES ANYONE STILL USE 12345 AS A PASSWORD?!
SO THEY WEREN'T REAL KIDS?
CYBORGS, CHAVEZ. THEY WERE C-Y-B-O-R-G-S.
WHATEVER-- THANK THE UNIVERSE IT'S OVER.
WE KILLED IT THOUGH.
SO IT WAS A ROUGH NIGHT, BUT WE'RE HERE TO CELEBRATE YOUR-- WAIT, WHAT IS THAT FREAKING *LIGHT?!*
LISA!
AMERICA!
LISA, BABY, WHERE ARE YOU?
I DON'T KNOW! I JUST WANNA GO HOME. PLEASE, CHAVEZ, THESE KIDS ARE HOLDING ME HOSTAGE!
STOP

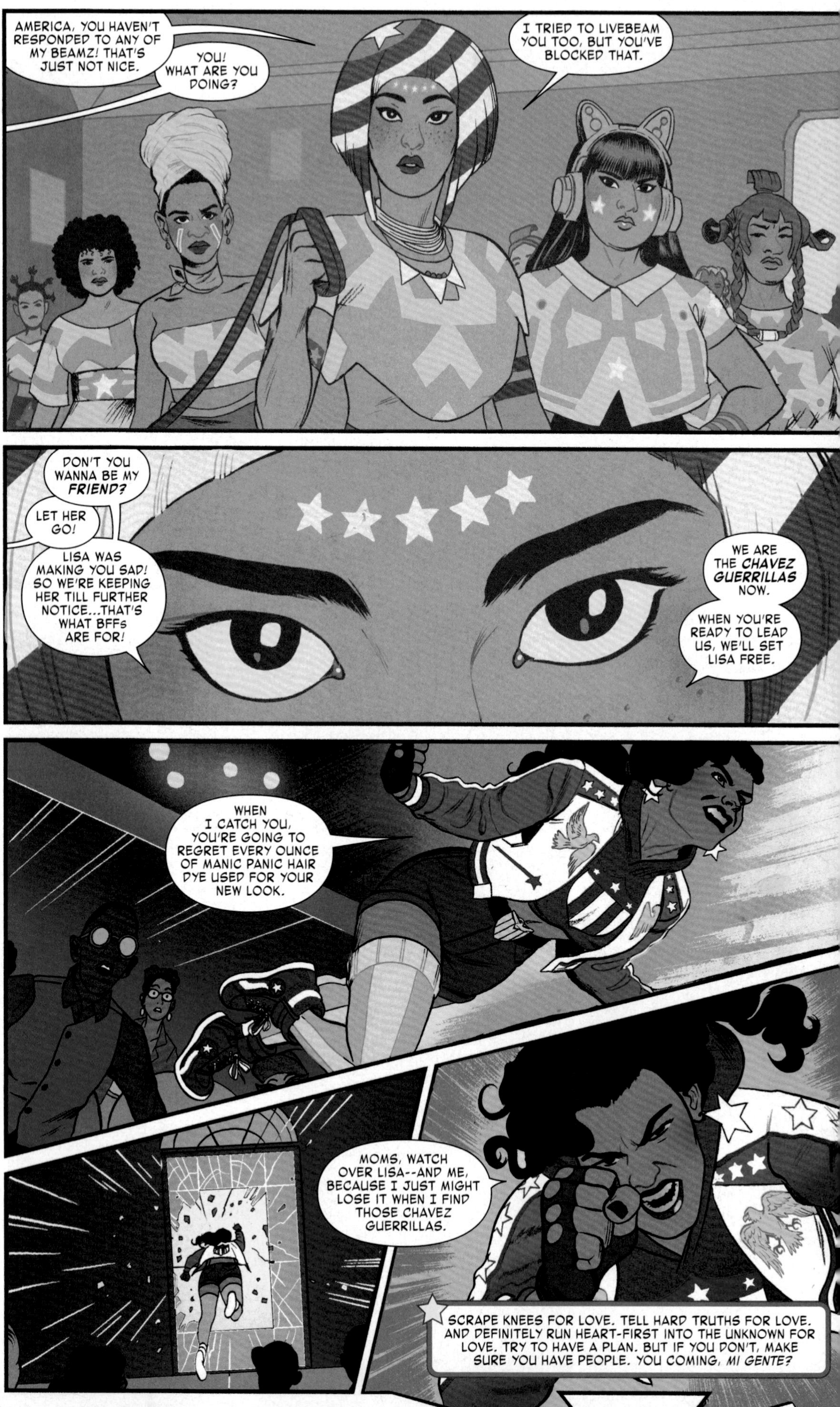
AMERICA, YOU HAVEN'T RESPONDED TO ANY OF MY BEAMZ! THAT'S JUST NOT NICE.
YOU! WHAT ARE YOU DOING?
I TRIED TO LIVEBEAM YOU TOO, BUT YOU'VE BLOCKED THAT.
DON'T YOU WANNA BE MY *FRIEND?*
LET HER GO!
LISA WAS MAKING YOU SAD! SO WE'RE KEEPING HER TILL FURTHER NOTICE...THAT'S WHAT BFFs ARE FOR!
WE ARE THE *CHAVEZ GUERRILLAS* NOW.
WHEN YOU'RE READY TO LEAD US, WE'LL SET LISA FREE.
WHEN I CATCH YOU, YOU'RE GOING TO REGRET EVERY OUNCE OF MANIC PANIC HAIR DYE USED FOR YOUR NEW LOOK.
MOMS, WATCH OVER LISA--AND ME, BECAUSE I JUST MIGHT LOSE IT WHEN I FIND THOSE CHAVEZ GUERRILLAS.
SCRAPE KNEES FOR LOVE. TELL HARD TRUTHS FOR LOVE. AND DEFINITELY RUN HEART-FIRST INTO THE UNKNOWN FOR LOVE. TRY TO HAVE A PLAN. BUT IF YOU DON'T, MAKE SURE YOU HAVE PEOPLE. YOU COMING, *MI GENTE?*

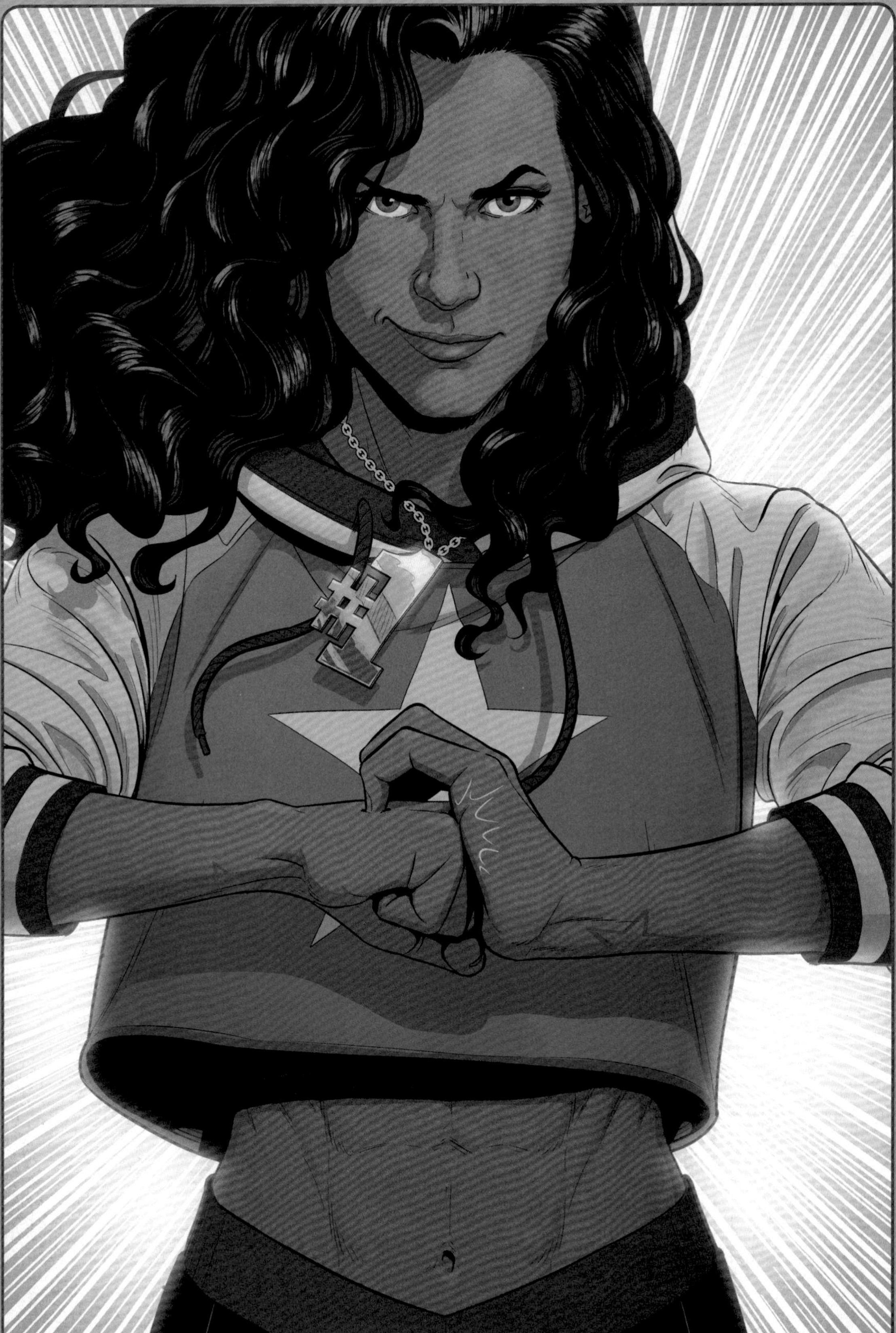

JAMIE McKELVIE & MATTHEW WILSON
#1 VARIANT

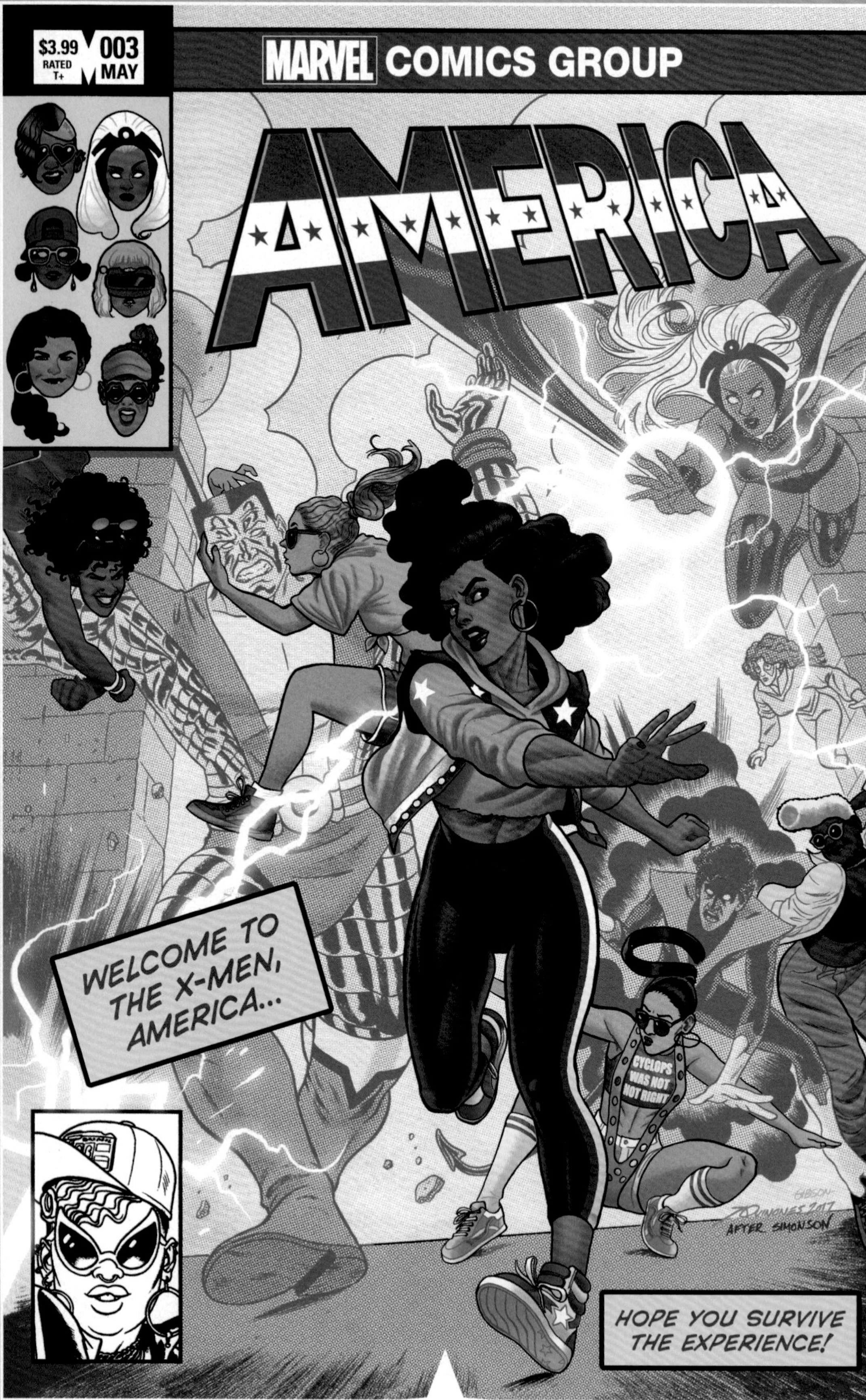

$3.99
RATED T+
003
MAY
MARVEL COMICS GROUP
AMERICA
WELCOME TO THE X-MEN, AMERICA...
CYCLOPS WAS NOT NOT RIGHT
GIBSON
JQUINONES 2017
AFTER SIMONSON
HOPE YOU SURVIVE THE EXPERIENCE!

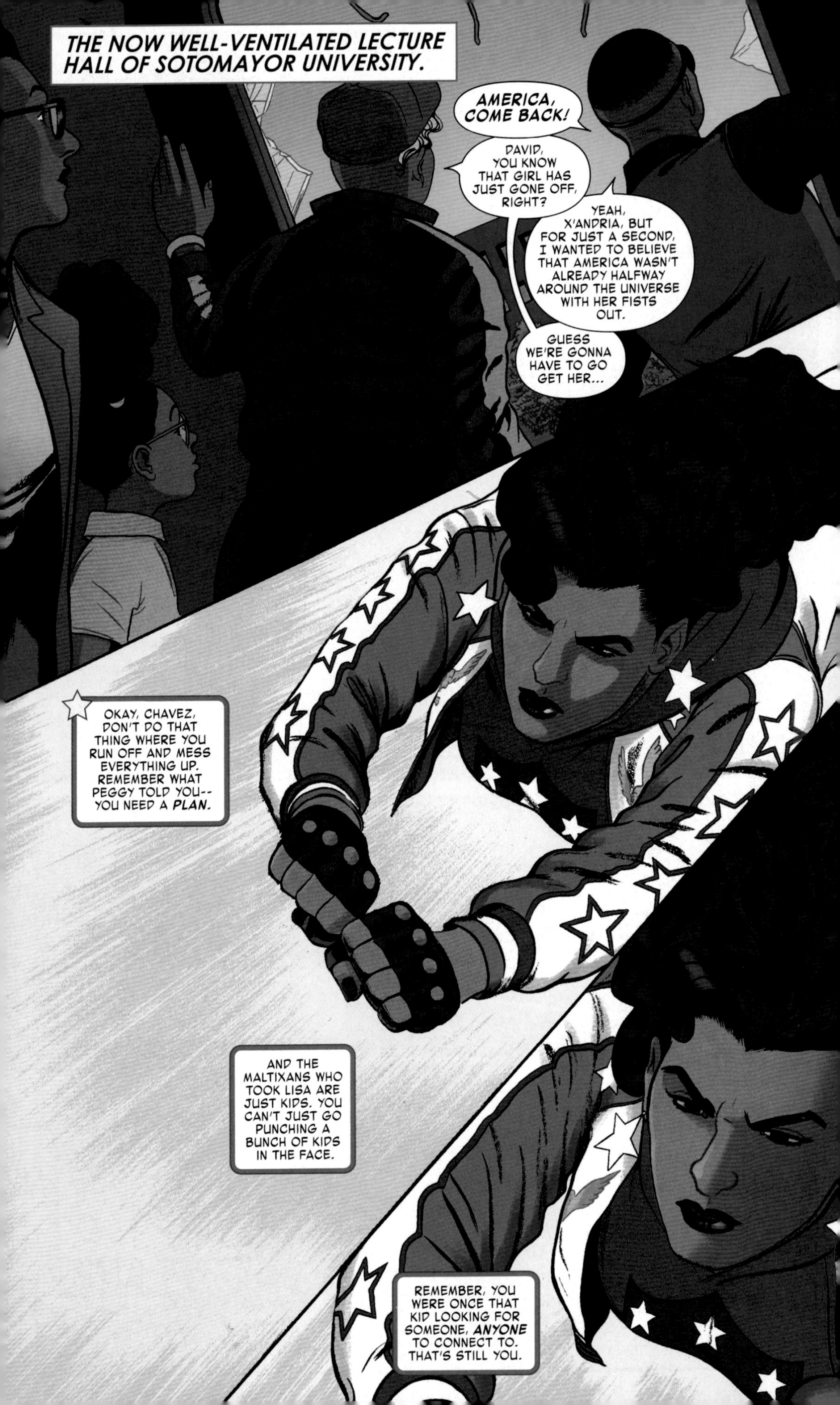
THE NOW WELL-VENTILATED LECTURE HALL OF SOTOMAYOR UNIVERSITY.
AMERICA, COME BACK!
DAVID, YOU KNOW THAT GIRL HAS JUST GONE OFF, RIGHT?
YEAH, X'ANDRIA, BUT FOR JUST A SECOND, I WANTED TO BELIEVE THAT AMERICA WASN'T ALREADY HALFWAY AROUND THE UNIVERSE WITH HER FISTS OUT.
GUESS WE'RE GONNA HAVE TO GO GET HER...
OKAY, CHAVEZ, DON'T DO THAT THING WHERE YOU RUN OFF AND MESS EVERYTHING UP. REMEMBER WHAT PEGGY TOLD YOU-- YOU NEED A PLAN.
AND THE MALTIXANS WHO TOOK LISA ARE JUST KIDS. YOU CAN'T JUST GO PUNCHING A BUNCH OF KIDS IN THE FACE.
REMEMBER, YOU WERE ONCE THAT KID LOOKING FOR SOMEONE, ANYONE TO CONNECT TO. THAT'S STILL YOU.

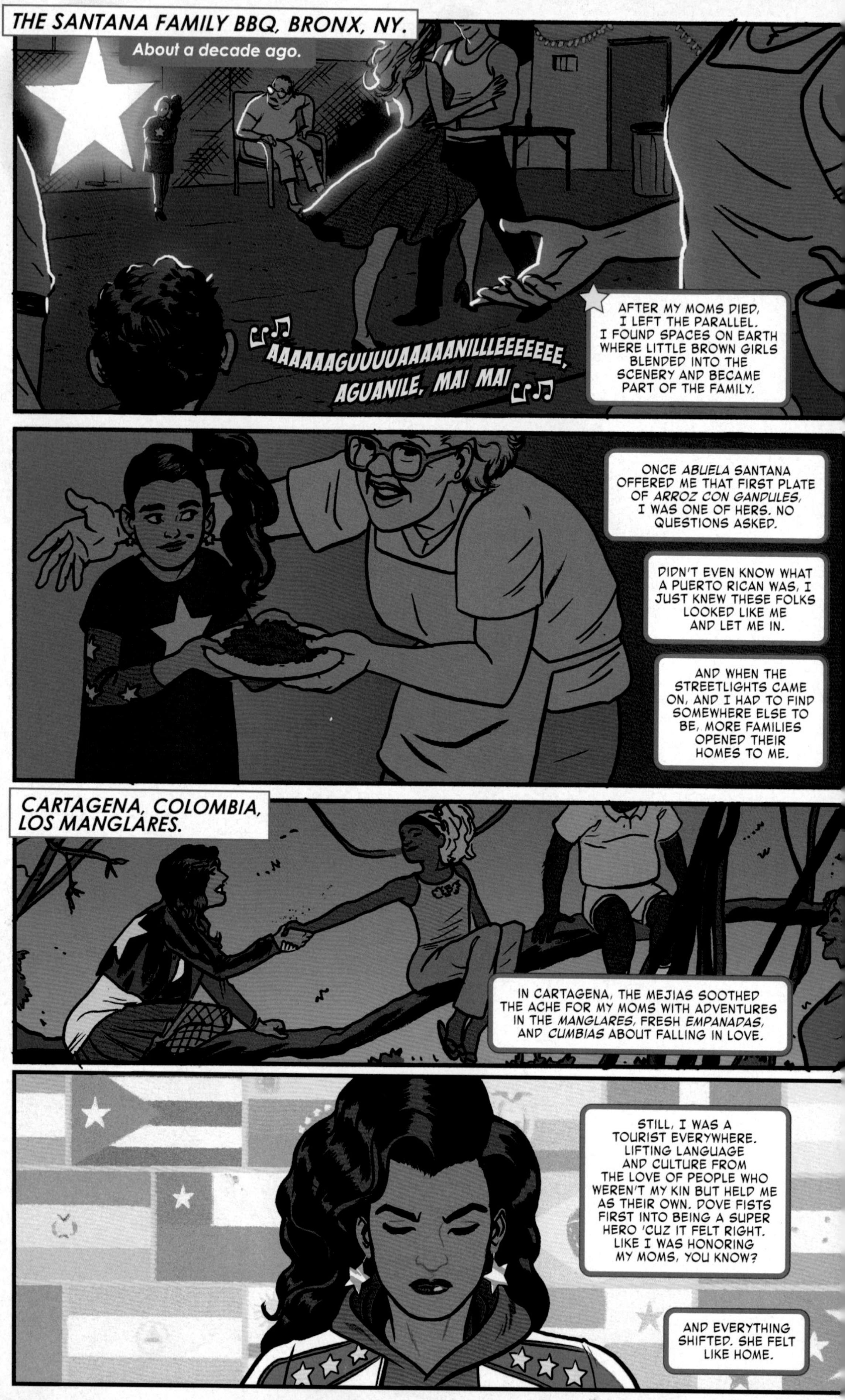
THE SANTANA FAMILY BBQ, BRONX, NY.
About a decade ago.
AAAAAAGUUUUAAAAANILLLEEEEEEE, AGUANILE, MAI MAI
AFTER MY MOMS DIED, I LEFT THE PARALLEL. I FOUND SPACES ON EARTH WHERE LITTLE BROWN GIRLS BLENDED INTO THE SCENERY AND BECAME PART OF THE FAMILY.
ONCE ABUELA SANTANA OFFERED ME THAT FIRST PLATE OF ARROZ CON GANDULES, I WAS ONE OF HERS. NO QUESTIONS ASKED.
DIDN'T EVEN KNOW WHAT A PUERTO RICAN WAS, I JUST KNEW THESE FOLKS LOOKED LIKE ME AND LET ME IN.
AND WHEN THE STREETLIGHTS CAME ON, AND I HAD TO FIND SOMEWHERE ELSE TO BE, MORE FAMILIES OPENED THEIR HOMES TO ME.
CARTAGENA, COLOMBIA, LOS MANGLARES.
IN CARTAGENA, THE MEJIAS SOOTHED THE ACHE FOR MY MOMS WITH ADVENTURES IN THE MANGLARES, FRESH EMPANADAS, AND CUMBIAS ABOUT FALLING IN LOVE.
STILL, I WAS A TOURIST EVERYWHERE. LIFTING LANGUAGE AND CULTURE FROM THE LOVE OF PEOPLE WHO WEREN'T MY KIN BUT HELD ME AS THEIR OWN. DOVE FISTS FIRST INTO BEING A SUPER HERO 'CUZ IT FELT RIGHT. LIKE I WAS HONORING MY MOMS, YOU KNOW?
AND EVERYTHING SHIFTED. SHE FELT LIKE HOME.

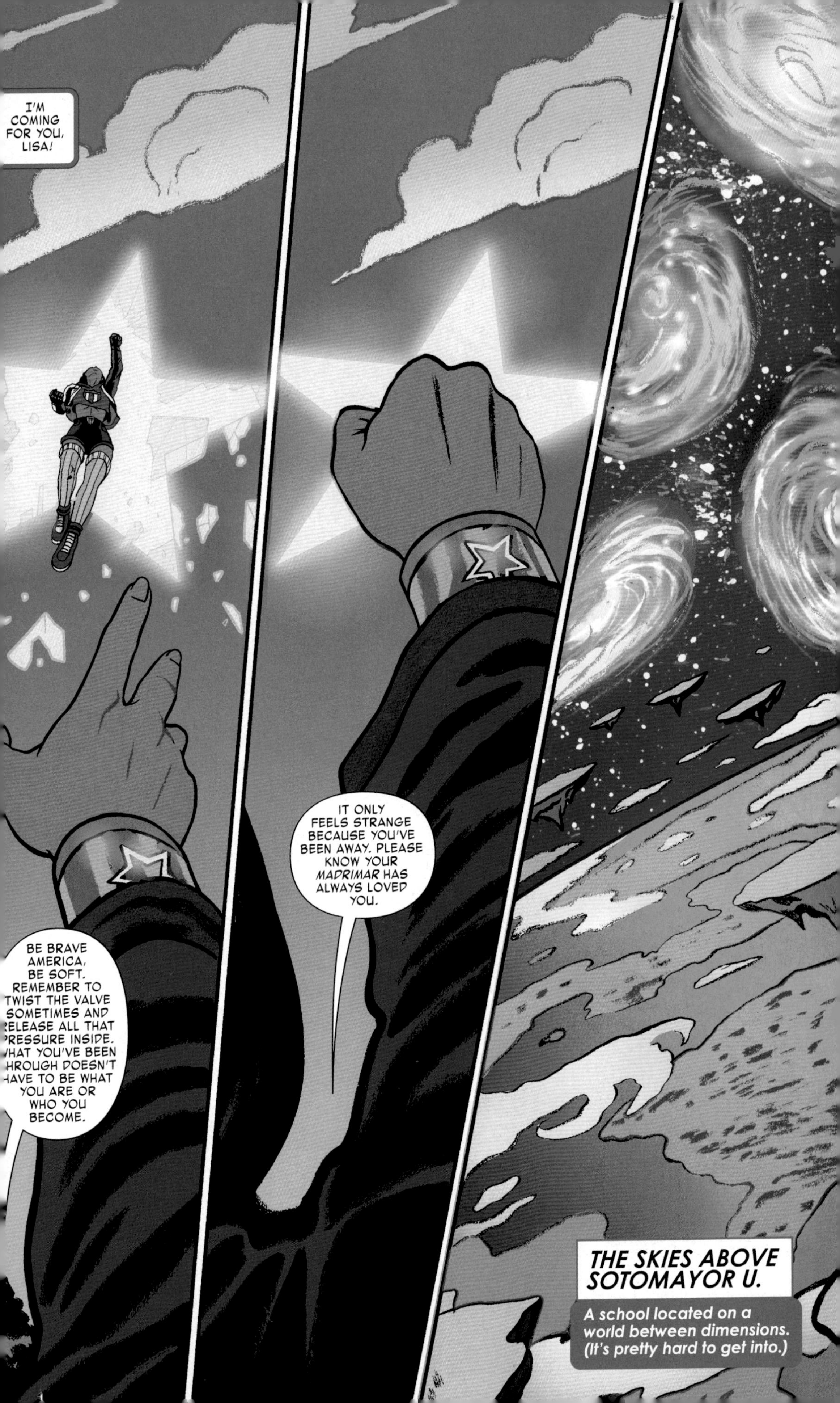

I'M COMING FOR YOU, LISA!
BE BRAVE AMERICA, BE SOFT. REMEMBER TO TWIST THE VALVE SOMETIMES AND RELEASE ALL THAT PRESSURE INSIDE. WHAT YOU'VE BEEN THROUGH DOESN'T HAVE TO BE WHAT YOU ARE OR WHO YOU BECOME.
IT ONLY FEELS STRANGE BECAUSE YOU'VE BEEN AWAY. PLEASE KNOW YOUR *MADRIMAR* HAS ALWAYS LOVED YOU.
THE SKIES ABOVE SOTOMAYOR U.
A school located on a world between dimensions. (It's pretty hard to get into.)

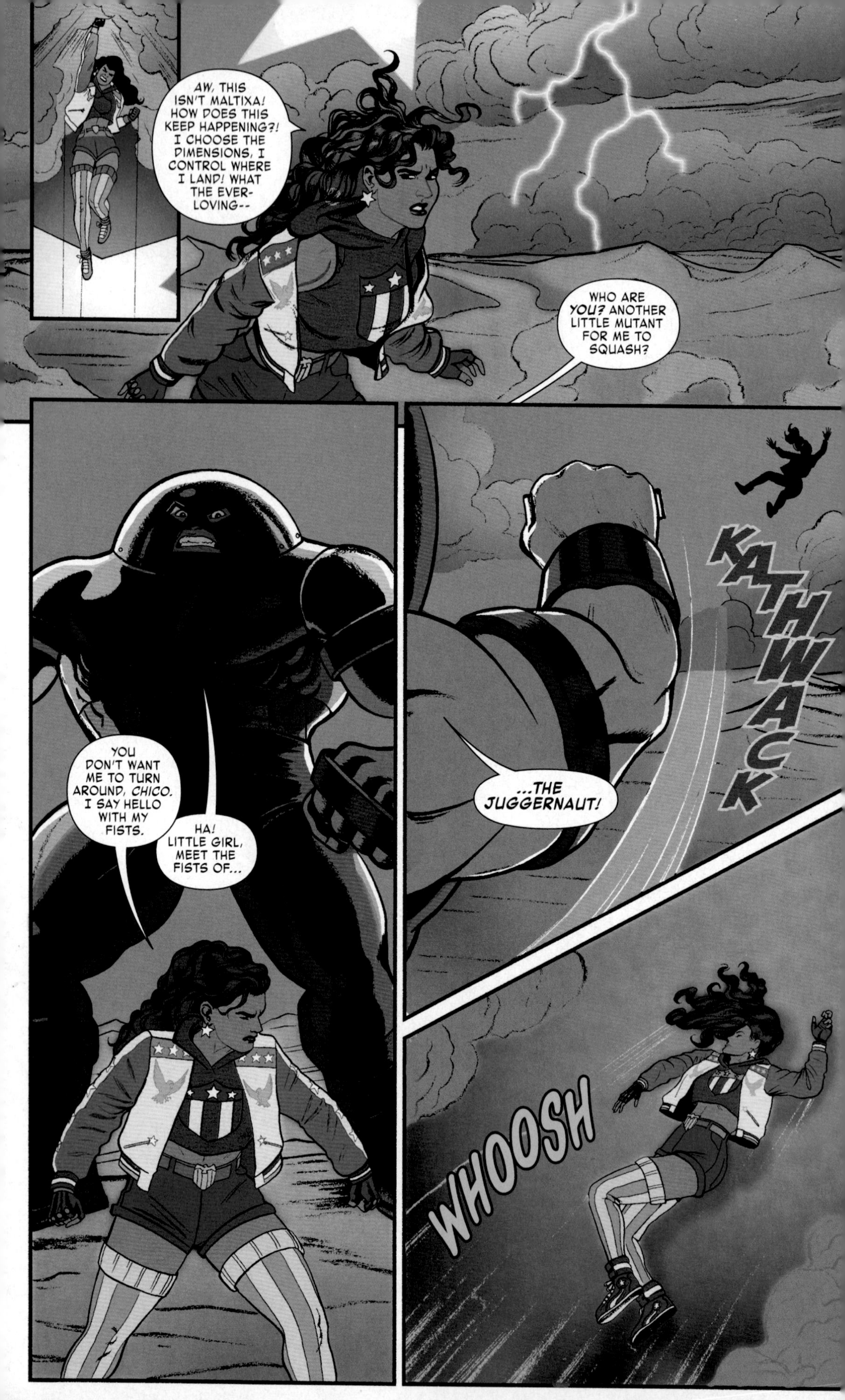
AW, THIS ISN'T MALTIXA! HOW DOES THIS KEEP HAPPENING?! I CHOOSE THE DIMENSIONS, I CONTROL WHERE I LAND! WHAT THE EVER-LOVING--
WHO ARE *YOU?* ANOTHER LITTLE MUTANT FOR ME TO SQUASH?
YOU DON'T WANT ME TO TURN AROUND, *CHICO.* I SAY HELLO WITH MY FISTS.
HA! LITTLE GIRL, MEET THE FISTS OF...
...THE JUGGERNAUT!
KATHWACK
WHOOSH

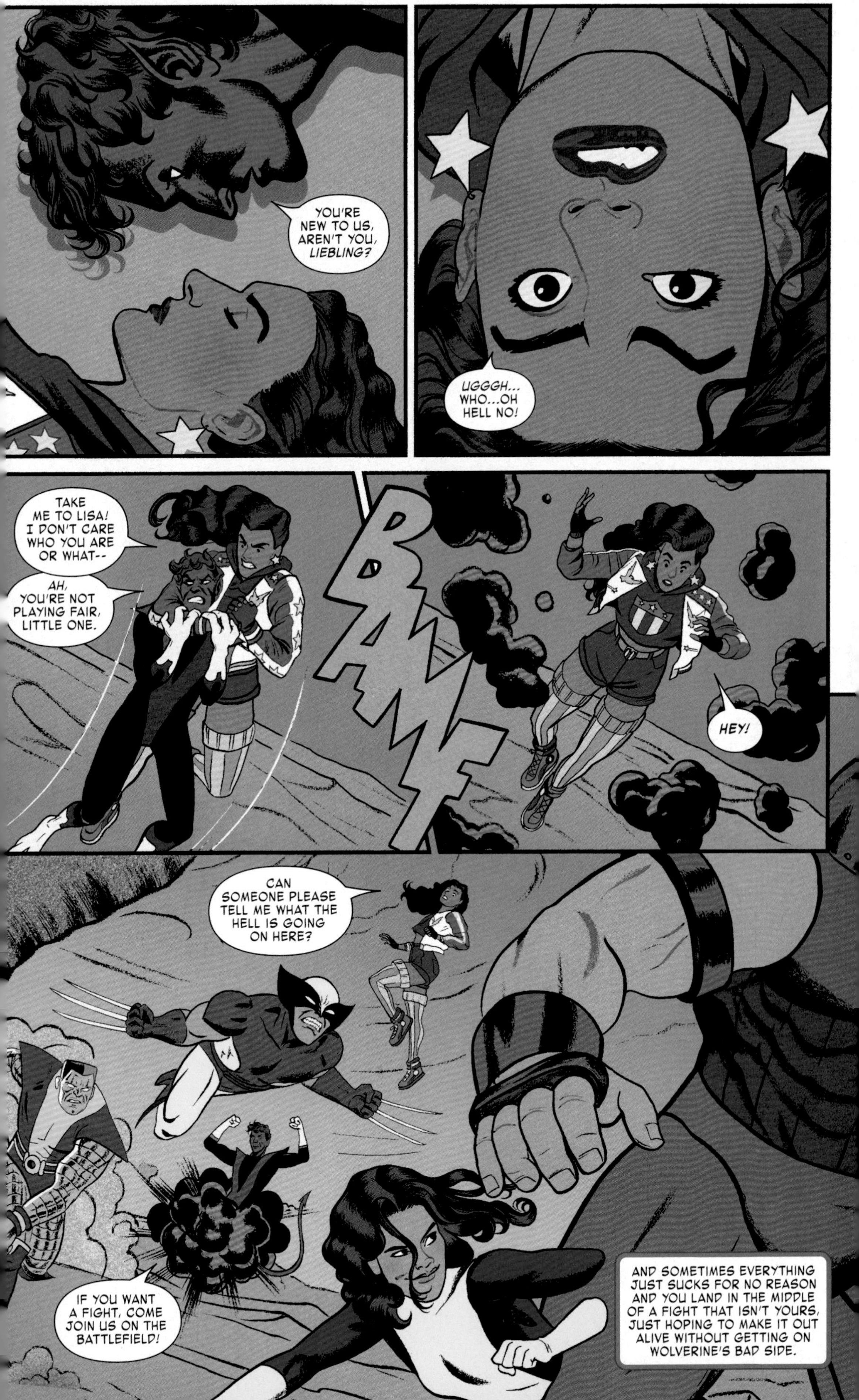
YOU'RE NEW TO US, AREN'T YOU, *LIEBLING*?
UGGGH... WHO...OH HELL NO!
TAKE ME TO LISA! I DON'T CARE WHO YOU ARE OR WHAT--
AH, YOU'RE NOT PLAYING FAIR, LITTLE ONE.
BAMF
HEY!
CAN SOMEONE PLEASE TELL ME WHAT THE HELL IS GOING ON HERE?
IF YOU WANT A FIGHT, COME JOIN US ON THE BATTLEFIELD!
AND SOMETIMES EVERYTHING JUST SUCKS FOR NO REASON AND YOU LAND IN THE MIDDLE OF A FIGHT THAT ISN'T YOURS, JUST HOPING TO MAKE IT OUT ALIVE WITHOUT GETTING ON WOLVERINE'S BAD SIDE.

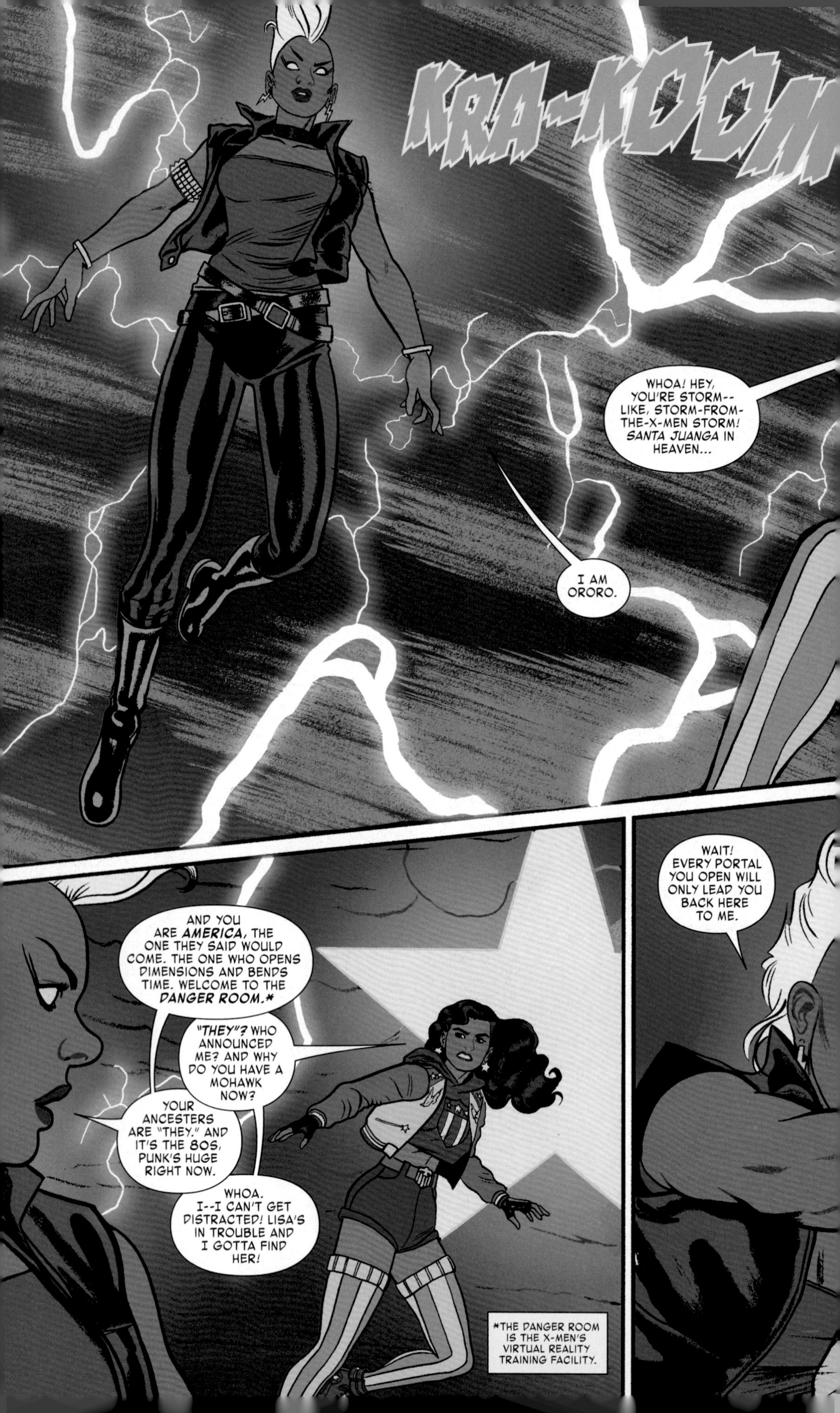
KRA-KOOM
WHOA! HEY, YOU'RE STORM-- LIKE, STORM-FROM-THE-X-MEN STORM! SANTA JUANGA IN HEAVEN...
I AM ORORO.
AND YOU ARE AMERICA, THE ONE THEY SAID WOULD COME. THE ONE WHO OPENS DIMENSIONS AND BENDS TIME. WELCOME TO THE DANGER ROOM.*
"THEY"? WHO ANNOUNCED ME? AND WHY DO YOU HAVE A MOHAWK NOW?
YOUR ANCESTERS ARE "THEY." AND IT'S THE 80S, PUNK'S HUGE RIGHT NOW.
WHOA. I--I CAN'T GET DISTRACTED! LISA'S IN TROUBLE AND I GOTTA FIND HER!
*THE DANGER ROOM IS THE X-MEN'S VIRTUAL REALITY TRAINING FACILITY.
WAIT! EVERY PORTAL YOU OPEN WILL ONLY LEAD YOU BACK HERE TO ME.

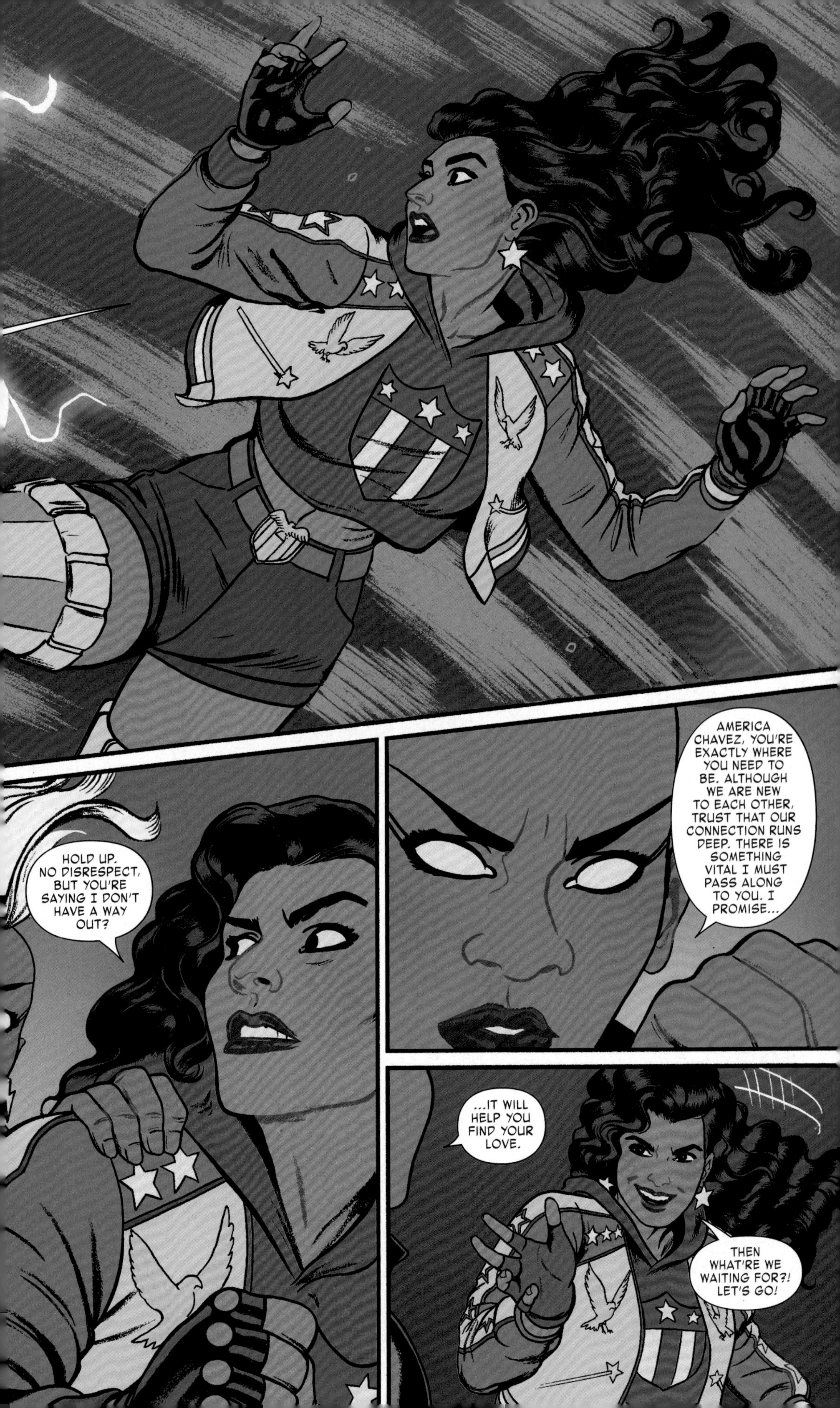
HOLD UP. NO DISRESPECT, BUT YOU'RE SAYING I DON'T HAVE A WAY OUT?
AMERICA CHAVEZ, YOU'RE EXACTLY WHERE YOU NEED TO BE. ALTHOUGH WE ARE NEW TO EACH OTHER, TRUST THAT OUR CONNECTION RUNS DEEP. THERE IS SOMETHING VITAL I MUST PASS ALONG TO YOU. I PROMISE...
...IT WILL HELP YOU FIND YOUR LOVE.
THEN WHAT'RE WE WAITING FOR?! LET'S GO!

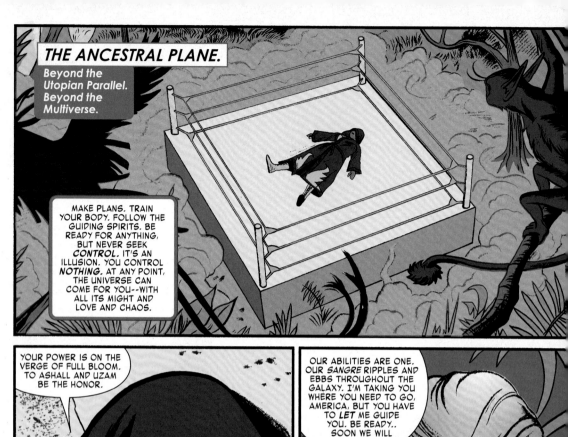

THE ANCESTRAL PLANE.

Beyond the Utopian Parallel. Beyond the Multiverse.

MAKE PLANS. TRAIN YOUR BODY. FOLLOW THE GUIDING SPIRITS. BE READY FOR ANYTHING, BUT NEVER SEEK *CONTROL.* IT'S AN ILLUSION. YOU CONTROL *NOTHING.* AT ANY POINT, THE UNIVERSE CAN COME FOR YOU--WITH ALL ITS MIGHT AND LOVE AND CHAOS.

YOUR POWER IS ON THE VERGE OF FULL BLOOM. TO ASHALL AND UZAM BE THE HONOR.

OUR ABILITIES ARE ONE. OUR *SANGRE* RIPPLES AND EBBS THROUGHOUT THE GALAXY. I'M TAKING YOU WHERE YOU NEED TO GO, AMERICA, BUT YOU HAVE TO *LET* ME GUIDE YOU. BE READY.. SOON WE WILL COLLIDE.

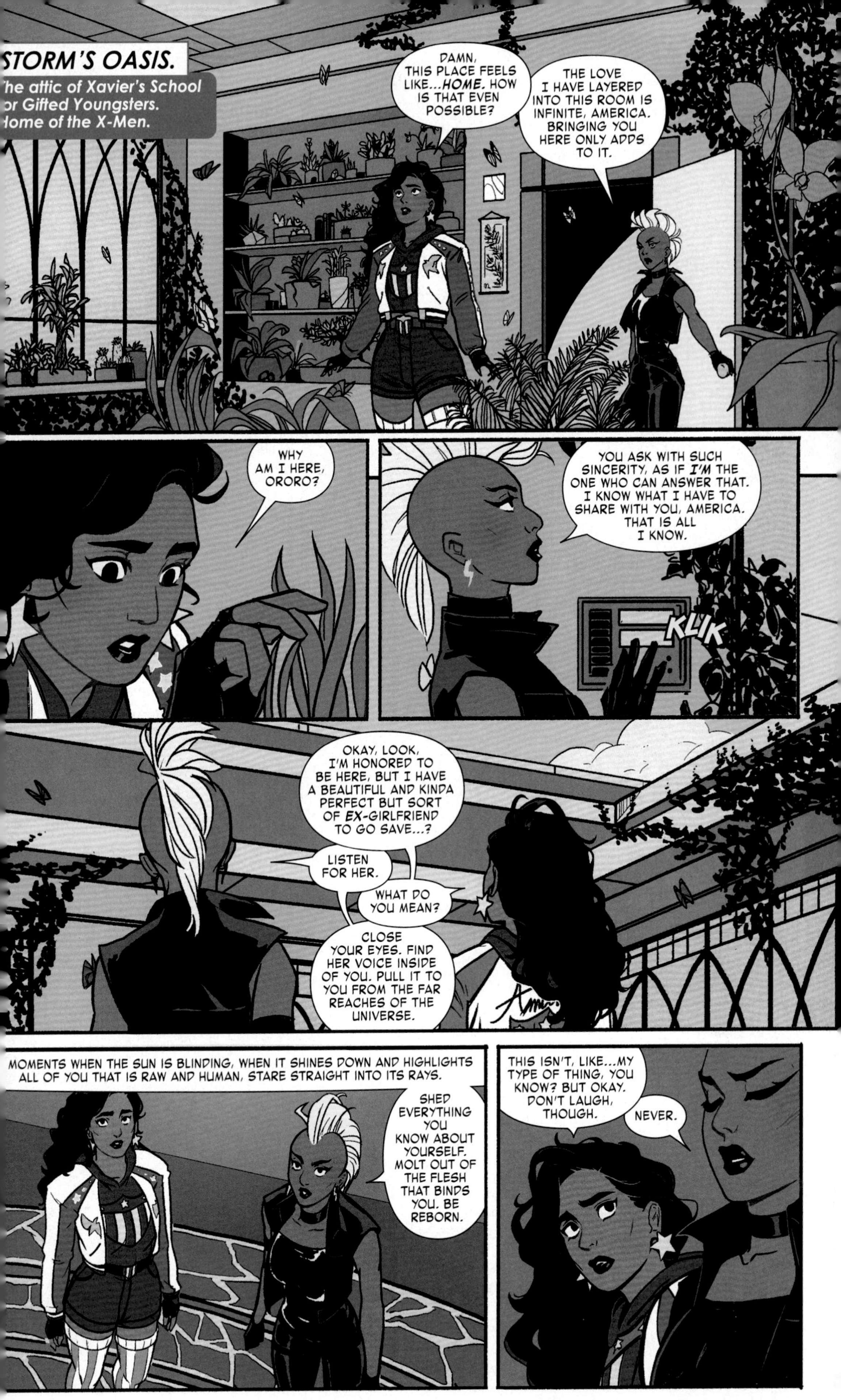

STORM'S OASIS.
The attic of Xavier's School for Gifted Youngsters. Home of the X-Men.
DAMN, THIS PLACE FEELS LIKE...HOME. HOW IS THAT EVEN POSSIBLE?
THE LOVE I HAVE LAYERED INTO THIS ROOM IS INFINITE, AMERICA. BRINGING YOU HERE ONLY ADDS TO IT.
WHY AM I HERE, ORORO?
YOU ASK WITH SUCH SINCERITY, AS IF I'M THE ONE WHO CAN ANSWER THAT. I KNOW WHAT I HAVE TO SHARE WITH YOU, AMERICA. THAT IS ALL I KNOW.
KLIK
OKAY, LOOK, I'M HONORED TO BE HERE, BUT I HAVE A BEAUTIFUL AND KINDA PERFECT BUT SORT OF EX-GIRLFRIEND TO GO SAVE...?
LISTEN FOR HER.
WHAT DO YOU MEAN?
CLOSE YOUR EYES. FIND HER VOICE INSIDE OF YOU. PULL IT TO YOU FROM THE FAR REACHES OF THE UNIVERSE.
MOMENTS WHEN THE SUN IS BLINDING, WHEN IT SHINES DOWN AND HIGHLIGHTS ALL OF YOU THAT IS RAW AND HUMAN, STARE STRAIGHT INTO ITS RAYS.
SHED EVERYTHING YOU KNOW ABOUT YOURSELF. MOLT OUT OF THE FLESH THAT BINDS YOU. BE REBORN.
THIS ISN'T, LIKE...MY TYPE OF THING, YOU KNOW? BUT OKAY. DON'T LAUGH, THOUGH.
NEVER.

LISA. THINK ABOUT LISA. FIND HER VOICE. ENGAGE WITH YOUR FEELINGS. WHAT DOES YOUR HEART SAY?

I CAN'T DO THIS.

MY POWERS DON'T WORK LIKE THIS! I DON'T DO TOUCHY-FEELY "HEAR YOUR INNER VOICE" STUFF, OKAY?!

HAVE YOU EVER CONSIDERED THAT YOUR POWERS MAY EXTEND BEYOND PORTALS AND PUNCHING? THAT YOU MAY BE CONNECTED TO THE MULTIVERSE IN WAYS YOU'VE NEVER IMAGINED, WAYS THAT NO PERSON OR ENTITY HAS EVER BEFORE?

I...I GUESS I'VE BEEN AFRAID. IN MY DREAMS, I'M A HYPERNOVA.

BUT WHEN I WAKE UP, I'M SOME FADED NEON SIGN BLINKING ON AN OFF. AND I HAVEN' FIGURED OUT THE WAY TO GET THERE TO BE THAT MEGA BLAST OF ENERGY YOU KNOW?

THERE'S NO SHAME IN BEING AFRAID. HARNESS THE FEAR. LET IT PROPEL YOU FORWARD. THIS ACT OF LISTENING FOR LISA WILL BRING YOU TO HER AND TO THE ANCESTORS YOU SEEK.

I HAVE ANCESTORS? LIKE FOR REAL?

DIVE INTO THE ENORMITY OF YOUR POWER, AMERICA. NOW'S THE TIME.

I CAN'T SIT STILL LIKE THIS, AMIDST BUTTERFLIES AND HAPPY SUNSHINE, AND CONCENTRATE. LOOK, THERE'S ONLY ONE WAY TO DO THIS--

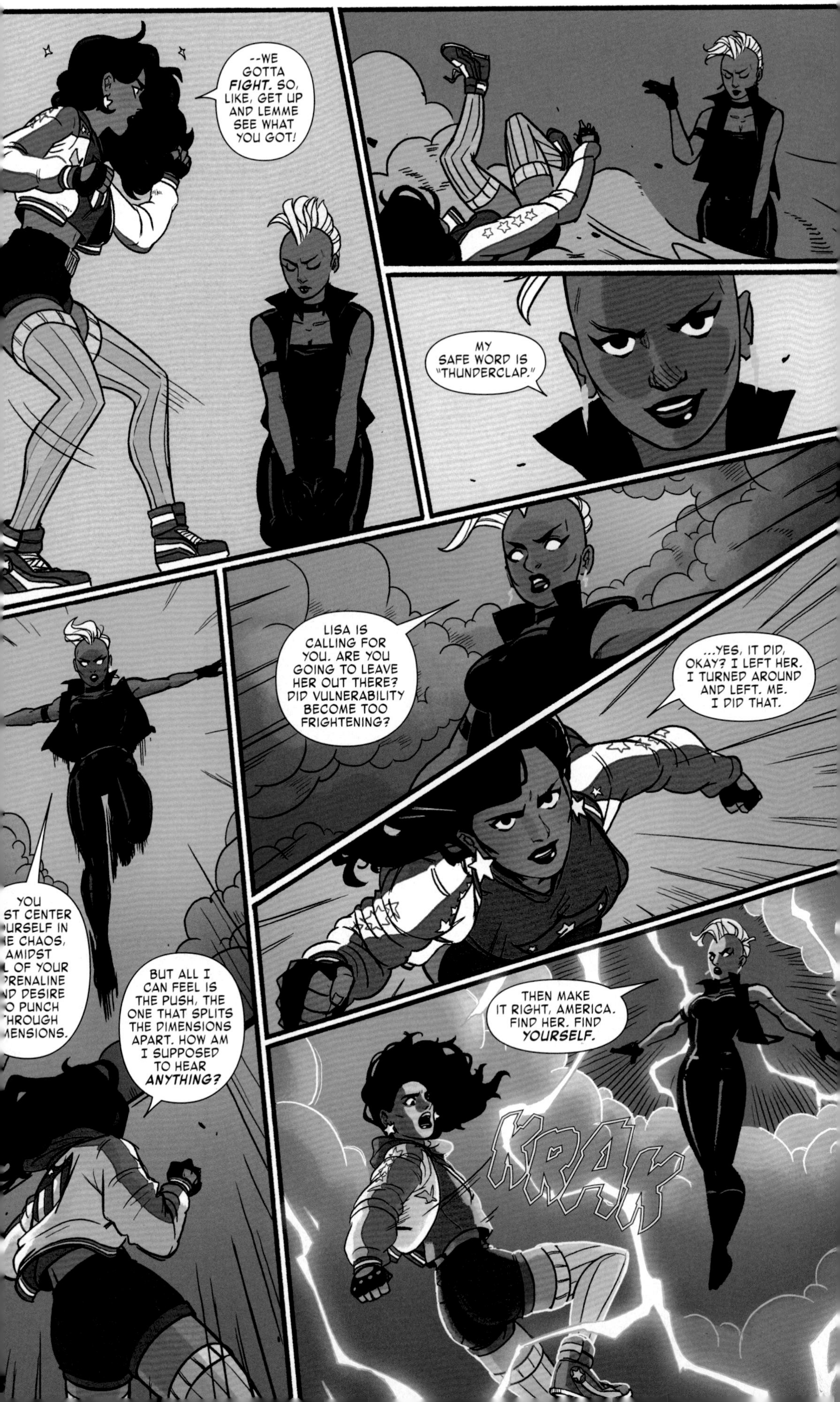
--WE GOTTA *FIGHT.* SO, LIKE, GET UP AND LEMME SEE WHAT YOU GOT!
MY SAFE WORD IS "THUNDERCLAP."
LISA IS CALLING FOR YOU. ARE YOU GOING TO LEAVE HER OUT THERE? DID VULNERABILITY BECOME TOO FRIGHTENING?
...YES, IT DID, OKAY? I LEFT HER. I TURNED AROUND AND LEFT. ME. I DID THAT.
YOU ST CENTER URSELF IN E CHAOS, AMIDST L OF YOUR RENALINE ND DESIRE O PUNCH THROUGH MENSIONS.
BUT ALL I CAN FEEL IS THE PUSH, THE ONE THAT SPLITS THE DIMENSIONS APART. HOW AM I SUPPOSED TO HEAR *ANYTHING?*
THEN MAKE IT RIGHT, AMERICA. FIND HER. FIND *YOURSELF.*
KRAK

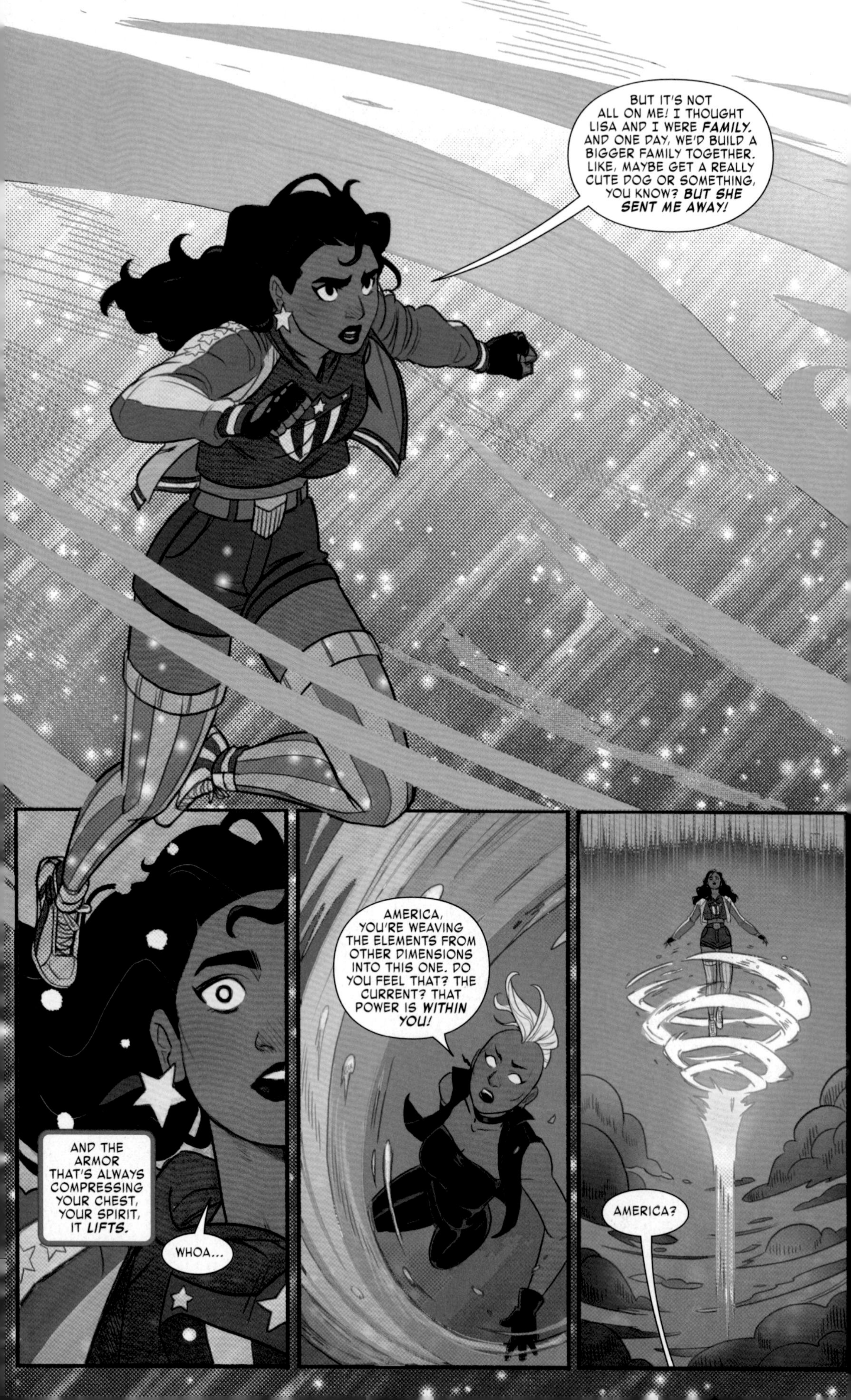
BUT IT'S NOT ALL ON ME! I THOUGHT LISA AND I WERE FAMILY. AND ONE DAY, WE'D BUILD A BIGGER FAMILY TOGETHER. LIKE, MAYBE GET A REALLY CUTE DOG OR SOMETHING, YOU KNOW? BUT SHE SENT ME AWAY!
AND THE ARMOR THAT'S ALWAYS COMPRESSING YOUR CHEST, YOUR SPIRIT, IT LIFTS.
WHOA...
AMERICA, YOU'RE WEAVING THE ELEMENTS FROM OTHER DIMENSIONS INTO THIS ONE. DO YOU FEEL THAT? THE CURRENT? THAT POWER IS WITHIN YOU!
AMERICA?

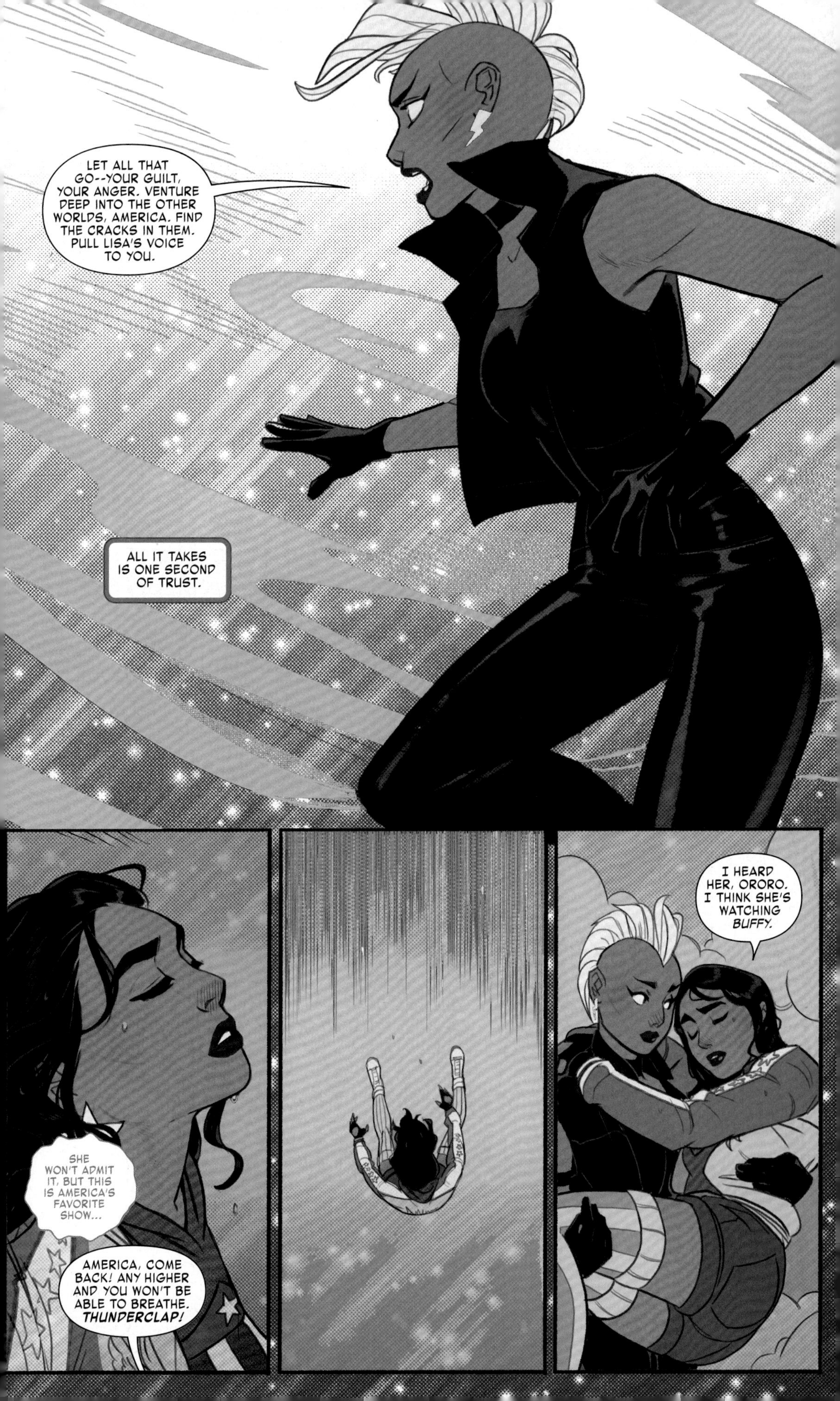
LET ALL THAT GO--YOUR GUILT, YOUR ANGER. VENTURE DEEP INTO THE OTHER WORLDS, AMERICA. FIND THE CRACKS IN THEM. PULL LISA'S VOICE TO YOU.
ALL IT TAKES IS ONE SECOND OF TRUST.
SHE WON'T ADMIT IT, BUT THIS IS AMERICA'S FAVORITE SHOW...
AMERICA, COME BACK! ANY HIGHER AND YOU WON'T BE ABLE TO BREATHE. *THUNDERCLAP!*
I HEARD HER, ORORO. I THINK SHE'S WATCHING *BUFFY.*

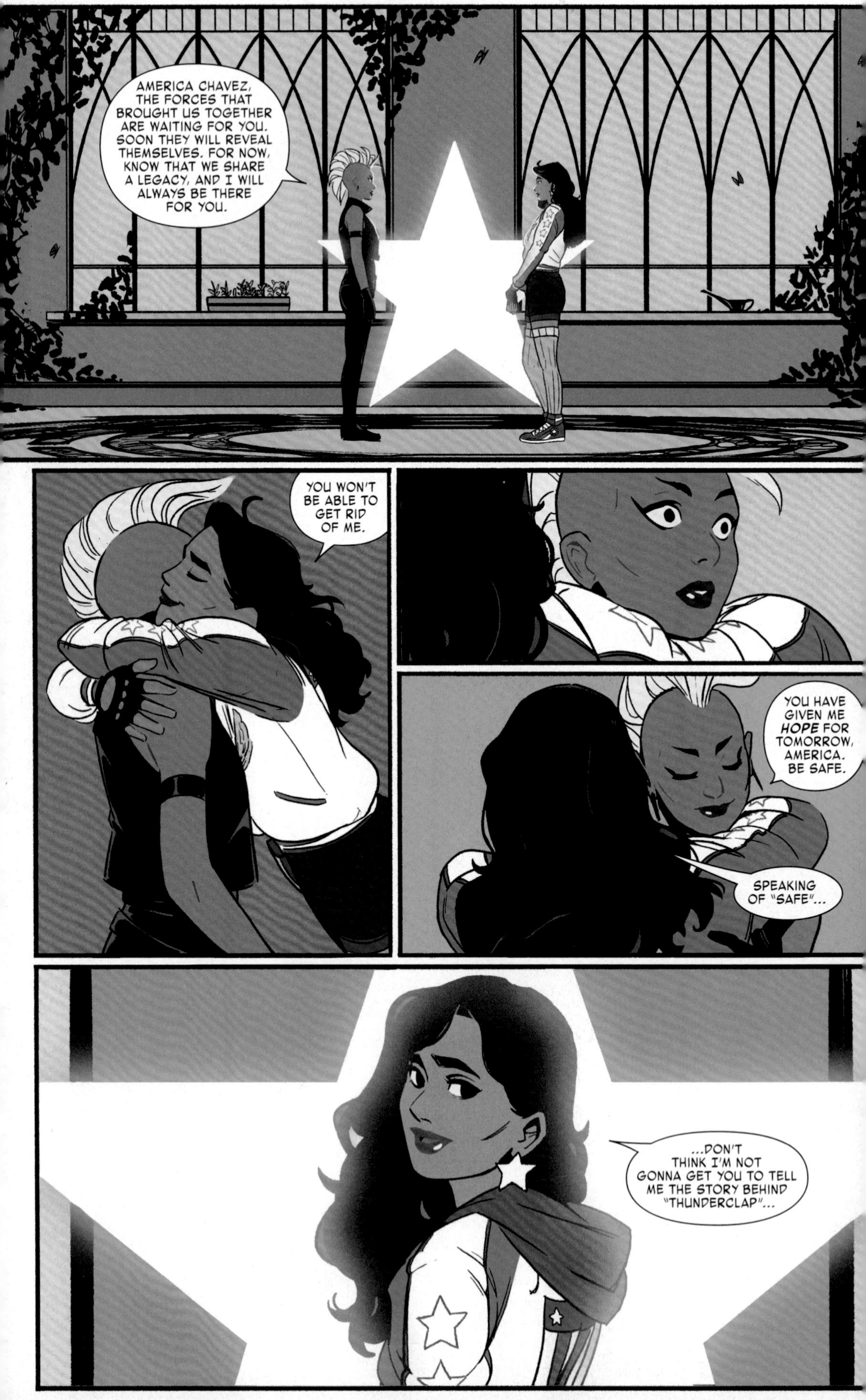

AMERICA CHAVEZ, THE FORCES THAT BROUGHT US TOGETHER ARE WAITING FOR YOU. SOON THEY WILL REVEAL THEMSELVES. FOR NOW, KNOW THAT WE SHARE A LEGACY, AND I WILL ALWAYS BE THERE FOR YOU.
YOU WON'T BE ABLE TO GET RID OF ME.
YOU HAVE GIVEN ME HOPE FOR TOMORROW, AMERICA. BE SAFE.
SPEAKING OF "SAFE"...
...DON'T THINK I'M NOT GONNA GET YOU TO TELL ME THE STORY BEHIND "THUNDERCLAP"...

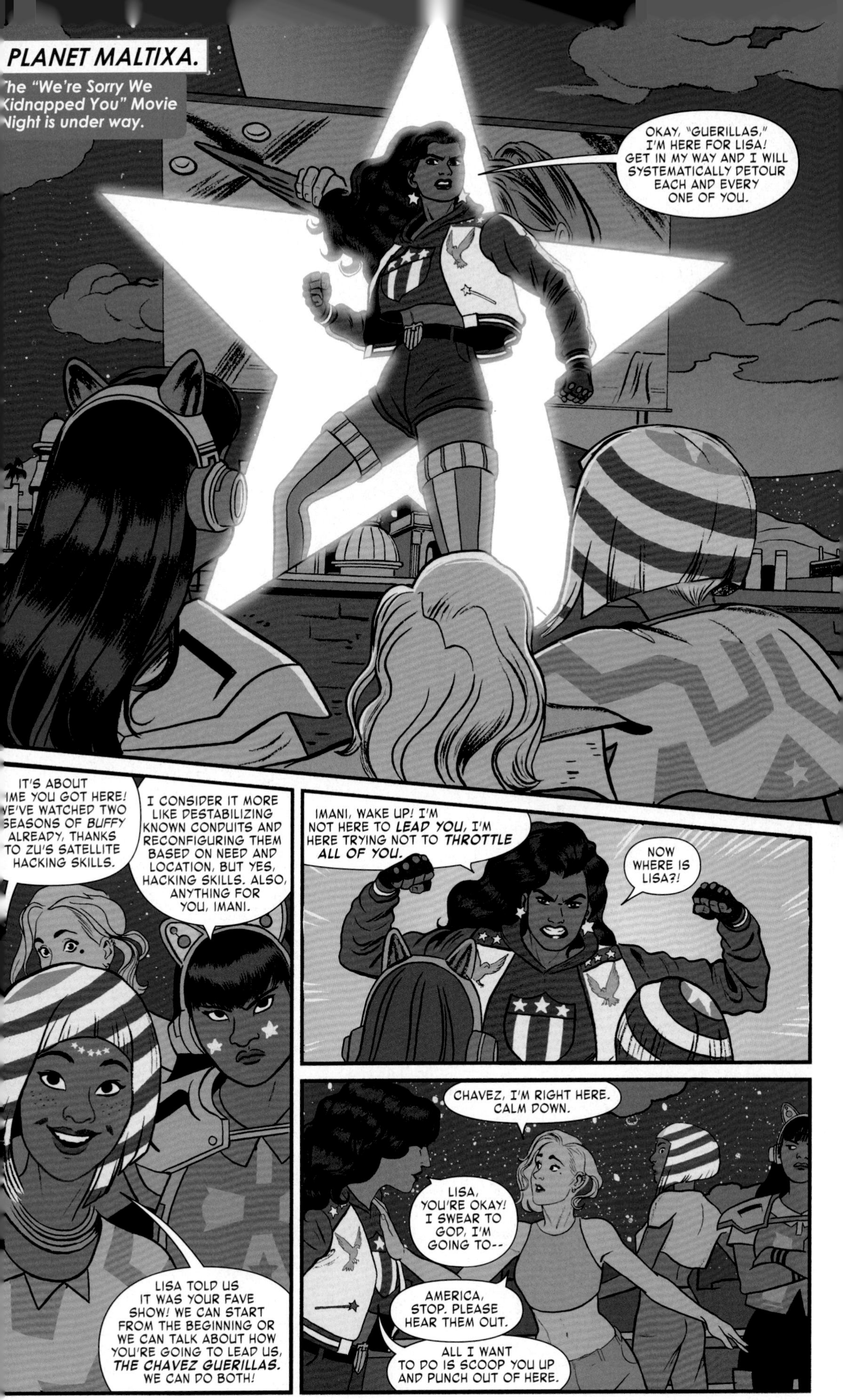
PLANET MALTIXA.
he "We're Sorry We
idnapped You" Movie
Night is under way.
OKAY, "GUERILLAS," I'M HERE FOR LISA! GET IN MY WAY AND I WILL SYSTEMATICALLY DETOUR EACH AND EVERY ONE OF YOU.
IT'S ABOUT IME YOU GOT HERE! E'VE WATCHED TWO SEASONS OF BUFFY ALREADY, THANKS TO ZU'S SATELLITE HACKING SKILLS.
I CONSIDER IT MORE LIKE DESTABILIZING KNOWN CONDUITS AND RECONFIGURING THEM BASED ON NEED AND LOCATION, BUT YES, HACKING SKILLS. ALSO, ANYTHING FOR YOU, IMANI.
LISA TOLD US IT WAS YOUR FAVE SHOW! WE CAN START FROM THE BEGINNING OR WE CAN TALK ABOUT HOW YOU'RE GOING TO LEAD US, THE CHAVEZ GUERILLAS. WE CAN DO BOTH!
IMANI, WAKE UP! I'M NOT HERE TO LEAD YOU, I'M HERE TRYING NOT TO THROTTLE ALL OF YOU.
NOW WHERE IS LISA?!
CHAVEZ, I'M RIGHT HERE. CALM DOWN.
LISA, YOU'RE OKAY! I SWEAR TO GOD, I'M GOING TO--
AMERICA, STOP. PLEASE HEAR THEM OUT.
ALL I WANT TO DO IS SCOOP YOU UP AND PUNCH OUT OF HERE.

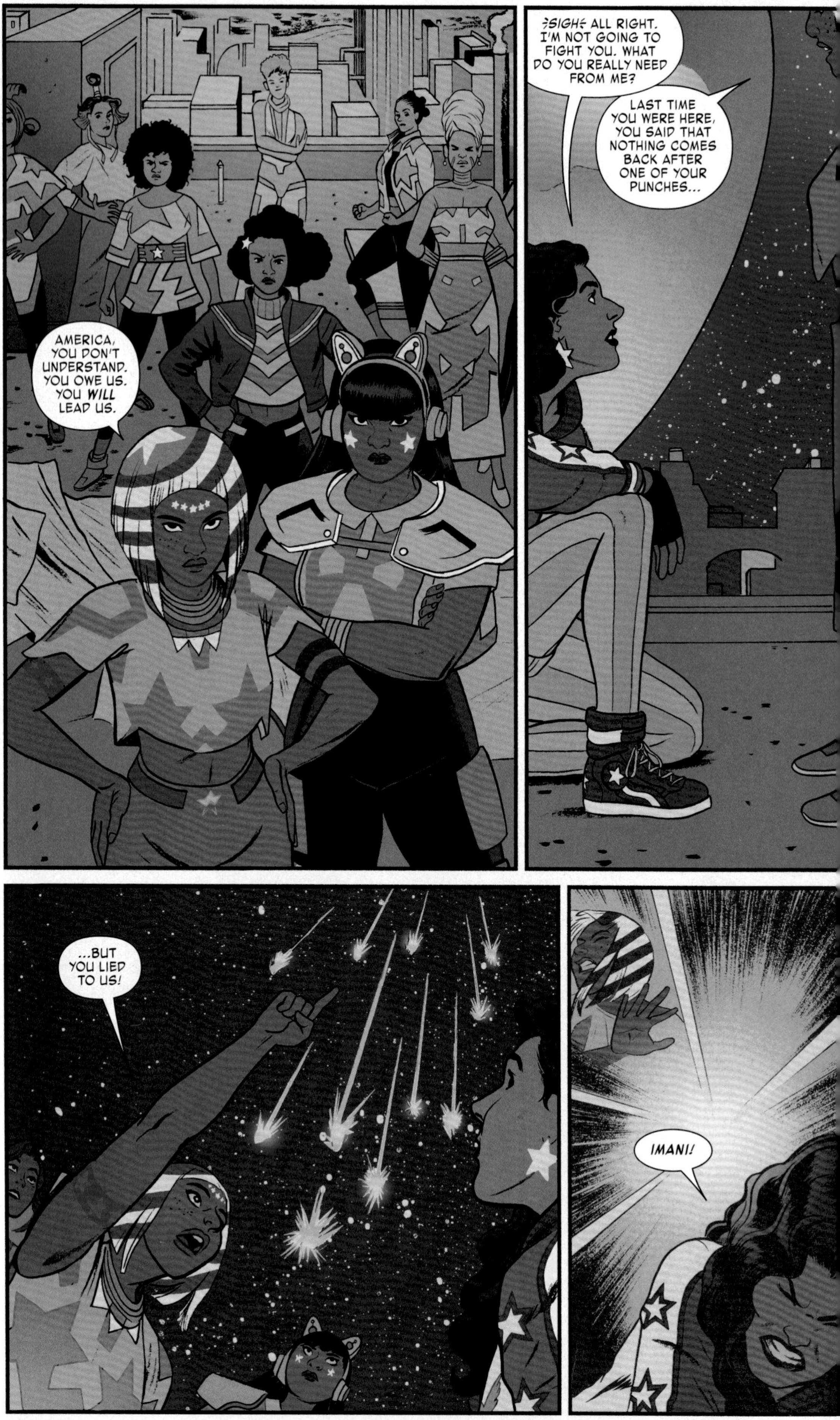

AMERICA, YOU DON'T UNDERSTAND. YOU OWE US. YOU *WILL* LEAD US.
SIGH ALL RIGHT. I'M NOT GOING TO FIGHT YOU. WHAT DO YOU REALLY NEED FROM ME?
LAST TIME YOU WERE HERE, YOU SAID THAT NOTHING COMES BACK AFTER ONE OF YOUR PUNCHES...
...BUT YOU LIED TO US!
IMANI!

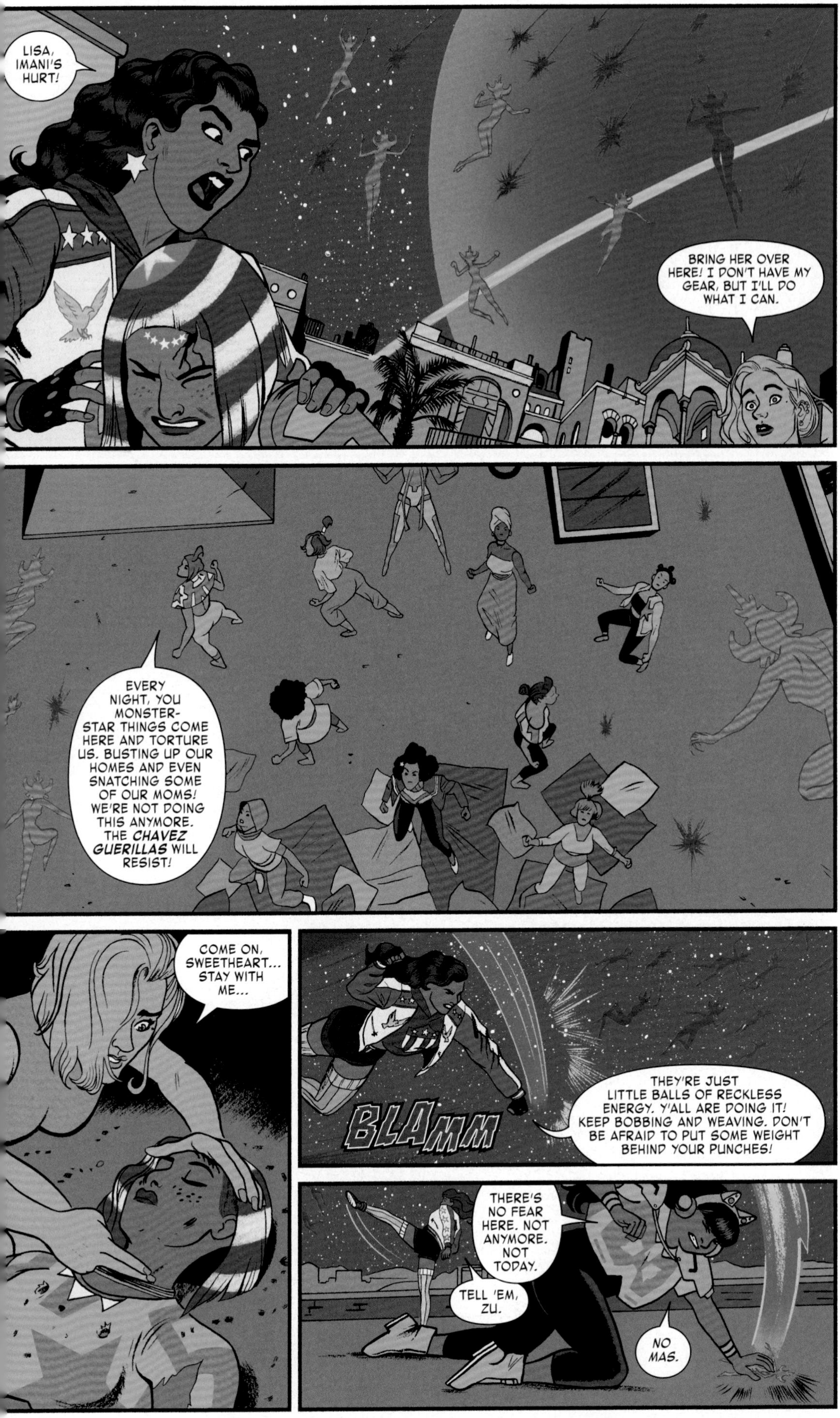
LISA, IMANI'S HURT!
BRING HER OVER HERE! I DON'T HAVE MY GEAR, BUT I'LL DO WHAT I CAN.
EVERY NIGHT, YOU MONSTER-STAR THINGS COME HERE AND TORTURE US. BUSTING UP OUR HOMES AND EVEN SNATCHING SOME OF OUR MOMS! WE'RE NOT DOING THIS ANYMORE. THE CHAVEZ GUERILLAS WILL RESIST!
COME ON, SWEETHEART... STAY WITH ME...
BLAMM
THEY'RE JUST LITTLE BALLS OF RECKLESS ENERGY. Y'ALL ARE DOING IT! KEEP BOBBING AND WEAVING. DON'T BE AFRAID TO PUT SOME WEIGHT BEHIND YOUR PUNCHES!
THERE'S NO FEAR HERE. NOT ANYMORE. NOT TODAY.
TELL 'EM, ZU.
NO MAS.

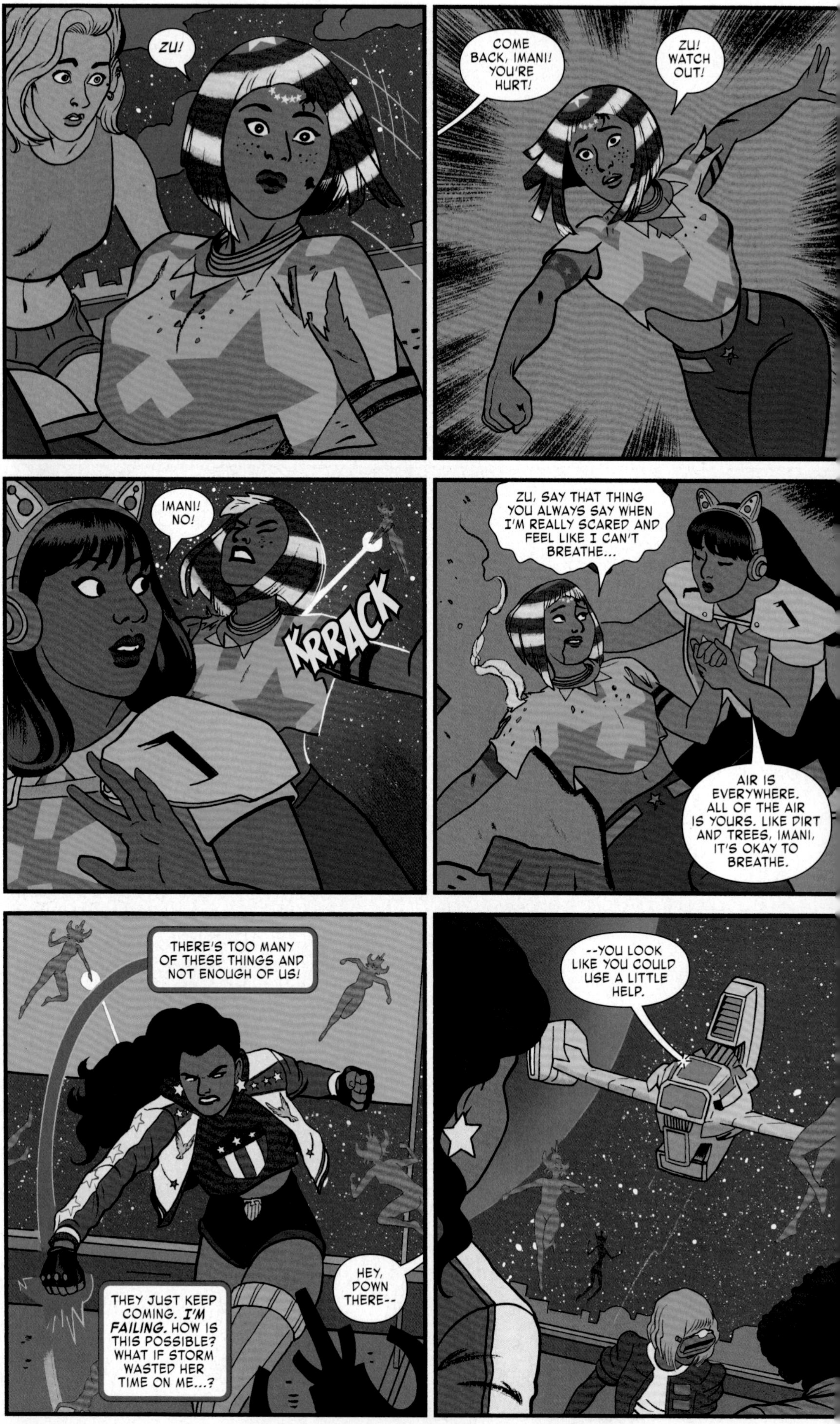
ZU!
COME BACK, IMANI! YOU'RE HURT!
ZU! WATCH OUT!
IMANI! NO!
KRRACK
ZU, SAY THAT THING YOU ALWAYS SAY WHEN I'M REALLY SCARED AND FEEL LIKE I CAN'T BREATHE...
AIR IS EVERYWHERE. ALL OF THE AIR IS YOURS. LIKE DIRT AND TREES, IMANI, IT'S OKAY TO BREATHE.
THERE'S TOO MANY OF THESE THINGS AND NOT ENOUGH OF US!
THEY JUST KEEP COMING. I'M FAILING. HOW IS THIS POSSIBLE? WHAT IF STORM WASTED HER TIME ON ME...?
HEY, DOWN THERE--
--YOU LOOK LIKE YOU COULD USE A LITTLE HELP.

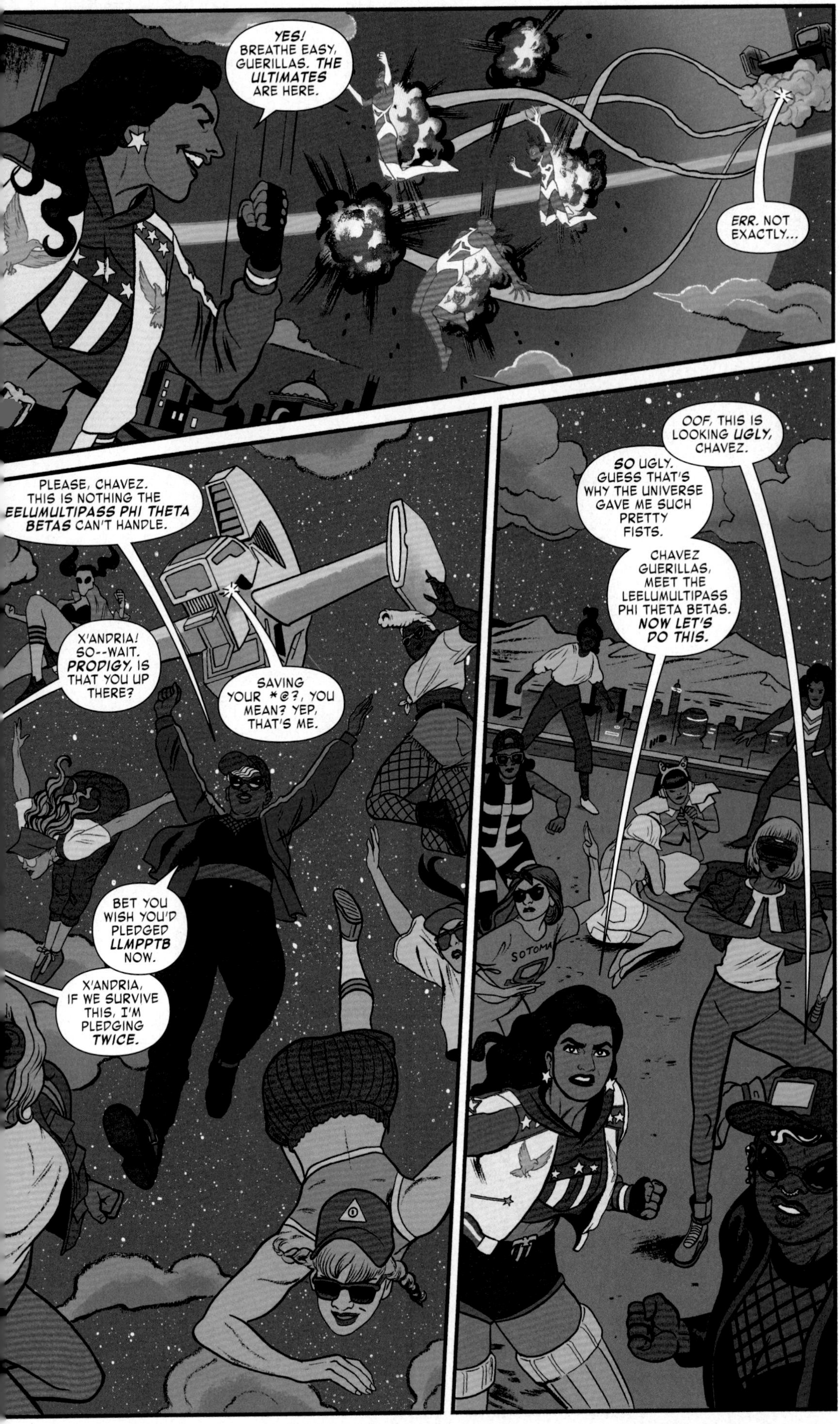
YES! BREATHE EASY, GUERILLAS. THE ULTIMATES ARE HERE.
ERR. NOT EXACTLY...
PLEASE, CHAVEZ. THIS IS NOTHING THE EELUMULTIPASS PHI THETA BETAS CAN'T HANDLE.
X'ANDRIA! SO--WAIT. PRODIGY, IS THAT YOU UP THERE?
SAVING YOUR *@?, YOU MEAN? YEP, THAT'S ME.
BET YOU WISH YOU'D PLEDGED LLMPPTB NOW.
X'ANDRIA, IF WE SURVIVE THIS, I'M PLEDGING TWICE.
OOF, THIS IS LOOKING UGLY, CHAVEZ.
SO UGLY. GUESS THAT'S WHY THE UNIVERSE GAVE ME SUCH PRETTY FISTS.
CHAVEZ GUERILLAS, MEET THE LEELUMULTIPASS PHI THETA BETAS. NOW LET'S DO THIS.
SOTOMA

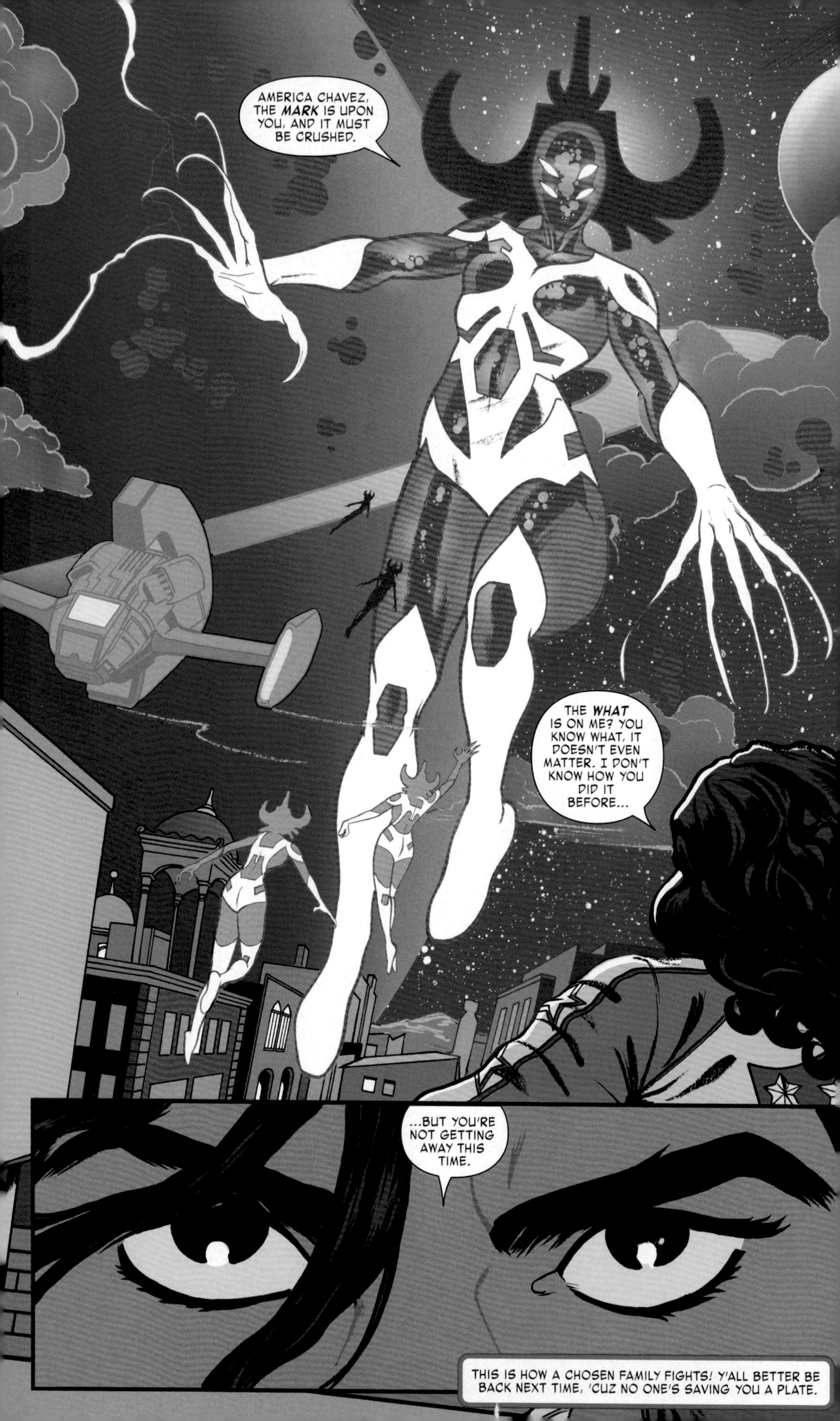
AMERICA CHAVEZ, THE MARK IS UPON YOU, AND IT MUST BE CRUSHED.
THE WHAT IS ON ME? YOU KNOW WHAT, IT DOESN'T EVEN MATTER. I DON'T KNOW HOW YOU DID IT BEFORE...
...BUT YOU'RE NOT GETTING AWAY THIS TIME.
THIS IS HOW A CHOSEN FAMILY FIGHTS! Y'ALL BETTER BE BACK NEXT TIME, 'CUZ NO ONE'S SAVING YOU A PLATE.

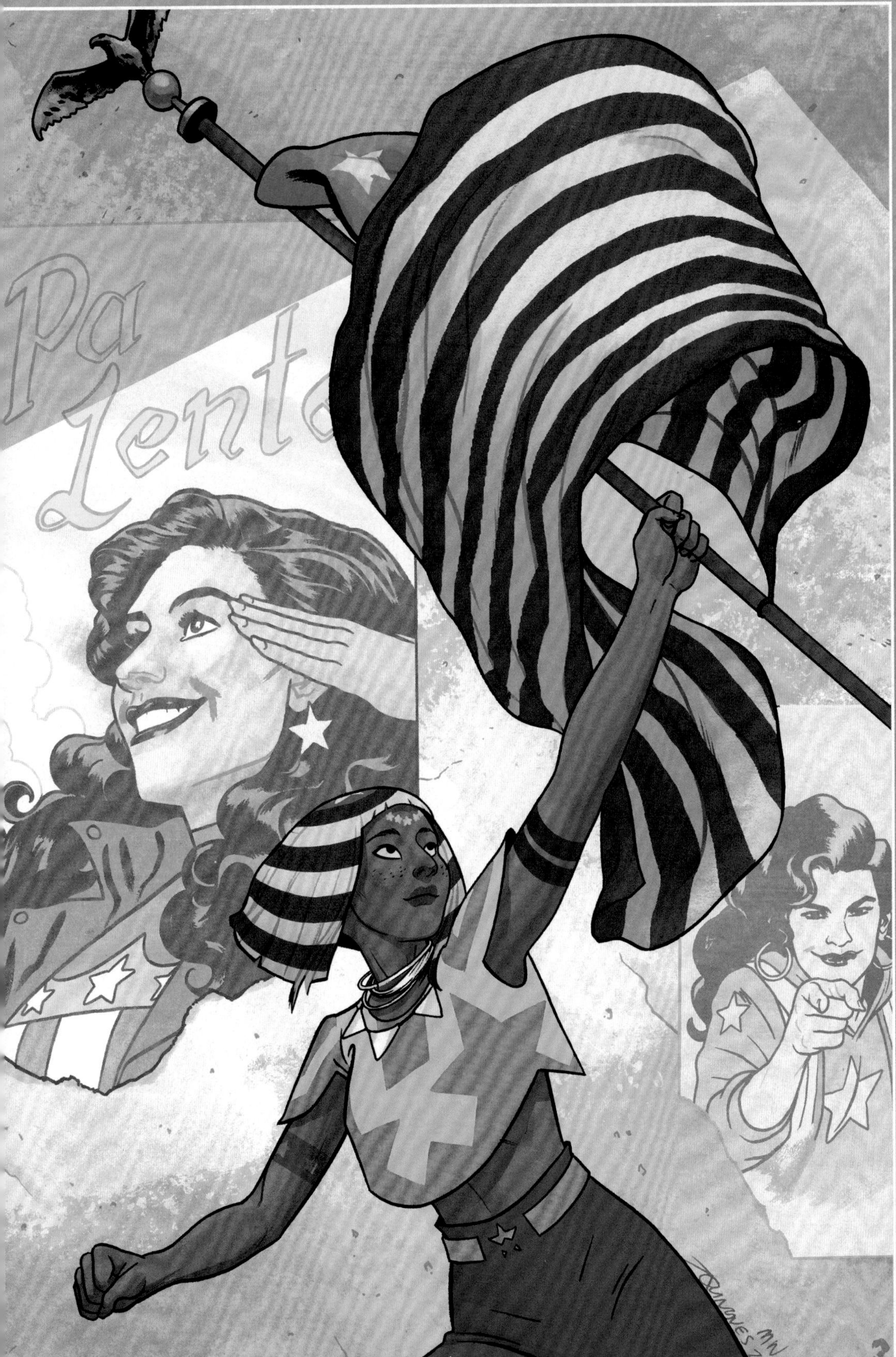

4

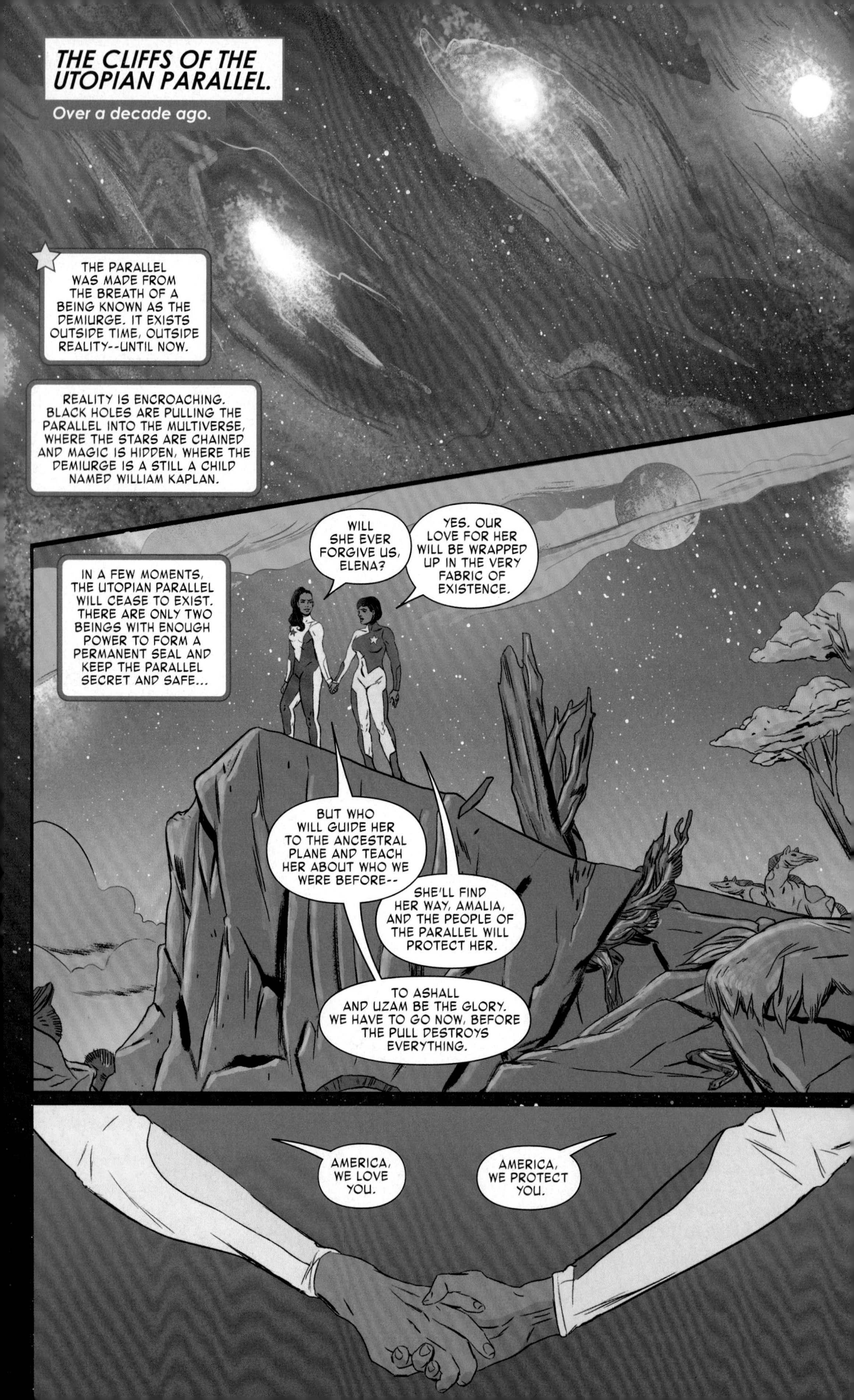
THE CLIFFS OF THE UTOPIAN PARALLEL.
Over a decade ago.
THE PARALLEL WAS MADE FROM THE BREATH OF A BEING KNOWN AS THE DEMIURGE. IT EXISTS OUTSIDE TIME, OUTSIDE REALITY--UNTIL NOW.
REALITY IS ENCROACHING. BLACK HOLES ARE PULLING THE PARALLEL INTO THE MULTIVERSE, WHERE THE STARS ARE CHAINED AND MAGIC IS HIDDEN, WHERE THE DEMIURGE IS A STILL A CHILD NAMED WILLIAM KAPLAN.
IN A FEW MOMENTS, THE UTOPIAN PARALLEL WILL CEASE TO EXIST. THERE ARE ONLY TWO BEINGS WITH ENOUGH POWER TO FORM A PERMANENT SEAL AND KEEP THE PARALLEL SECRET AND SAFE...
WILL SHE EVER FORGIVE US, ELENA?
YES. OUR LOVE FOR HER WILL BE WRAPPED UP IN THE VERY FABRIC OF EXISTENCE.
BUT WHO WILL GUIDE HER TO THE ANCESTRAL PLANE AND TEACH HER ABOUT WHO WE WERE BEFORE--
SHE'LL FIND HER WAY, AMALIA, AND THE PEOPLE OF THE PARALLEL WILL PROTECT HER.
TO ASHALL AND UZAM BE THE GLORY. WE HAVE TO GO NOW, BEFORE THE PULL DESTROYS EVERYTHING.
AMERICA, WE LOVE YOU.
AMERICA, WE PROTECT YOU.

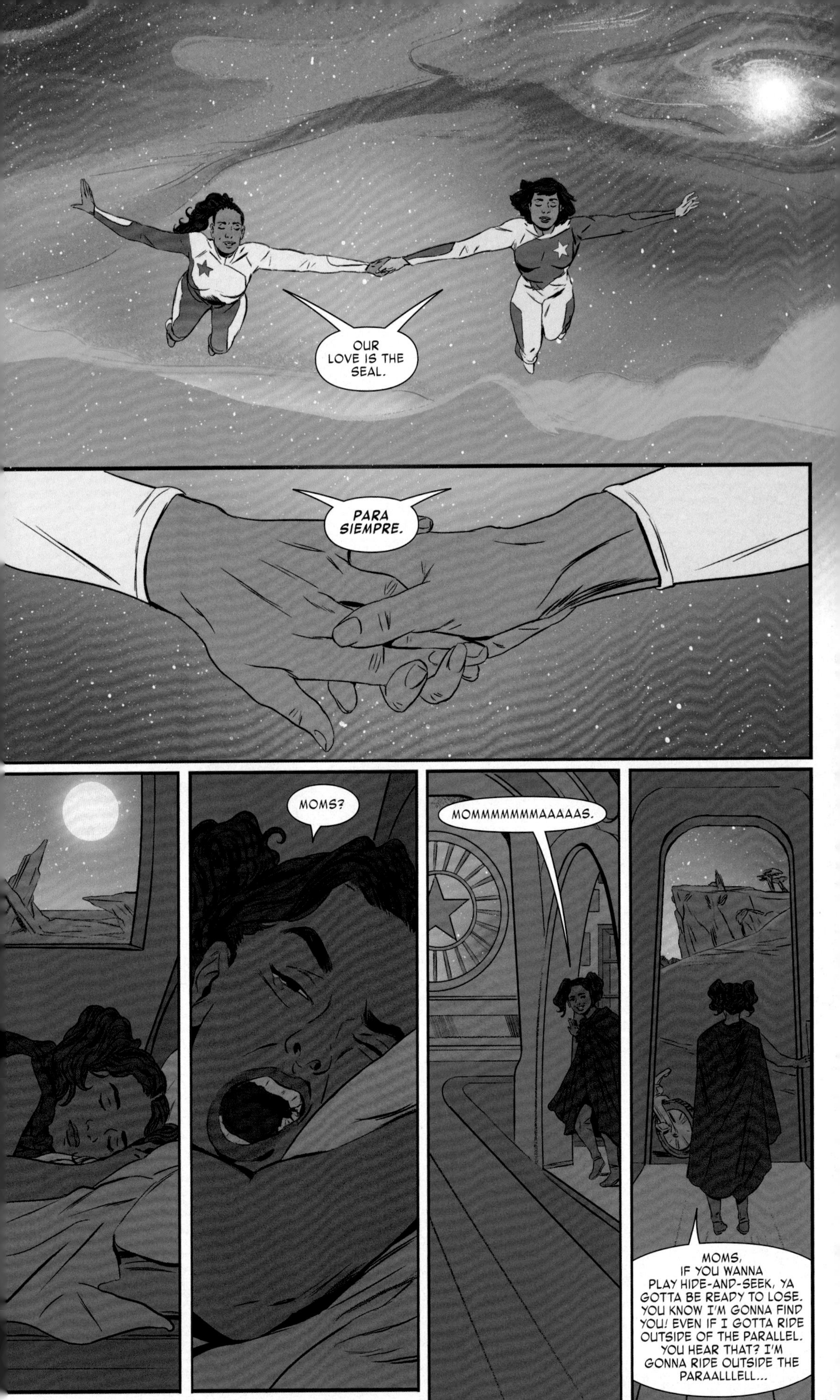
OUR LOVE IS THE SEAL.
PARA SIEMPRE.
MOMS?
MOMMMMMMMAAAAAS.
MOMS, IF YOU WANNA PLAY HIDE-AND-SEEK, YA GOTTA BE READY TO LOSE. YOU KNOW I'M GONNA FIND YOU! EVEN IF I GOTTA RIDE OUTSIDE OF THE PARALLEL. YOU HEAR THAT? I'M GONNA RIDE OUTSIDE THE PARAALLLELL...

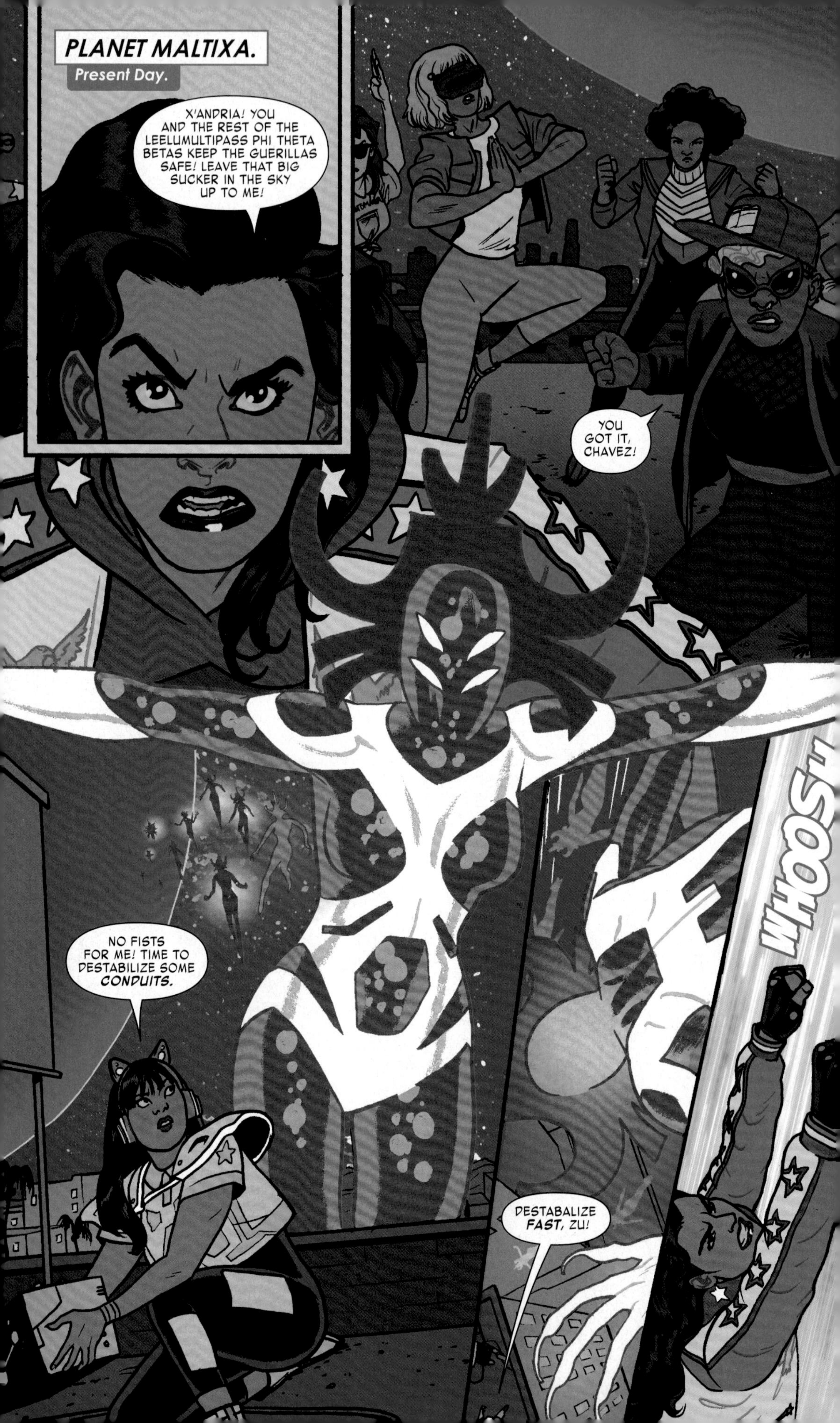
PLANET MALTIXA.
Present Day.
X'ANDRIA! YOU AND THE REST OF THE LEELUMULTIPASS PHI THETA BETAS KEEP THE GUERILLAS SAFE! LEAVE THAT BIG SUCKER IN THE SKY UP TO ME!
YOU GOT IT, CHAVEZ!
NO FISTS FOR ME! TIME TO DESTABILIZE SOME CONDUITS.
DESTABALIZE FAST, ZU!
WHOOSH

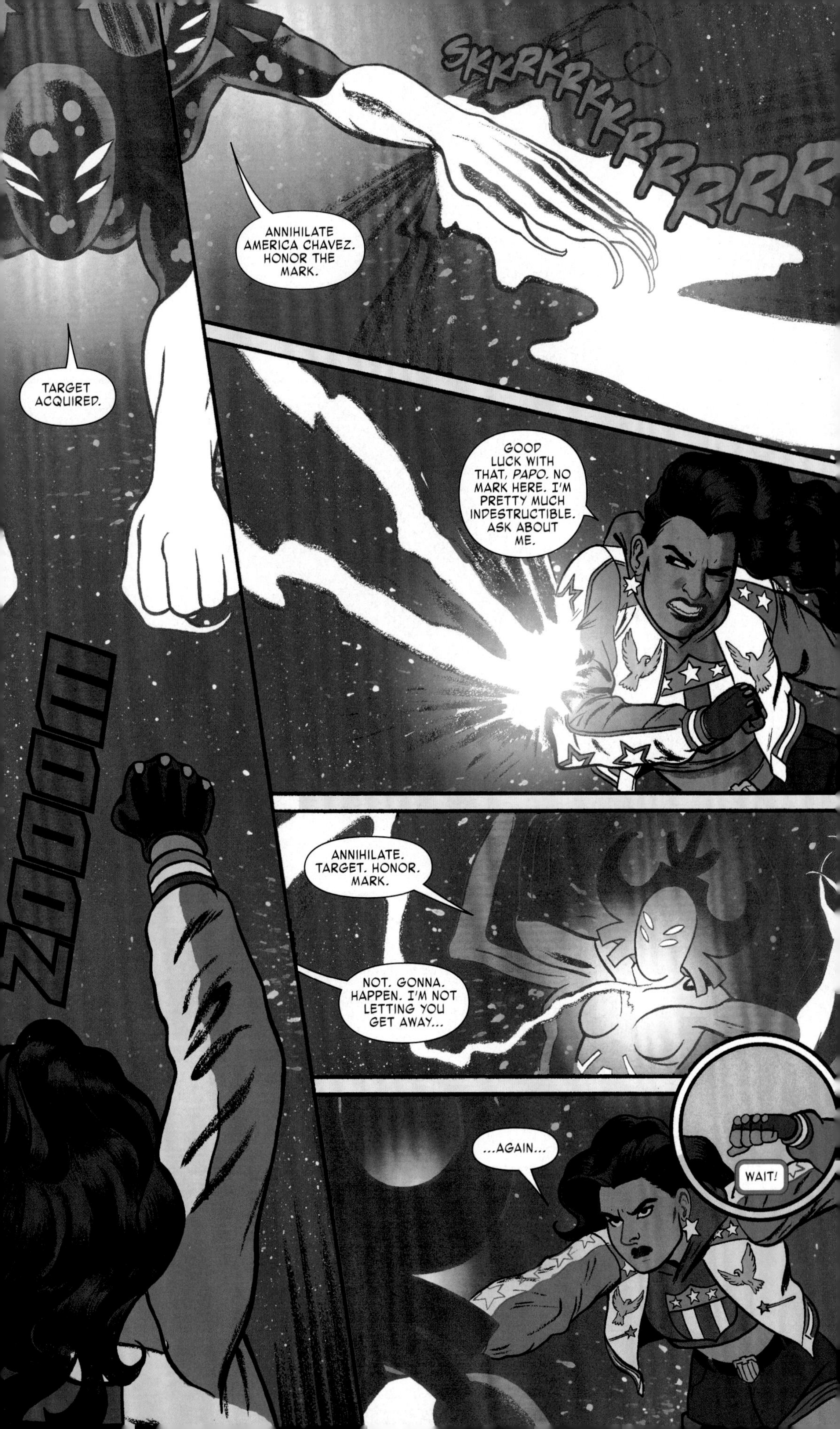
SKKRKRKKRRRRR
ANNIHILATE AMERICA CHAVEZ. HONOR THE MARK.
TARGET ACQUIRED.
GOOD LUCK WITH THAT, *PAPO.* NO MARK HERE. I'M PRETTY MUCH INDESTRUCTIBLE. ASK ABOUT ME.
ZOOOOOM
ANNIHILATE. TARGET. HONOR. MARK.
NOT. GONNA. HAPPEN. I'M NOT LETTING YOU GET AWAY...
...AGAIN...
WAIT!

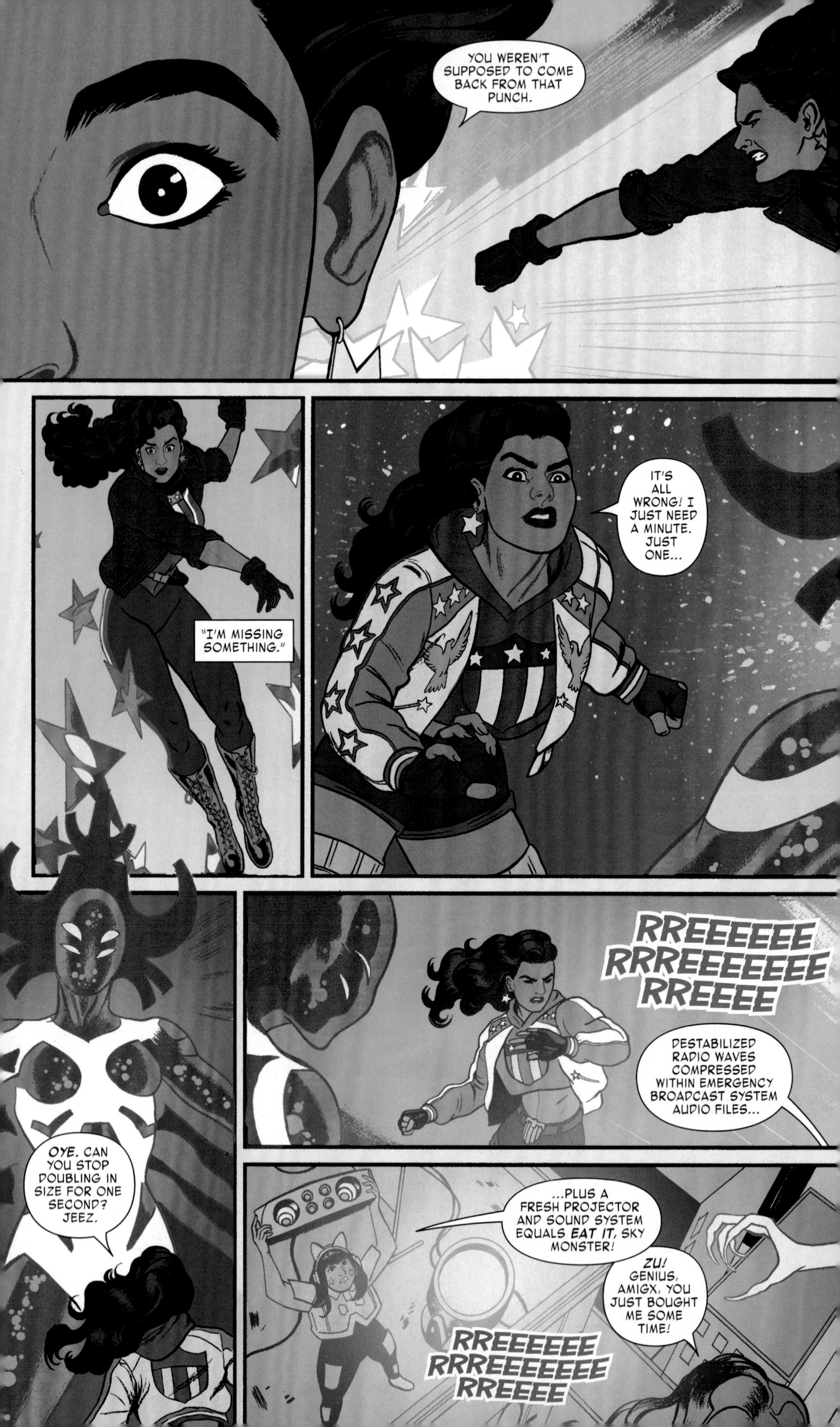
YOU WEREN'T SUPPOSED TO COME BACK FROM THAT PUNCH.
"I'M MISSING SOMETHING."
IT'S ALL WRONG! I JUST NEED A MINUTE. JUST ONE...
RREEEEEE RRREEEEEEE RREEEE
DESTABILIZED RADIO WAVES COMPRESSED WITHIN EMERGENCY BROADCAST SYSTEM AUDIO FILES...
OYE. CAN YOU STOP DOUBLING IN SIZE FOR ONE SECOND? JEEZ.
...PLUS A FRESH PROJECTOR AND SOUND SYSTEM EQUALS EAT IT, SKY MONSTER!
ZU! GENIUS, AMIGX, YOU JUST BOUGHT ME SOME TIME!
RREEEEEE RRREEEEEEE RREEEE

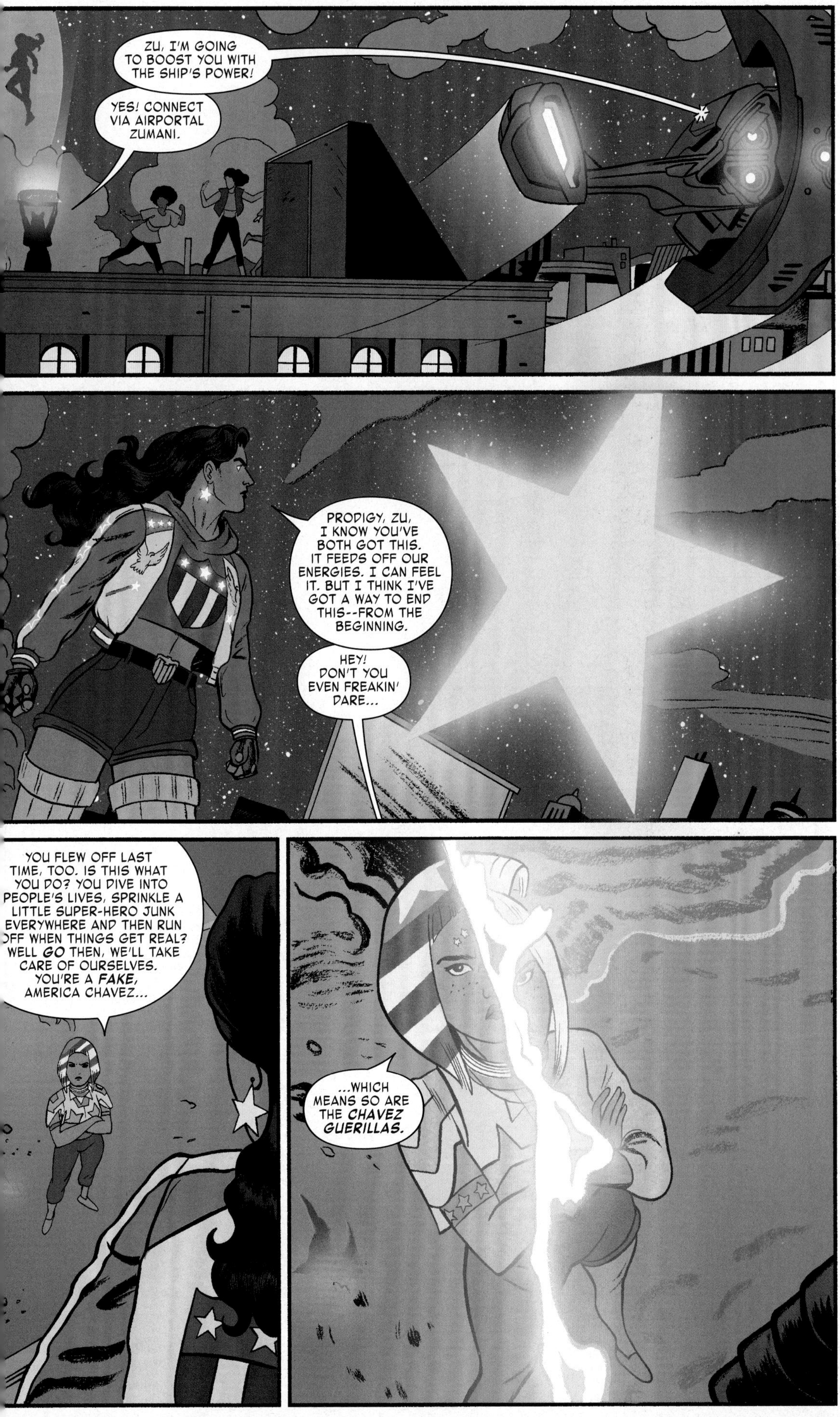
ZU, I'M GOING TO BOOST YOU WITH THE SHIP'S POWER!
YES! CONNECT VIA AIRPORTAL ZUMANI.
PRODIGY, ZU, I KNOW YOU'VE BOTH GOT THIS. IT FEEDS OFF OUR ENERGIES. I CAN FEEL IT. BUT I THINK I'VE GOT A WAY TO END THIS--FROM THE BEGINNING.
HEY! DON'T YOU EVEN FREAKIN' DARE...
YOU FLEW OFF LAST TIME, TOO. IS THIS WHAT YOU DO? YOU DIVE INTO PEOPLE'S LIVES, SPRINKLE A LITTLE SUPER-HERO JUNK EVERYWHERE AND THEN RUN OFF WHEN THINGS GET REAL? WELL GO THEN, WE'LL TAKE CARE OF OURSELVES. YOU'RE A FAKE, AMERICA CHAVEZ...
...WHICH MEANS SO ARE THE CHAVEZ GUERILLAS.

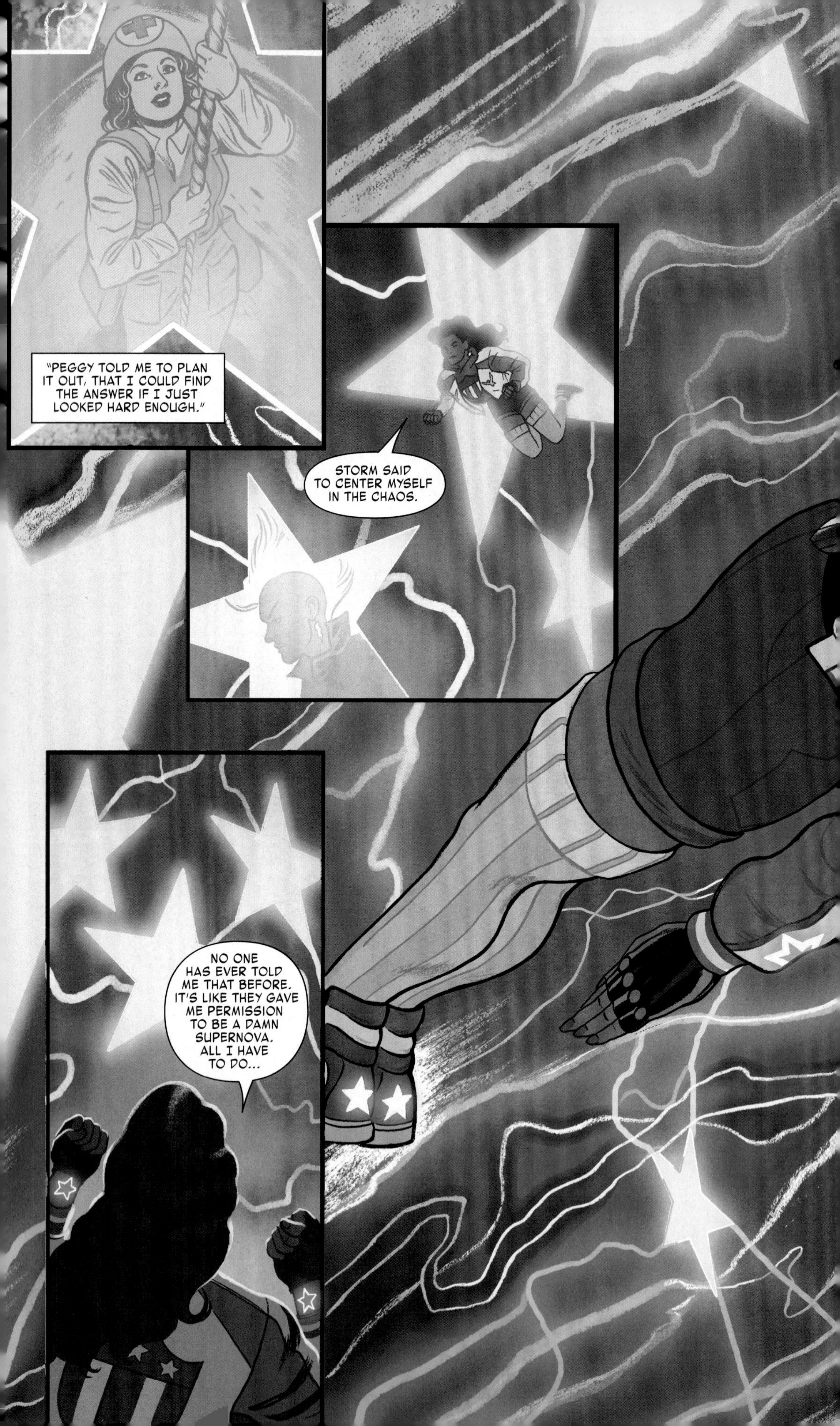
"PEGGY TOLD ME TO PLAN IT OUT, THAT I COULD FIND THE ANSWER IF I JUST LOOKED HARD ENOUGH."
STORM SAID TO CENTER MYSELF IN THE CHAOS.
NO ONE HAS EVER TOLD ME THAT BEFORE. IT'S LIKE THEY GAVE ME PERMISSION TO BE A DAMN SUPERNOVA. ALL I HAVE TO DO...

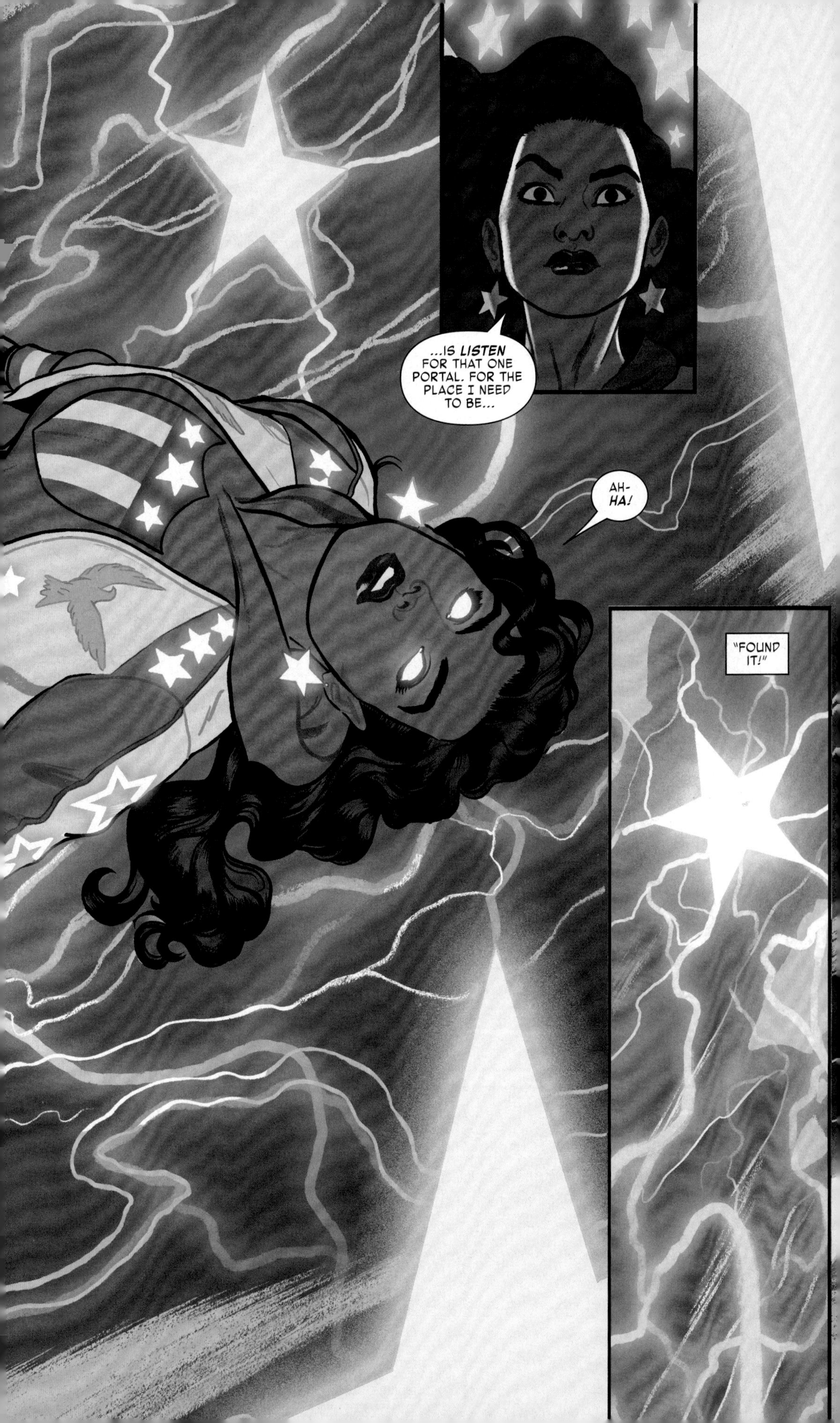
...IS LISTEN FOR THAT ONE PORTAL. FOR THE PLACE I NEED TO BE...
AH-HA!
"FOUND IT!"

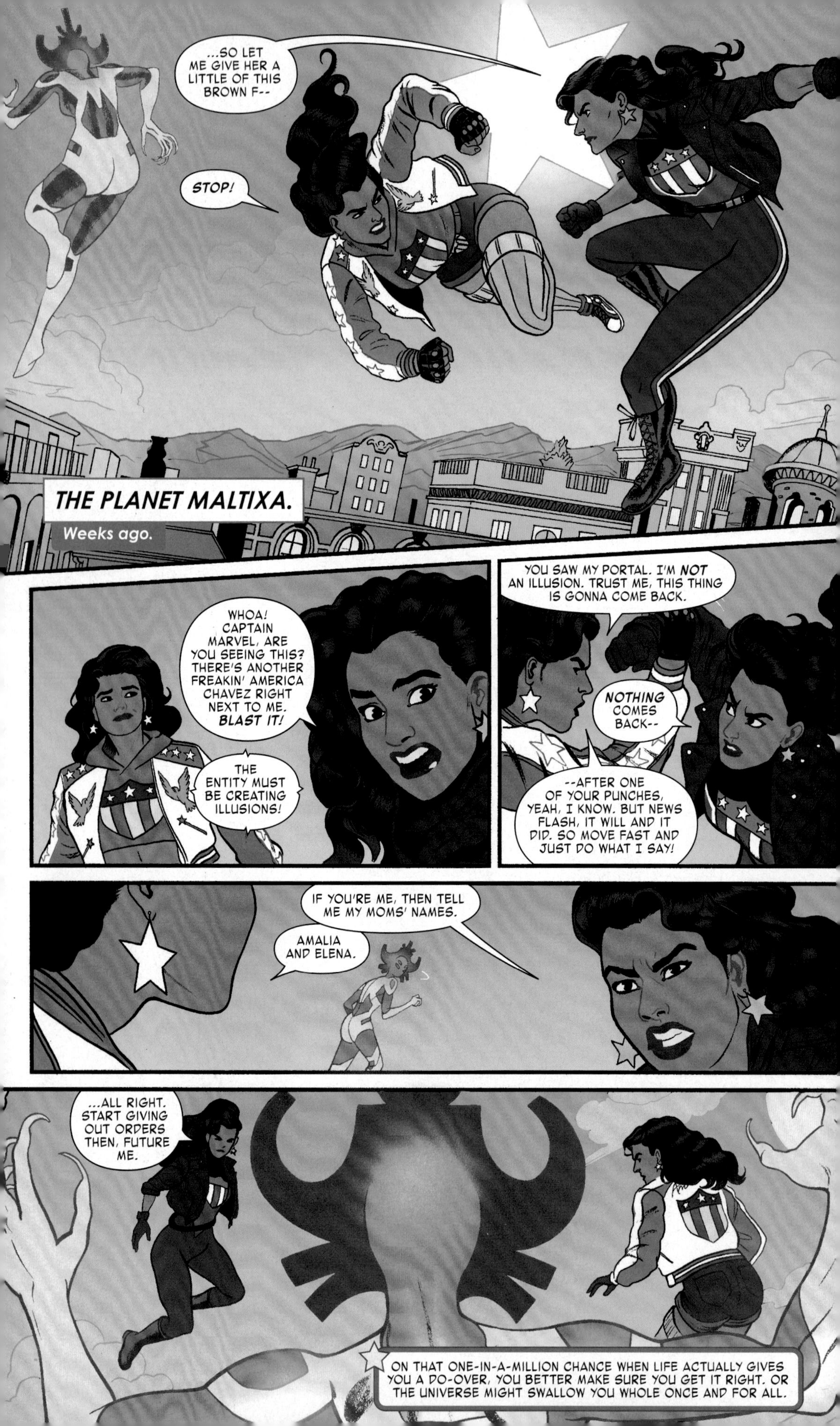

...SO LET ME GIVE HER A LITTLE OF THIS BROWN F--
STOP!
THE PLANET MALTIXA.
Weeks ago.
WHOA! CAPTAIN MARVEL, ARE YOU SEEING THIS? THERE'S ANOTHER FREAKIN' AMERICA CHAVEZ RIGHT NEXT TO ME. BLAST IT!
THE ENTITY MUST BE CREATING ILLUSIONS!
YOU SAW MY PORTAL. I'M NOT AN ILLUSION. TRUST ME, THIS THING IS GONNA COME BACK.
NOTHING COMES BACK--
--AFTER ONE OF YOUR PUNCHES, YEAH, I KNOW. BUT NEWS FLASH, IT WILL AND IT DID. SO MOVE FAST AND JUST DO WHAT I SAY!
IF YOU'RE ME, THEN TELL ME MY MOMS' NAMES.
AMALIA AND ELENA.
...ALL RIGHT. START GIVING OUT ORDERS THEN, FUTURE ME.
ON THAT ONE-IN-A-MILLION CHANCE WHEN LIFE ACTUALLY GIVES YOU A DO-OVER, YOU BETTER MAKE SURE YOU GET IT RIGHT. OR THE UNIVERSE MIGHT SWALLOW YOU WHOLE ONCE AND FOR ALL.

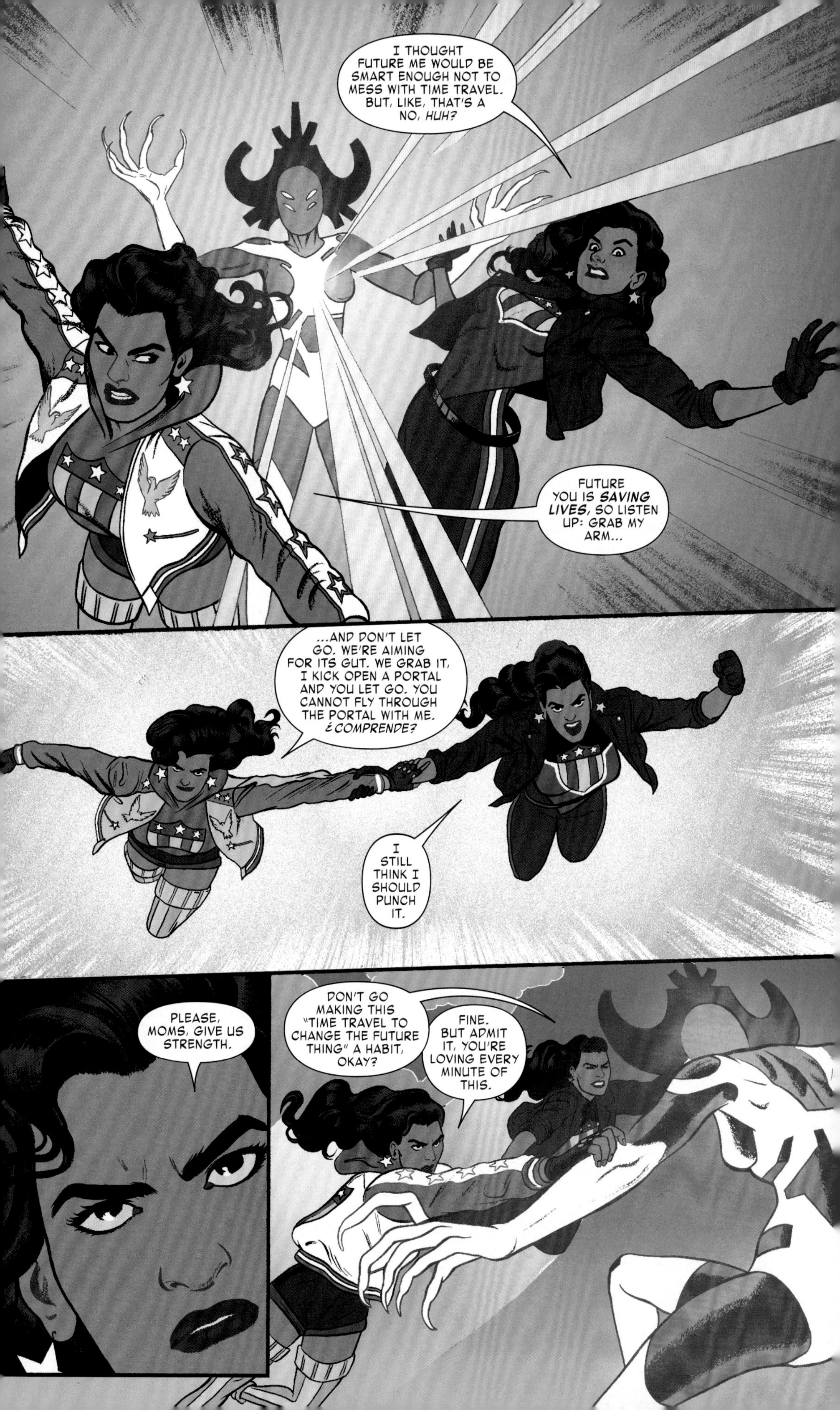
I THOUGHT FUTURE ME WOULD BE SMART ENOUGH NOT TO MESS WITH TIME TRAVEL. BUT, LIKE, THAT'S A NO, *HUH?*
FUTURE YOU IS ***SAVING LIVES,*** SO LISTEN UP: GRAB MY ARM...
...AND DON'T LET GO. WE'RE AIMING FOR ITS GUT. WE GRAB IT, I KICK OPEN A PORTAL AND YOU LET GO. YOU CANNOT FLY THROUGH THE PORTAL WITH ME. *¿COMPRENDE?*
I STILL THINK I SHOULD PUNCH IT.
PLEASE, MOMS, GIVE US STRENGTH.
DON'T GO MAKING THIS "TIME TRAVEL TO CHANGE THE FUTURE THING" A HABIT, OKAY?
FINE. BUT ADMIT IT, YOU'RE LOVING EVERY MINUTE OF THIS.

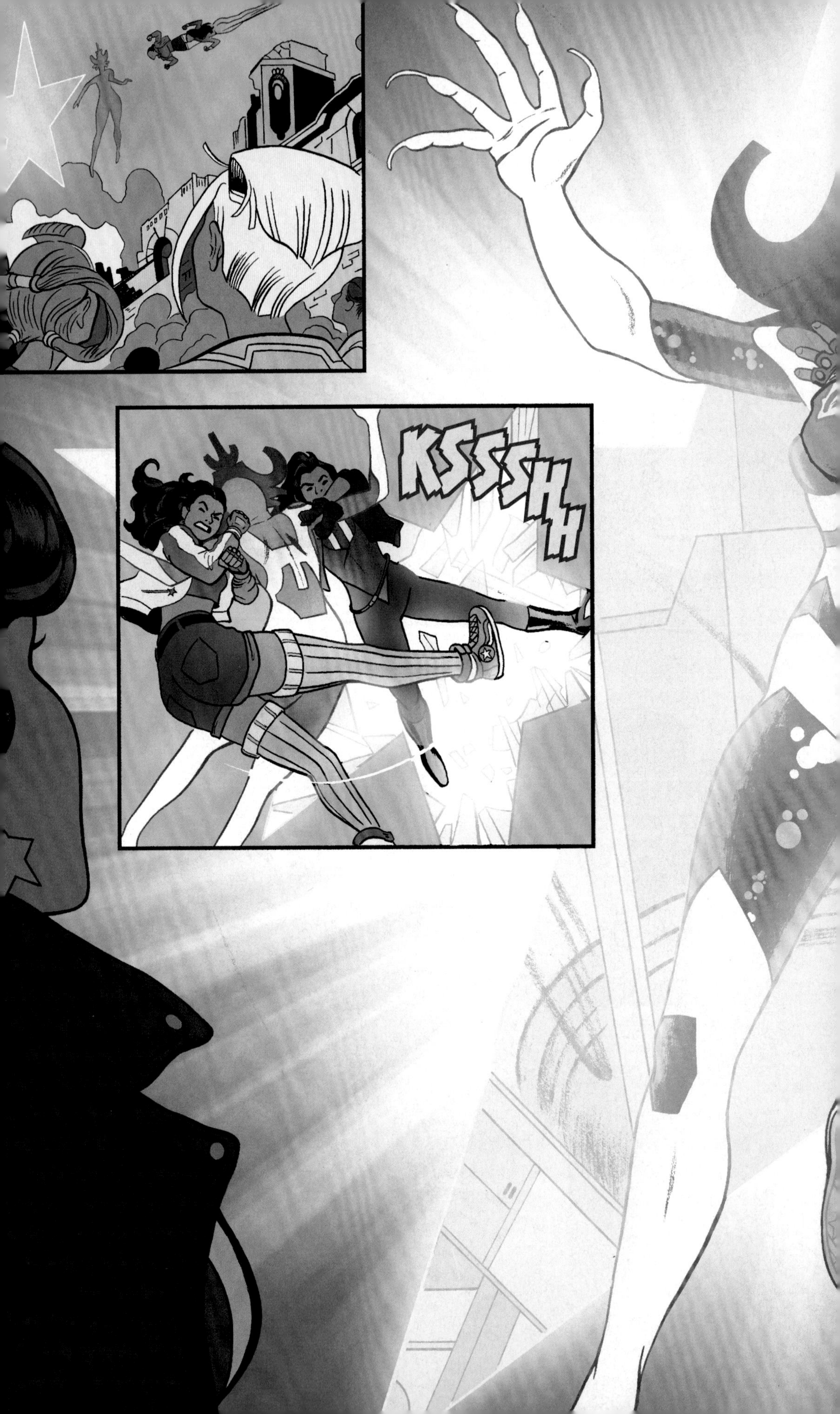
KSSSHH

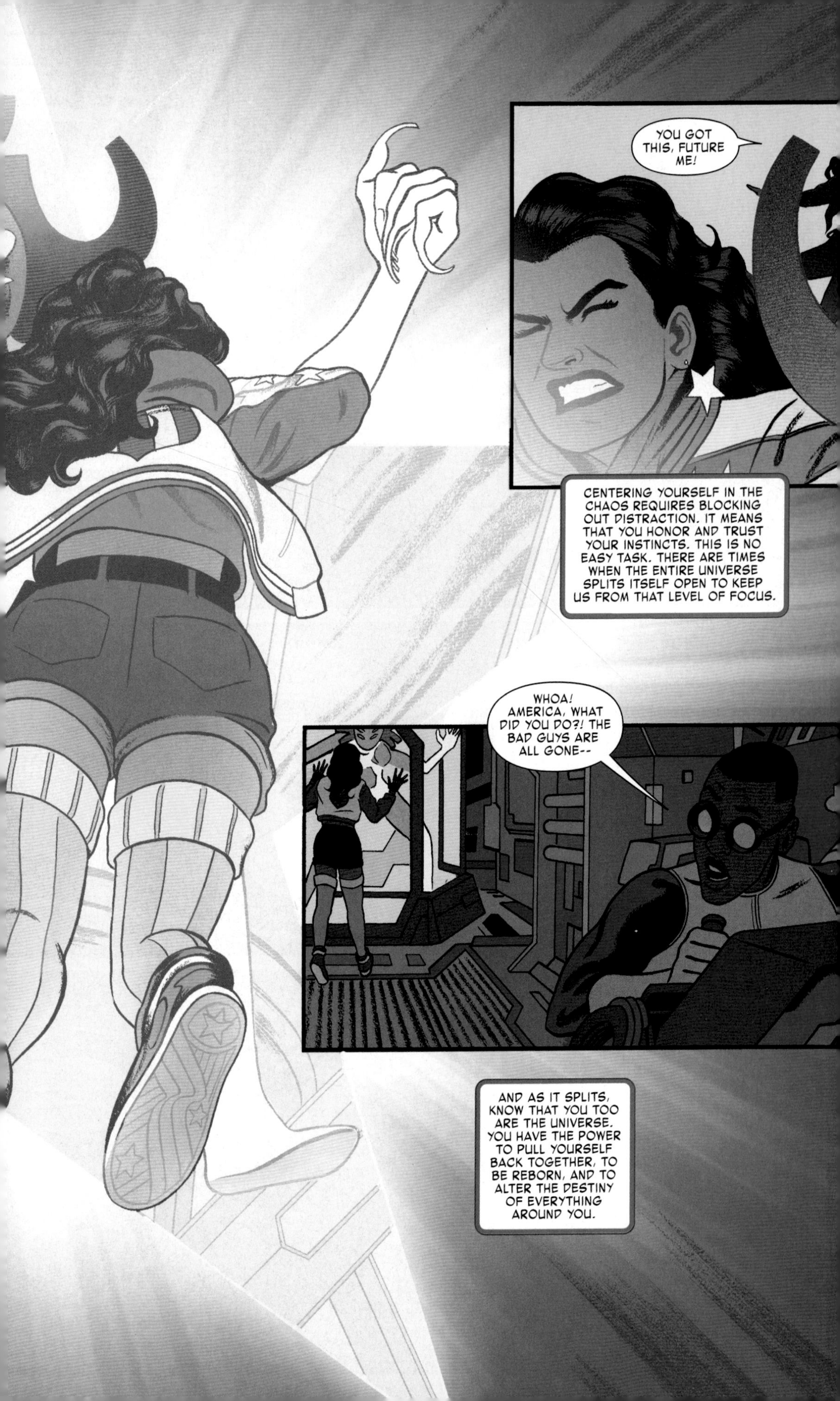
YOU GOT THIS, FUTURE ME!
CENTERING YOURSELF IN THE CHAOS REQUIRES BLOCKING OUT DISTRACTION. IT MEANS THAT YOU HONOR AND TRUST YOUR INSTINCTS. THIS IS NO EASY TASK. THERE ARE TIMES WHEN THE ENTIRE UNIVERSE SPLITS ITSELF OPEN TO KEEP US FROM THAT LEVEL OF FOCUS.
WHOA! AMERICA, WHAT DID YOU DO?! THE BAD GUYS ARE ALL GONE--
AND AS IT SPLITS, KNOW THAT YOU TOO ARE THE UNIVERSE. YOU HAVE THE POWER TO PULL YOURSELF BACK TOGETHER, TO BE REBORN, AND TO ALTER THE DESTINY OF EVERYTHING AROUND YOU.

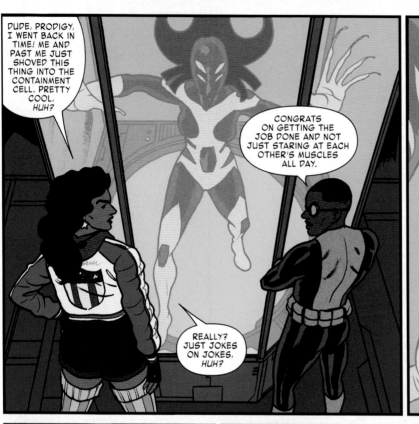

DUDE, PRODIGY, I WENT BACK IN TIME! ME AND PAST ME JUST SHOVED THIS THING INTO THE CONTAINMENT CELL. PRETTY COOL, *HUH?*

CONGRATS ON GETTING THE JOB DONE AND NOT JUST STARING AT EACH OTHER'S MUSCLES ALL DAY.

REALLY? JUST JOKES ON JOKES, *HUH?*

WHATEVER YOU ARE, THIS IS YOUR LAST CHANCE TO TELL US WHO SENT YOU AND WHY YOU'VE BEEN TERRORIZING MALTIXA.

SINCE YOU DROPPED IT IN, I'VE BEEN TAKING READINGS. IT DOESN'T SEEM LIKE A CREATURE ORGANIC TO ANY KNOWN ENVIRONMENT. SOMEONE *CREATED* THIS THING.

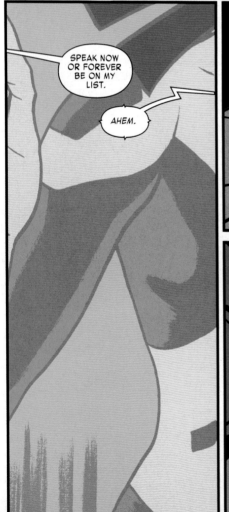

SPEAK NOW OR FOREVER BE ON MY LIST.

AHEM.

MR. ALLEYNE, WILL YOU KINDLY RETURN THE AIRCRAFT YOU SO DEFTLY LIBERATED TO THE TRISKELION-- AT ONCE?

LITERALLY WAS GOING TO BE MY NEXT MOVE, DR. BRASHEAR.

BLUE MARVEL! GOOD TO SEE YOU. WILL YOU KEEP THE ENTITY UNDER OBSERVATION FOR ME?

INDEED, AS LONG AS YOU COMMIT A THOROUGH INVESTIGATION OF ITS ORIGINS.

ON IT. GOTTA KEEP MY PROMISES TO THE MALTIXANS, TOO.

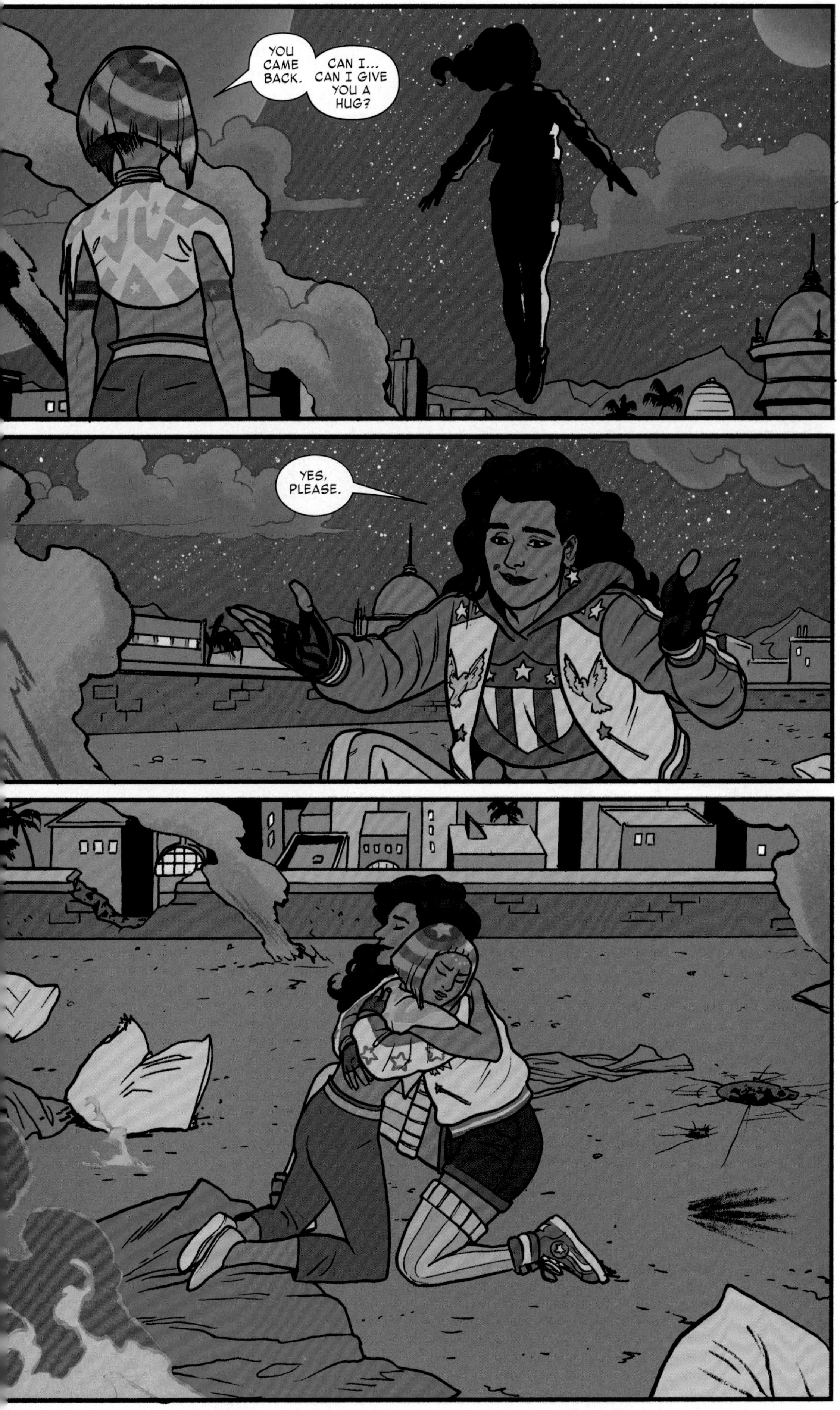

YOU CAME BACK.
CAN I... CAN I GIVE YOU A HUG?
YES, PLEASE.

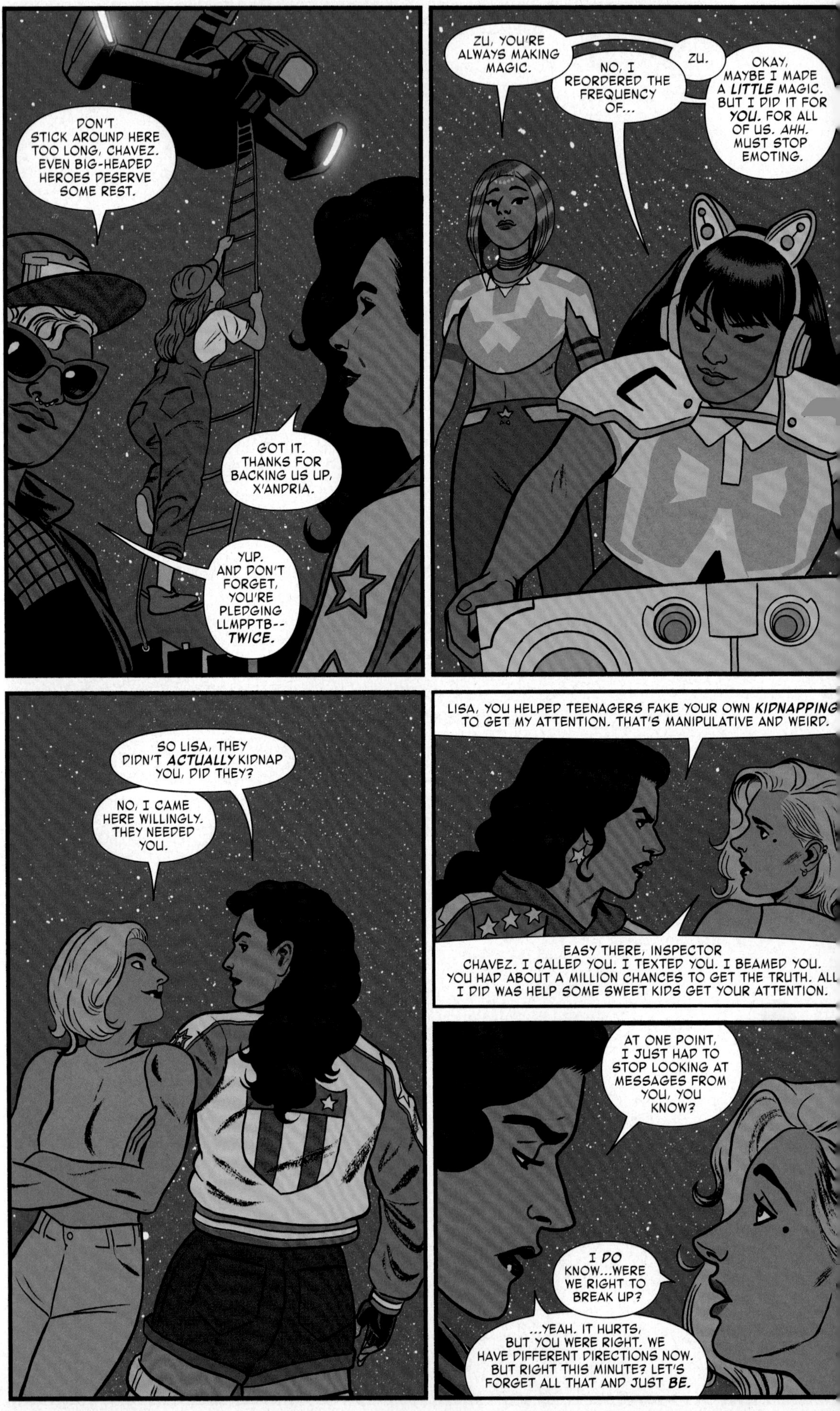
DON'T STICK AROUND HERE TOO LONG, CHAVEZ. EVEN BIG-HEADED HEROES DESERVE SOME REST.
GOT IT. THANKS FOR BACKING US UP, X'ANDRIA.
YUP. AND DON'T FORGET, YOU'RE PLEDGING LLMPPTB-- TWICE.
ZU, YOU'RE ALWAYS MAKING MAGIC.
NO, I REORDERED THE FREQUENCY OF...
ZU.
OKAY, MAYBE I MADE A LITTLE MAGIC. BUT I DID IT FOR YOU. FOR ALL OF US. AHH. MUST STOP EMOTING.
SO LISA, THEY DIDN'T ACTUALLY KIDNAP YOU, DID THEY?
NO, I CAME HERE WILLINGLY. THEY NEEDED YOU.
LISA, YOU HELPED TEENAGERS FAKE YOUR OWN KIDNAPPING TO GET MY ATTENTION. THAT'S MANIPULATIVE AND WEIRD.
EASY THERE, INSPECTOR CHAVEZ. I CALLED YOU. I TEXTED YOU. I BEAMED YOU. YOU HAD ABOUT A MILLION CHANCES TO GET THE TRUTH. ALL I DID WAS HELP SOME SWEET KIDS GET YOUR ATTENTION.
AT ONE POINT, I JUST HAD TO STOP LOOKING AT MESSAGES FROM YOU, YOU KNOW?
I DO KNOW...WERE WE RIGHT TO BREAK UP?
...YEAH. IT HURTS, BUT YOU WERE RIGHT. WE HAVE DIFFERENT DIRECTIONS NOW. BUT RIGHT THIS MINUTE? LET'S FORGET ALL THAT AND JUST BE.

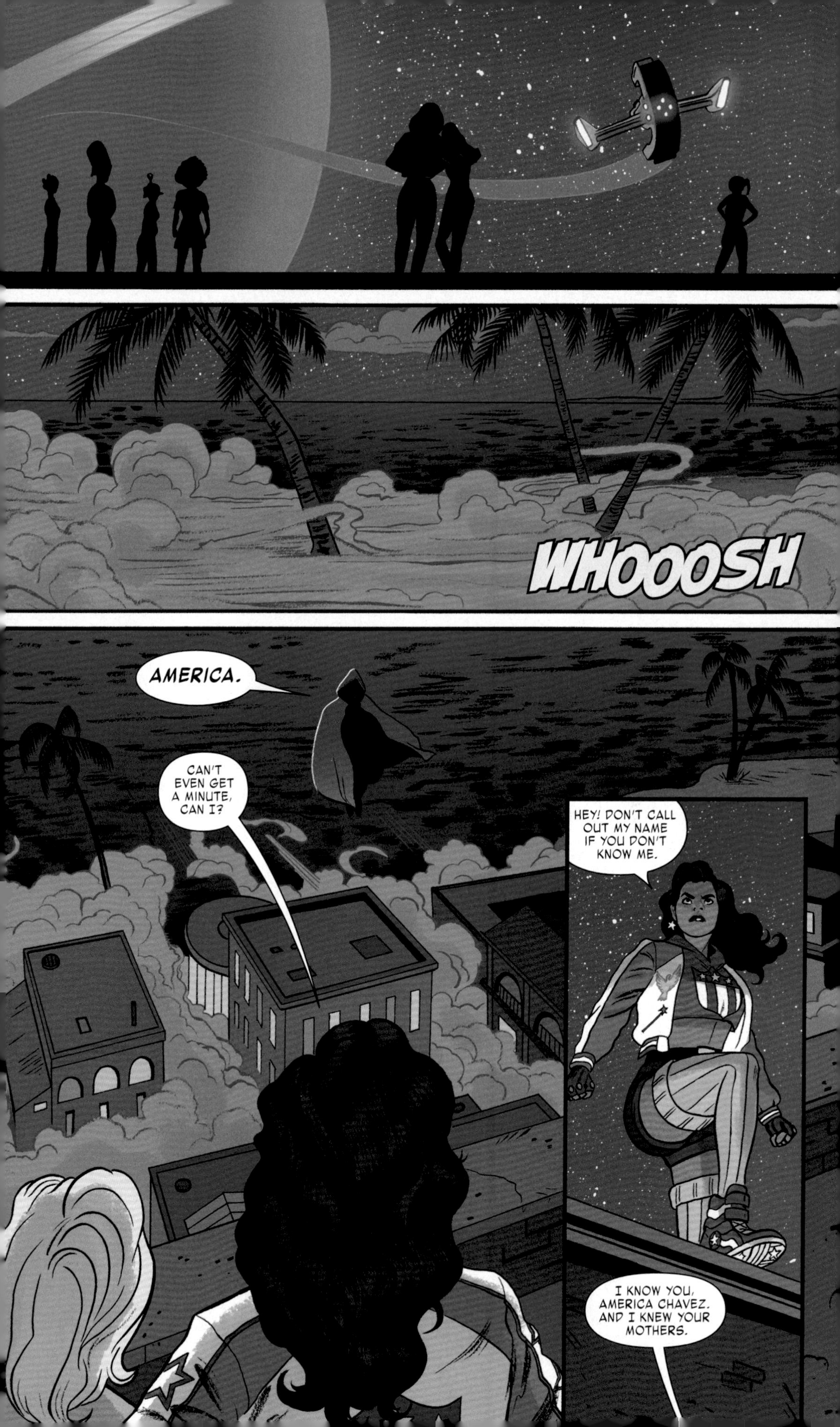
WHOOOSH
AMERICA.
CAN'T EVEN GET A MINUTE, CAN I?
HEY! DON'T CALL OUT MY NAME IF YOU DON'T KNOW ME.
I KNOW YOU, AMERICA CHAVEZ. AND I KNEW YOUR MOTHERS.

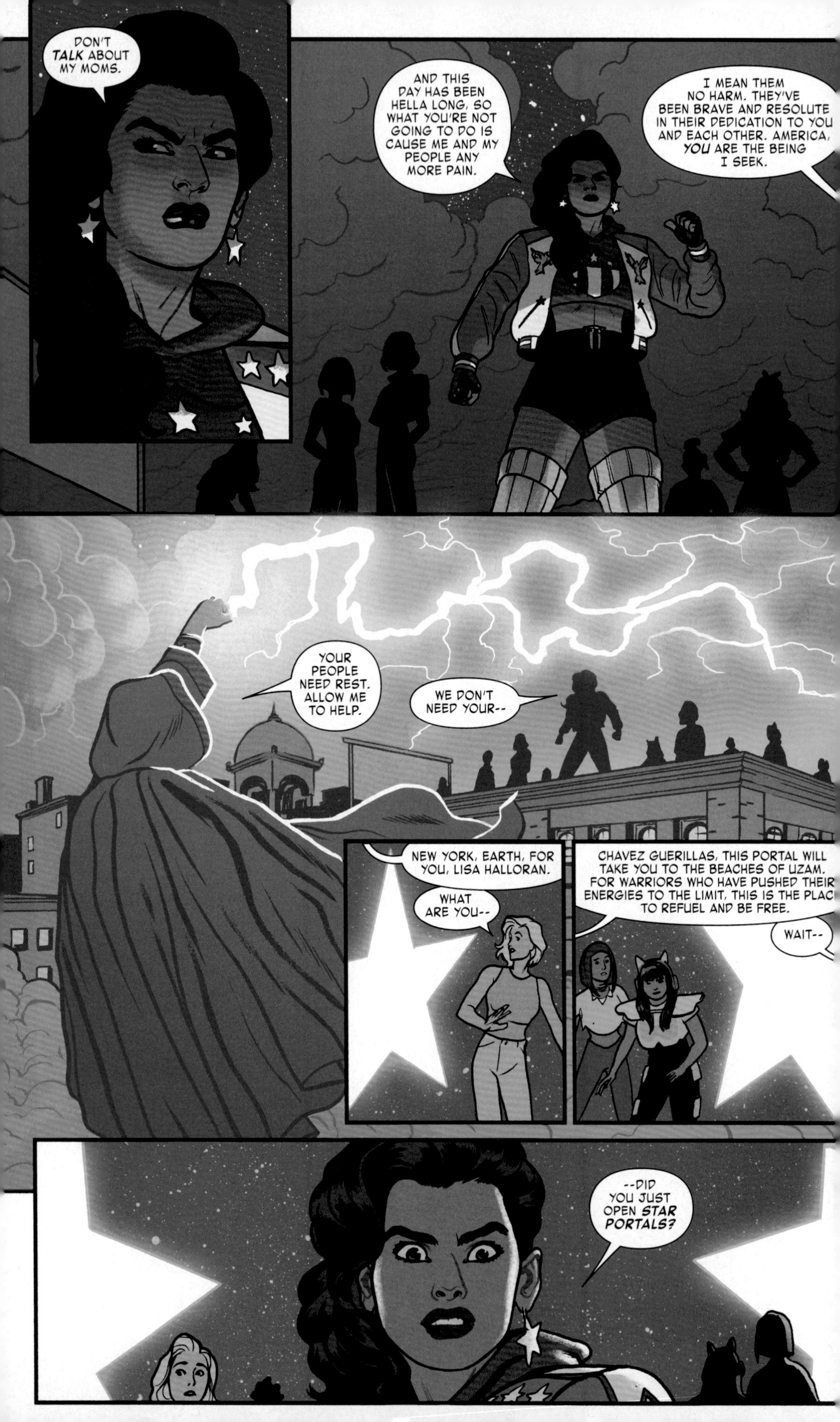
DON'T TALK ABOUT MY MOMS.
AND THIS DAY HAS BEEN HELLA LONG, SO WHAT YOU'RE NOT GOING TO DO IS CAUSE ME AND MY PEOPLE ANY MORE PAIN.
I MEAN THEM NO HARM. THEY'VE BEEN BRAVE AND RESOLUTE IN THEIR DEDICATION TO YOU AND EACH OTHER. AMERICA, YOU ARE THE BEING I SEEK.
YOUR PEOPLE NEED REST. ALLOW ME TO HELP.
WE DON'T NEED YOUR--
NEW YORK, EARTH, FOR YOU, LISA HALLORAN.
WHAT ARE YOU--
CHAVEZ GUERILLAS, THIS PORTAL WILL TAKE YOU TO THE BEACHES OF UZAM. FOR WARRIORS WHO HAVE PUSHED THEIR ENERGIES TO THE LIMIT, THIS IS THE PLAC TO REFUEL AND BE FREE.
WAIT--
--DID YOU JUST OPEN STAR PORTALS?

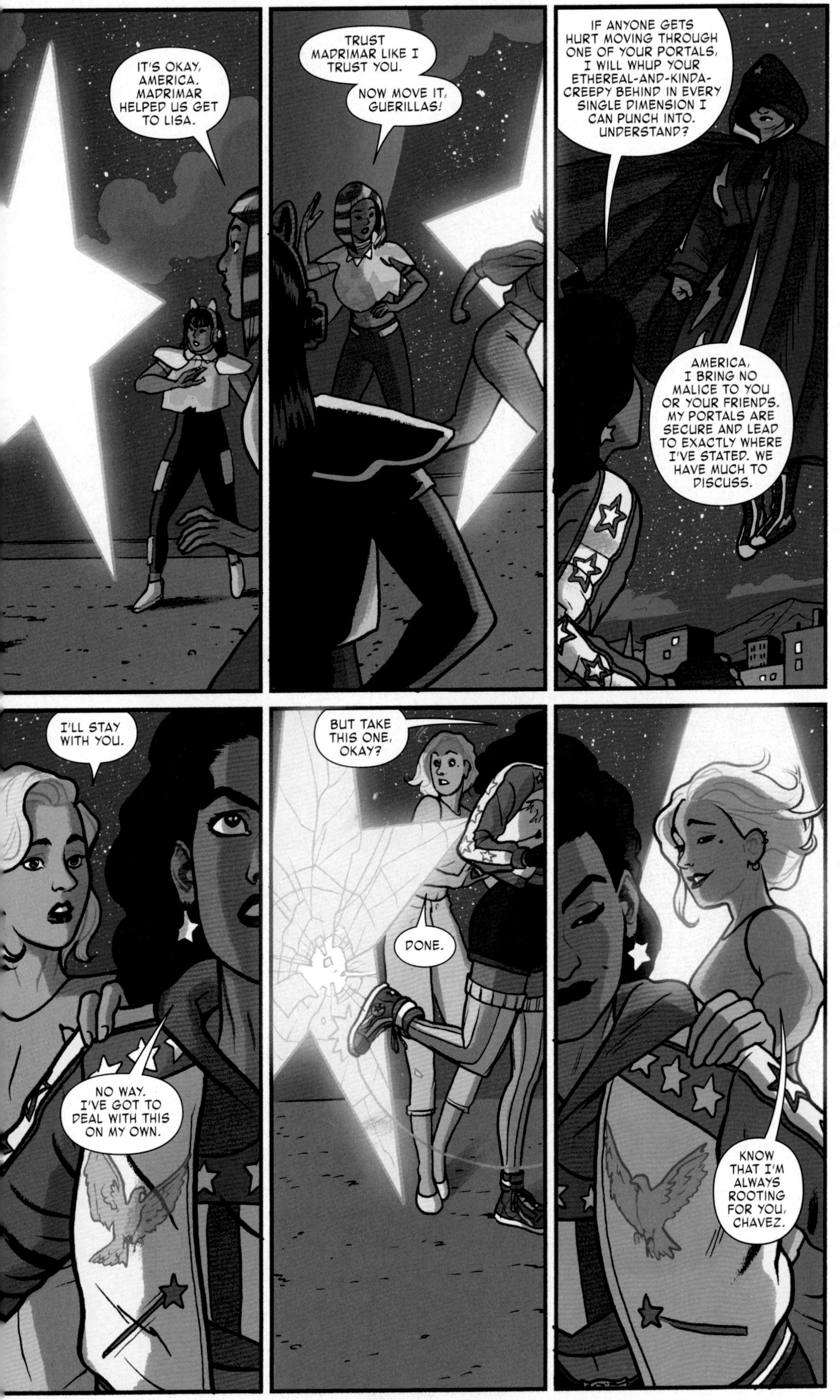
IT'S OKAY, AMERICA. MADRIMAR HELPED US GET TO LISA.
TRUST MADRIMAR LIKE I TRUST YOU.
NOW MOVE IT, GUERILLAS!
IF ANYONE GETS HURT MOVING THROUGH ONE OF YOUR PORTALS, I WILL WHUP YOUR ETHEREAL-AND-KINDA-CREEPY BEHIND IN EVERY SINGLE DIMENSION I CAN PUNCH INTO. UNDERSTAND?
AMERICA, I BRING NO MALICE TO YOU OR YOUR FRIENDS. MY PORTALS ARE SECURE AND LEAD TO EXACTLY WHERE I'VE STATED. WE HAVE MUCH TO DISCUSS.
I'LL STAY WITH YOU.
NO WAY. I'VE GOT TO DEAL WITH THIS ON MY OWN.
BUT TAKE THIS ONE, OKAY?
DONE.
KNOW THAT I'M ALWAYS ROOTING FOR YOU, CHAVEZ.

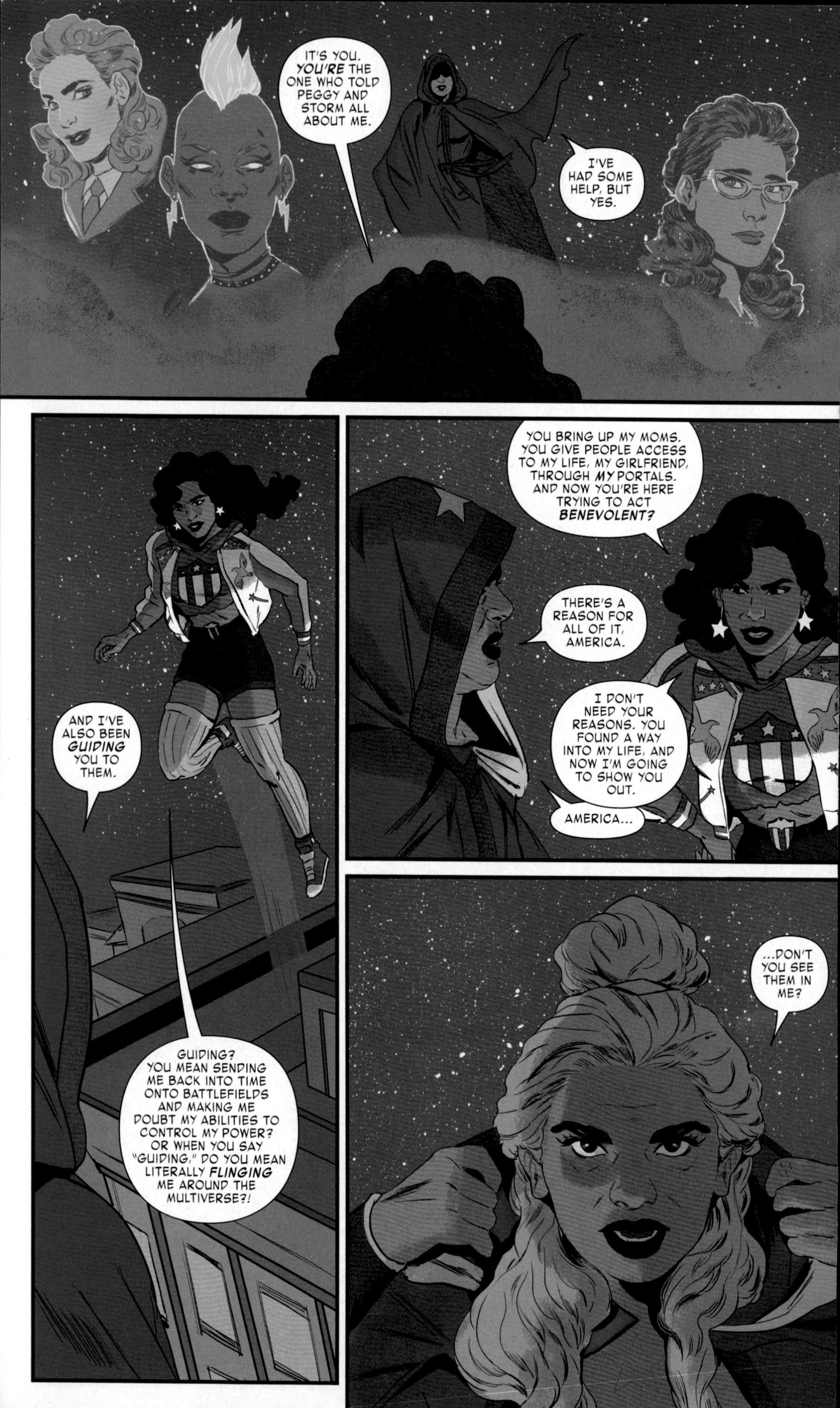

IT'S YOU. YOU'RE THE ONE WHO TOLD PEGGY AND STORM ALL ABOUT ME.
I'VE HAD SOME HELP, BUT YES.
AND I'VE ALSO BEEN GUIDING YOU TO THEM.
GUIDING? YOU MEAN SENDING ME BACK INTO TIME ONTO BATTLEFIELDS AND MAKING ME DOUBT MY ABILITIES TO CONTROL MY POWER? OR WHEN YOU SAY "GUIDING," DO YOU MEAN LITERALLY FLINGING ME AROUND THE MULTIVERSE?!
YOU BRING UP MY MOMS. YOU GIVE PEOPLE ACCESS TO MY LIFE, MY GIRLFRIEND, THROUGH MY PORTALS. AND NOW YOU'RE HERE TRYING TO ACT BENEVOLENT?
THERE'S A REASON FOR ALL OF IT, AMERICA.
I DON'T NEED YOUR REASONS. YOU FOUND A WAY INTO MY LIFE, AND NOW I'M GOING TO SHOW YOU OUT.
AMERICA...
...DON'T YOU SEE THEM IN ME?

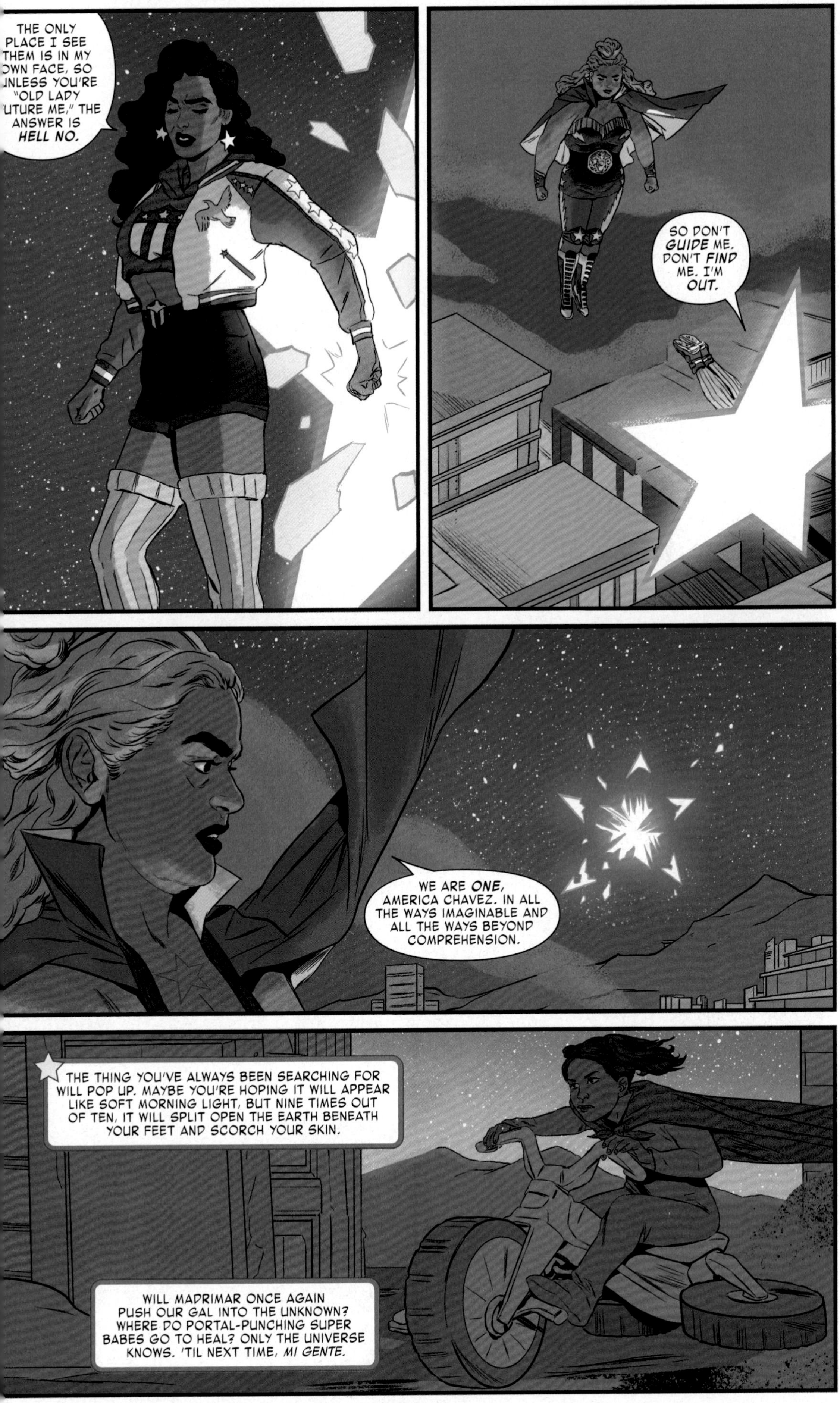
THE ONLY PLACE I SEE THEM IS IN MY OWN FACE, SO UNLESS YOU'RE "OLD LADY FUTURE ME," THE ANSWER IS *HELL NO.*
SO DON'T *GUIDE* ME. DON'T *FIND* ME. I'M *OUT.*
WE ARE *ONE,* AMERICA CHAVEZ. IN ALL THE WAYS IMAGINABLE AND ALL THE WAYS BEYOND COMPREHENSION.
THE THING YOU'VE ALWAYS BEEN SEARCHING FOR WILL POP UP. MAYBE YOU'RE HOPING IT WILL APPEAR LIKE SOFT MORNING LIGHT, BUT NINE TIMES OUT OF TEN, IT WILL SPLIT OPEN THE EARTH BENEATH YOUR FEET AND SCORCH YOUR SKIN.
WILL MADRIMAR ONCE AGAIN PUSH OUR GAL INTO THE UNKNOWN? WHERE DO PORTAL-PUNCHING SUPER BABES GO TO HEAL? ONLY THE UNIVERSE KNOWS. 'TIL NEXT TIME, *MI GENTE.*

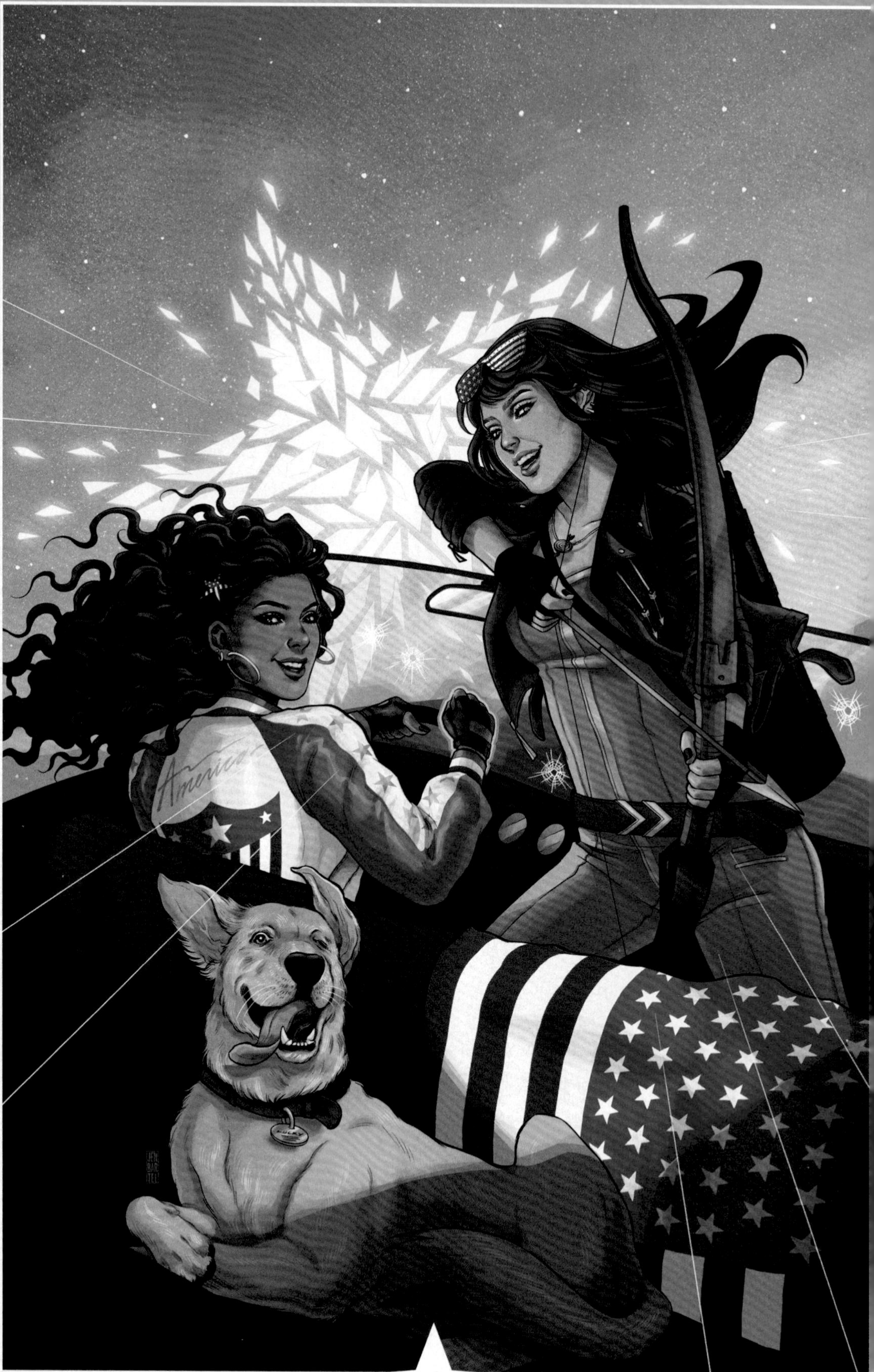

5

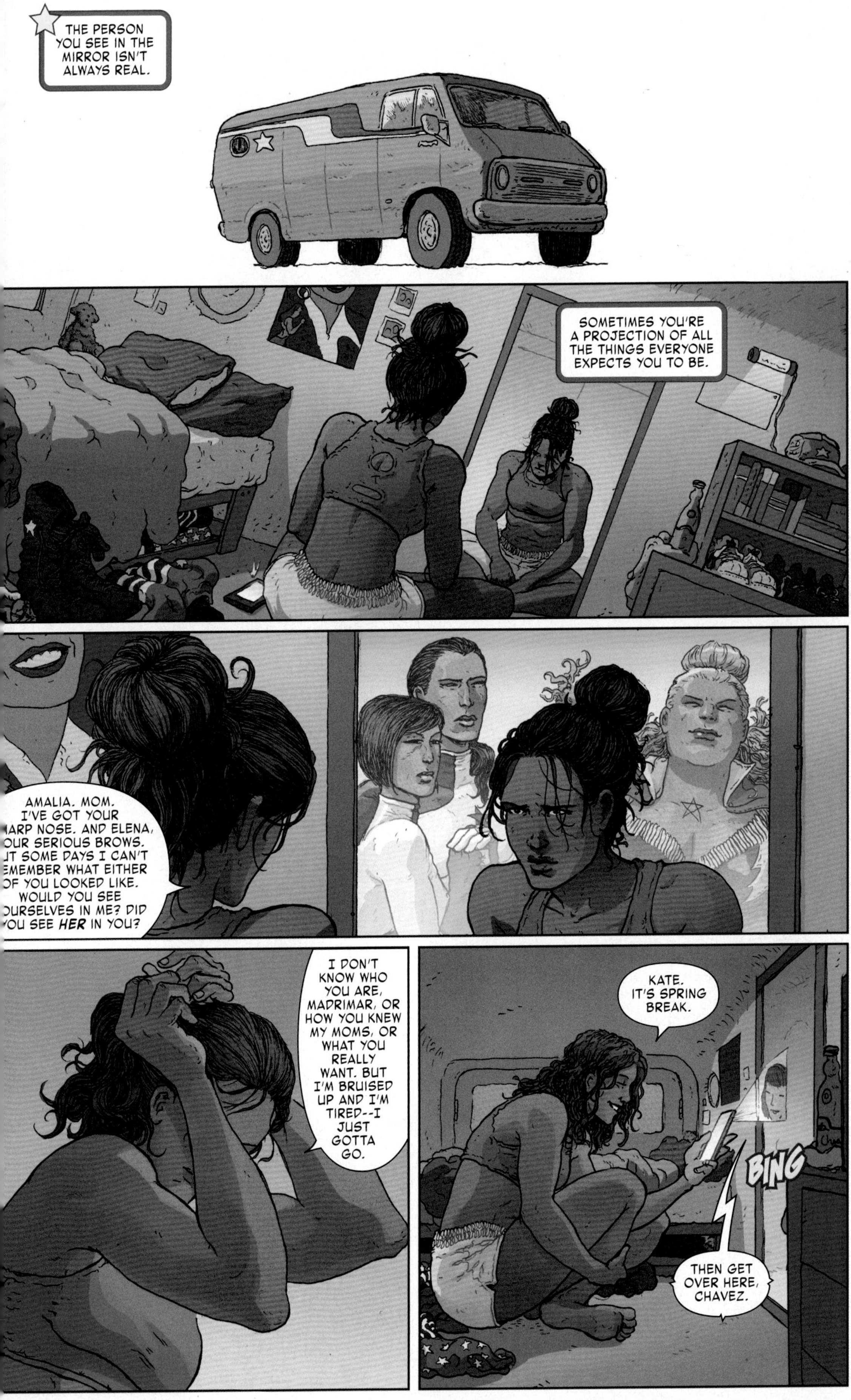
THE PERSON YOU SEE IN THE MIRROR ISN'T ALWAYS REAL.
SOMETIMES YOU'RE A PROJECTION OF ALL THE THINGS EVERYONE EXPECTS YOU TO BE.
AMALIA. MOM. I'VE GOT YOUR ARP NOSE. AND ELENA, OUR SERIOUS BROWS. UT SOME DAYS I CAN'T EMEMBER WHAT EITHER OF YOU LOOKED LIKE. WOULD YOU SEE OURSELVES IN ME? DID YOU SEE *HER* IN YOU?
I DON'T KNOW WHO YOU ARE, MADRIMAR, OR HOW YOU KNEW MY MOMS, OR WHAT YOU REALLY WANT. BUT I'M BRUISED UP AND I'M TIRED--I JUST GOTTA GO.
KATE. IT'S SPRING BREAK.
BING
THEN GET OVER HERE, CHAVEZ.

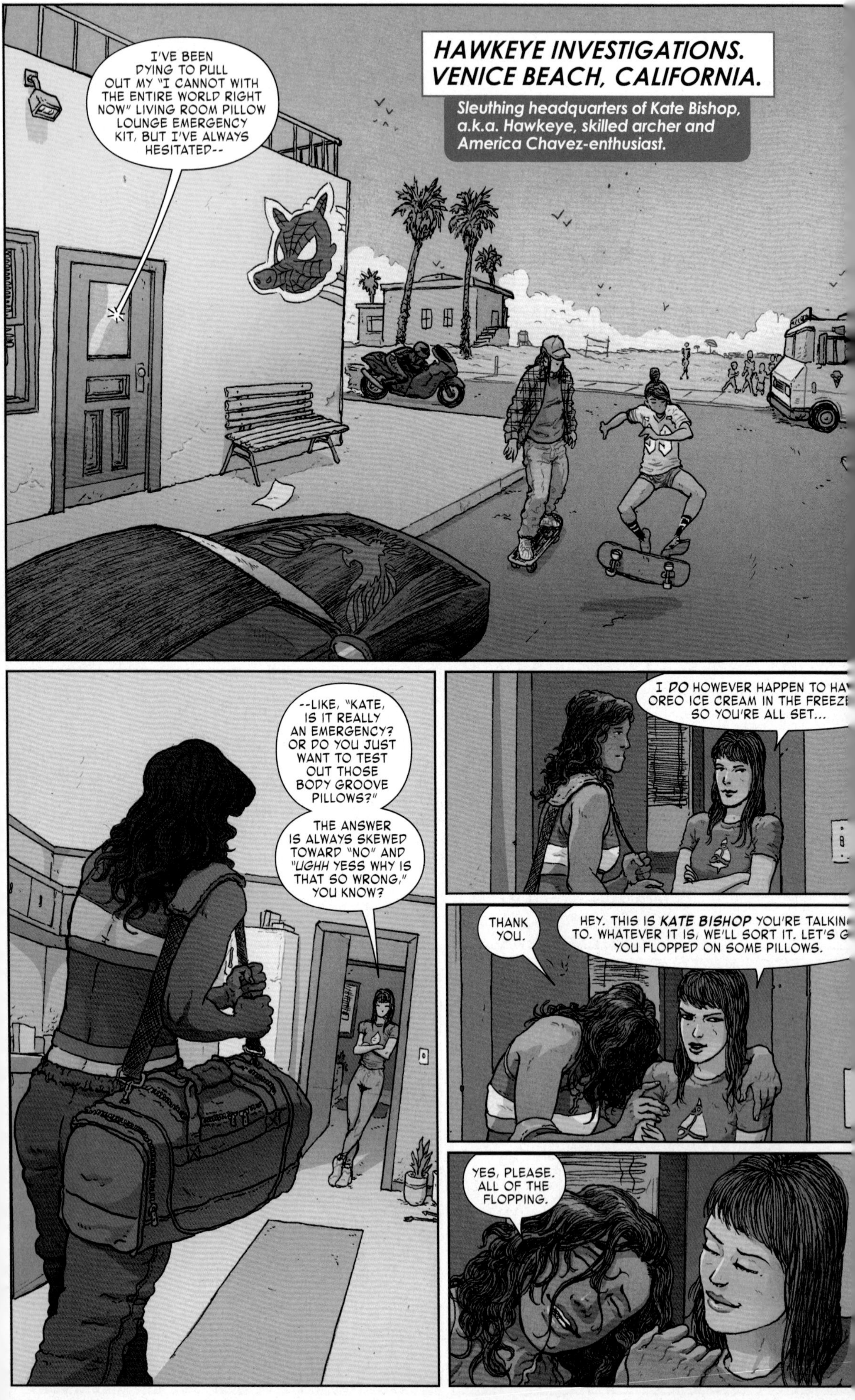
HAWKEYE INVESTIGATIONS. VENICE BEACH, CALIFORNIA.
Sleuthing headquarters of Kate Bishop, a.k.a. Hawkeye, skilled archer and America Chavez-enthusiast.
I'VE BEEN DYING TO PULL OUT MY "I CANNOT WITH THE ENTIRE WORLD RIGHT NOW" LIVING ROOM PILLOW LOUNGE EMERGENCY KIT, BUT I'VE ALWAYS HESITATED--
--LIKE, "KATE, IS IT REALLY AN EMERGENCY? OR DO YOU JUST WANT TO TEST OUT THOSE BODY GROOVE PILLOWS?"
THE ANSWER IS ALWAYS SKEWED TOWARD "NO" AND "UGHH YESS WHY IS THAT SO WRONG," YOU KNOW?
I DO HOWEVER HAPPEN TO HA OREO ICE CREAM IN THE FREEZ SO YOU'RE ALL SET...
THANK YOU.
HEY. THIS IS KATE BISHOP YOU'RE TALKIN TO. WHATEVER IT IS, WE'LL SORT IT. LET'S G YOU FLOPPED ON SOME PILLOWS.
YES, PLEASE. ALL OF THE FLOPPING.

THERE ARE THOSE CONNECTIONS THAT REMAIN CONSTANT NO MATTER WHAT DIMENSION YOU'RE IN.

WHEN EVERYTHING IS SWIRLING WITH DANGER AND CHAOS, BE BRAVE TOGETHER.

SLAY MONSTERS, THE PATRIARCHY, AND EXTRA-LARGE PIZZAS.

I THOUGHT THAT PULLING OUT *ALL* OF MY PILLOWS FOR YOU MIGHT BE OVERKILL, BUT...

NOPE, EXACT RIGHT AMOUNT OF PILLOWS. GOOD JOB.

T SAUCE FOR FILES ON THE ERIOUS ENTITY D ITS WEIRD RKINGS FOR YOU.

YOU BROUGHT ME A *CASE?* IN THE MIDDLE OF ALL YOUR SAD, LOST, HEARTACHE ENNUI...YOU BROUGHT ME A *CASE.* THAT, AMERICA CHAVEZ, IS HOW I KNOW YOU LIKE ME, YOU REALLY, REALLY LIKE ME.

PLEASE, KEEP THAT BETWEEN US.

NOTED. SO, LIKE, HOW ARE YOU *REALLY* DOING?

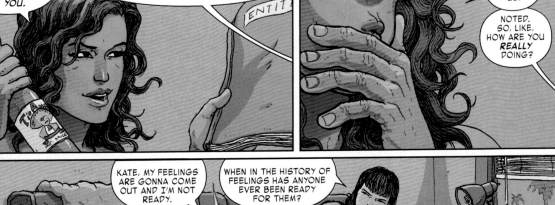

KATE, MY FEELINGS ARE GONNA COME OUT AND I'M NOT READY.

WHEN IN THE HISTORY OF FEELINGS HAS ANYONE EVER BEEN READY FOR THEM?

BING

UGH, NEVER, THAT'S WHEN. DO YOU MIND IF I PUT UP A PULL-UP BAR?

WHATEVER YA GOTTA DO, CHAVEZ.

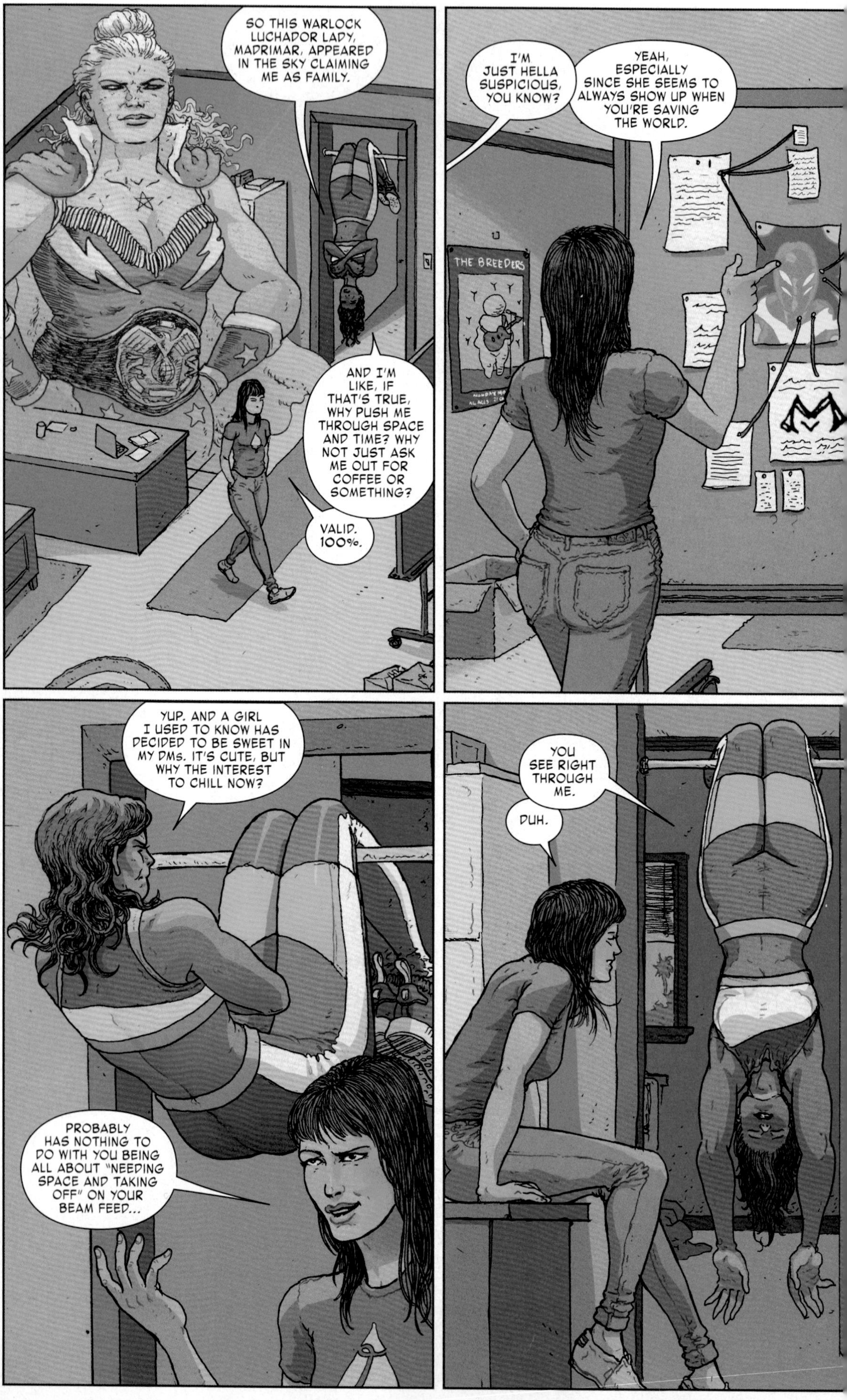
SO THIS WARLOCK LUCHADOR LADY, MADRIMAR, APPEARED IN THE SKY CLAIMING ME AS FAMILY.
AND I'M LIKE, IF THAT'S TRUE, WHY PUSH ME THROUGH SPACE AND TIME? WHY NOT JUST ASK ME OUT FOR COFFEE OR SOMETHING?
VALID. 100%.
I'M JUST HELLA SUSPICIOUS, YOU KNOW?
YEAH, ESPECIALLY SINCE SHE SEEMS TO ALWAYS SHOW UP WHEN YOU'RE SAVING THE WORLD.
THE BREEDERS
YUP. AND A GIRL I USED TO KNOW HAS DECIDED TO BE SWEET IN MY DMs. IT'S CUTE, BUT WHY THE INTEREST TO CHILL NOW?
PROBABLY HAS NOTHING TO DO WITH YOU BEING ALL ABOUT "NEEDING SPACE AND TAKING OFF" ON YOUR BEAM FEED...
YOU SEE RIGHT THROUGH ME.
DUH.

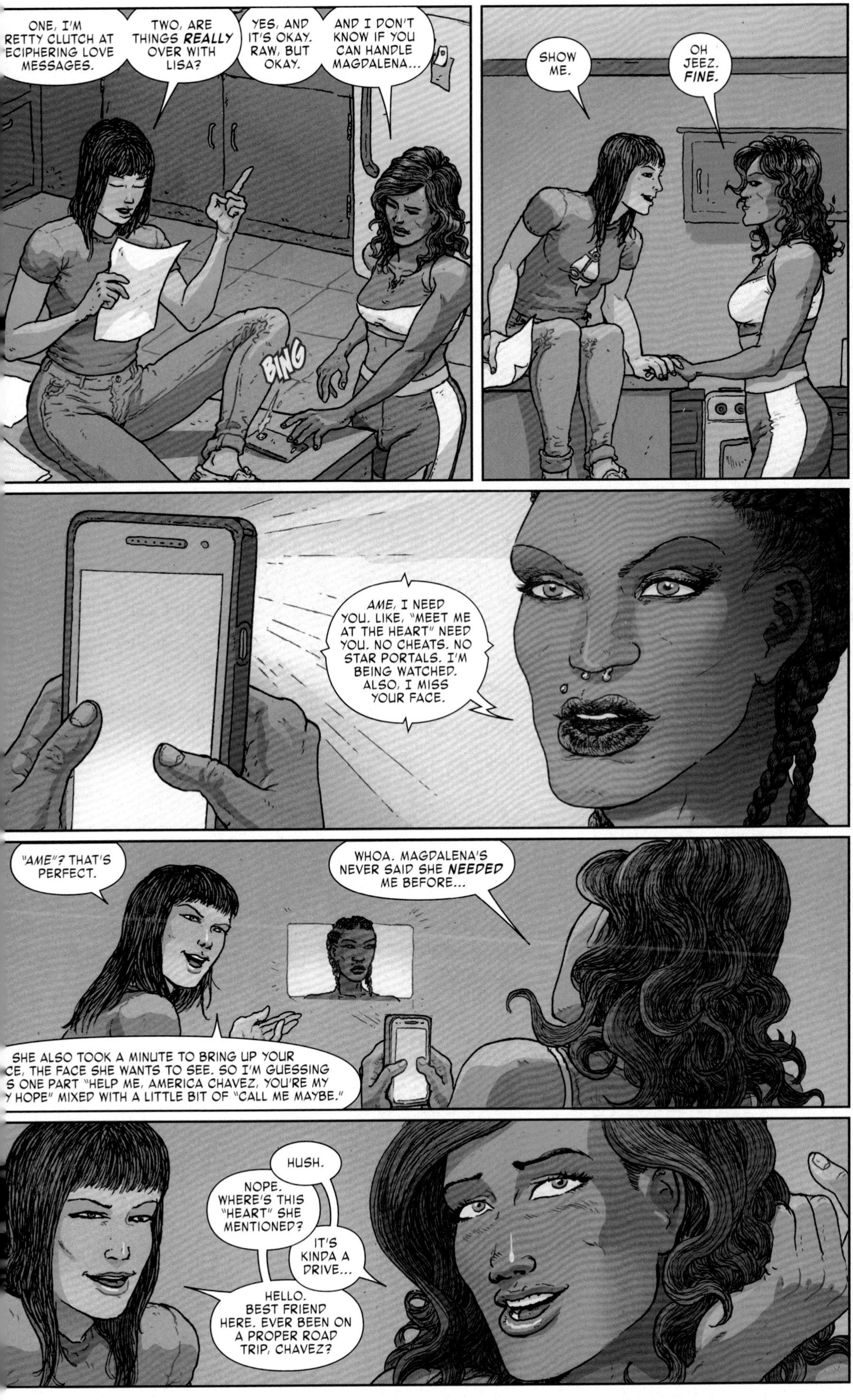
ONE, I'M
RETTY CLUTCH AT
ECIPHERING LOVE
MESSAGES.
TWO, ARE
THINGS REALLY
OVER WITH
LISA?
YES, AND
IT'S OKAY.
RAW, BUT
OKAY.
AND I DON'T
KNOW IF YOU
CAN HANDLE
MAGDALENA...
BING
SHOW
ME.
OH
JEEZ.
FINE.
AME, I NEED YOU. LIKE, "MEET ME AT THE HEART" NEED YOU. NO CHEATS. NO STAR PORTALS. I'M BEING WATCHED. ALSO, I MISS YOUR FACE.
"AME"? THAT'S PERFECT.
WHOA. MAGDALENA'S NEVER SAID SHE NEEDED ME BEFORE...
SHE ALSO TOOK A MINUTE TO BRING UP YOUR
CE, THE FACE SHE WANTS TO SEE. SO I'M GUESSING
S ONE PART "HELP ME, AMERICA CHAVEZ, YOU'RE MY
Y HOPE" MIXED WITH A LITTLE BIT OF "CALL ME MAYBE."
HUSH.
NOPE. WHERE'S THIS "HEART" SHE MENTIONED?
IT'S KINDA A DRIVE...
HELLO. BEST FRIEND HERE. EVER BEEN ON A PROPER ROAD TRIP, CHAVEZ?

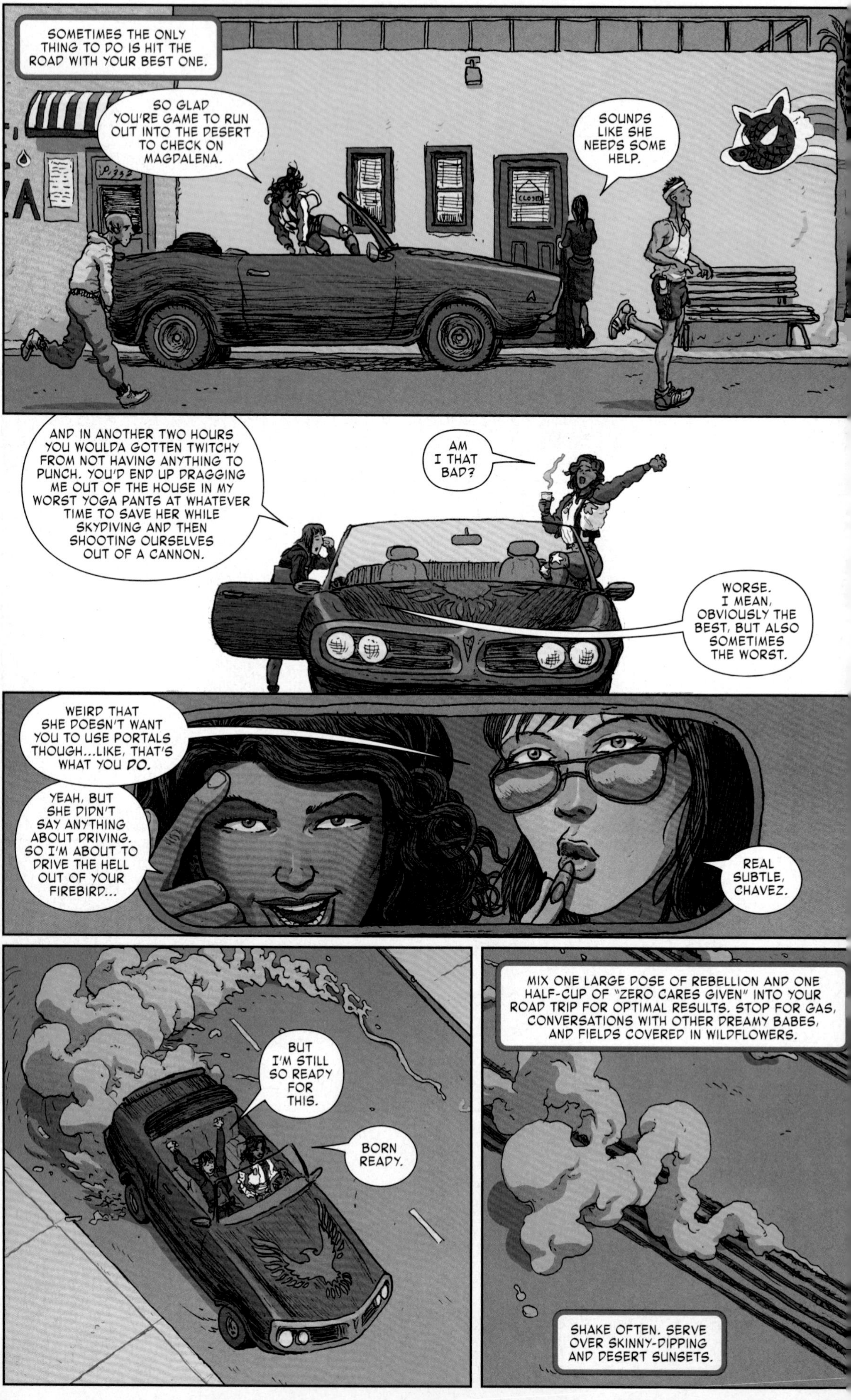
SOMETIMES THE ONLY THING TO DO IS HIT THE ROAD WITH YOUR BEST ONE.
SO GLAD YOU'RE GAME TO RUN OUT INTO THE DESERT TO CHECK ON MAGDALENA.
SOUNDS LIKE SHE NEEDS SOME HELP.
CLOSED
AND IN ANOTHER TWO HOURS YOU WOULDA GOTTEN TWITCHY FROM NOT HAVING ANYTHING TO PUNCH. YOU'D END UP DRAGGING ME OUT OF THE HOUSE IN MY WORST YOGA PANTS AT WHATEVER TIME TO SAVE HER WHILE SKYDIVING AND THEN SHOOTING OURSELVES OUT OF A CANNON.
AM I THAT BAD?
WORSE. I MEAN, OBVIOUSLY THE BEST, BUT ALSO SOMETIMES THE WORST.
WEIRD THAT SHE DOESN'T WANT YOU TO USE PORTALS THOUGH...LIKE, THAT'S WHAT YOU *DO.*
YEAH, BUT SHE DIDN'T SAY ANYTHING ABOUT DRIVING. SO I'M ABOUT TO DRIVE THE HELL OUT OF YOUR FIREBIRD...
REAL SUBTLE, CHAVEZ.
BUT I'M STILL SO READY FOR THIS.
BORN READY.
MIX ONE LARGE DOSE OF REBELLION AND ONE HALF-CUP OF "ZERO CARES GIVEN" INTO YOUR ROAD TRIP FOR OPTIMAL RESULTS. STOP FOR GAS, CONVERSATIONS WITH OTHER DREAMY BABES, AND FIELDS COVERED IN WILDFLOWERS.
SHAKE OFTEN. SERVE OVER SKINNY-DIPPING AND DESERT SUNSETS.

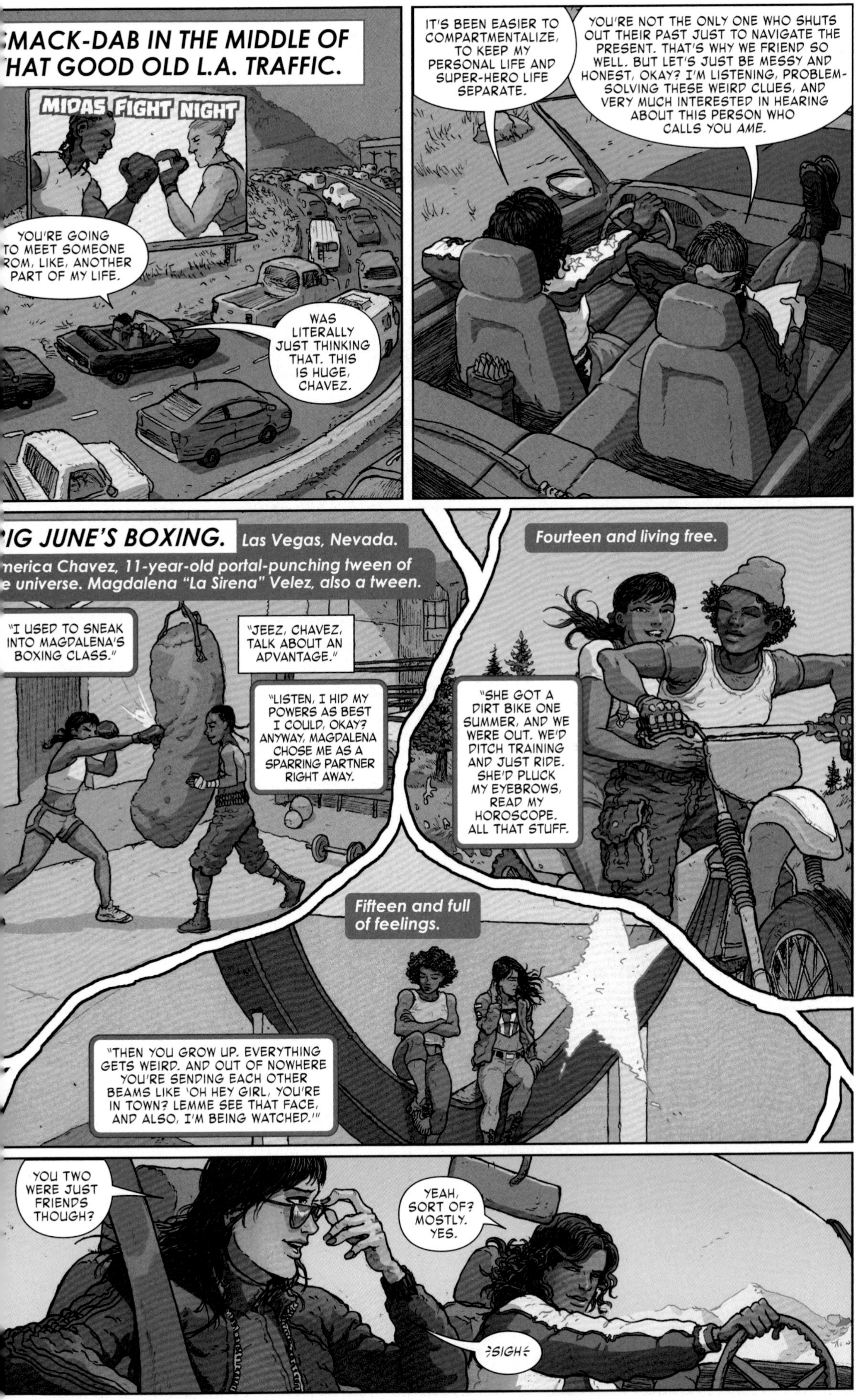
SMACK-DAB IN THE MIDDLE OF THAT GOOD OLD L.A. TRAFFIC.
MIDAS FIGHT NIGHT
YOU'RE GOING TO MEET SOMEONE FROM, LIKE, ANOTHER PART OF MY LIFE.
WAS LITERALLY JUST THINKING THAT. THIS IS HUGE, CHAVEZ.
IT'S BEEN EASIER TO COMPARTMENTALIZE, TO KEEP MY PERSONAL LIFE AND SUPER-HERO LIFE SEPARATE.
YOU'RE NOT THE ONLY ONE WHO SHUTS OUT THEIR PAST JUST TO NAVIGATE THE PRESENT. THAT'S WHY WE FRIEND SO WELL. BUT LET'S JUST BE MESSY AND HONEST, OKAY? I'M LISTENING, PROBLEM-SOLVING THESE WEIRD CLUES, AND VERY MUCH INTERESTED IN HEARING ABOUT THIS PERSON WHO CALLS YOU AME.
BIG JUNE'S BOXING. Las Vegas, Nevada.
America Chavez, 11-year-old portal-punching tween of the universe. Magdalena "La Sirena" Velez, also a tween.
"I USED TO SNEAK INTO MAGDALENA'S BOXING CLASS."
"JEEZ, CHAVEZ, TALK ABOUT AN ADVANTAGE."
"LISTEN, I HID MY POWERS AS BEST I COULD, OKAY? ANYWAY, MAGDALENA CHOSE ME AS A SPARRING PARTNER RIGHT AWAY.
Fourteen and living free.
"SHE GOT A DIRT BIKE ONE SUMMER, AND WE WERE OUT. WE'D DITCH TRAINING AND JUST RIDE. SHE'D PLUCK MY EYEBROWS, READ MY HOROSCOPE. ALL THAT STUFF.
Fifteen and full of feelings.
"THEN YOU GROW UP. EVERYTHING GETS WEIRD. AND OUT OF NOWHERE YOU'RE SENDING EACH OTHER BEAMS LIKE 'OH HEY GIRL, YOU'RE IN TOWN? LEMME SEE THAT FACE, AND ALSO, I'M BEING WATCHED.'"
YOU TWO WERE JUST FRIENDS THOUGH?
YEAH, SORT OF? MOSTLY. YES.
SIGH

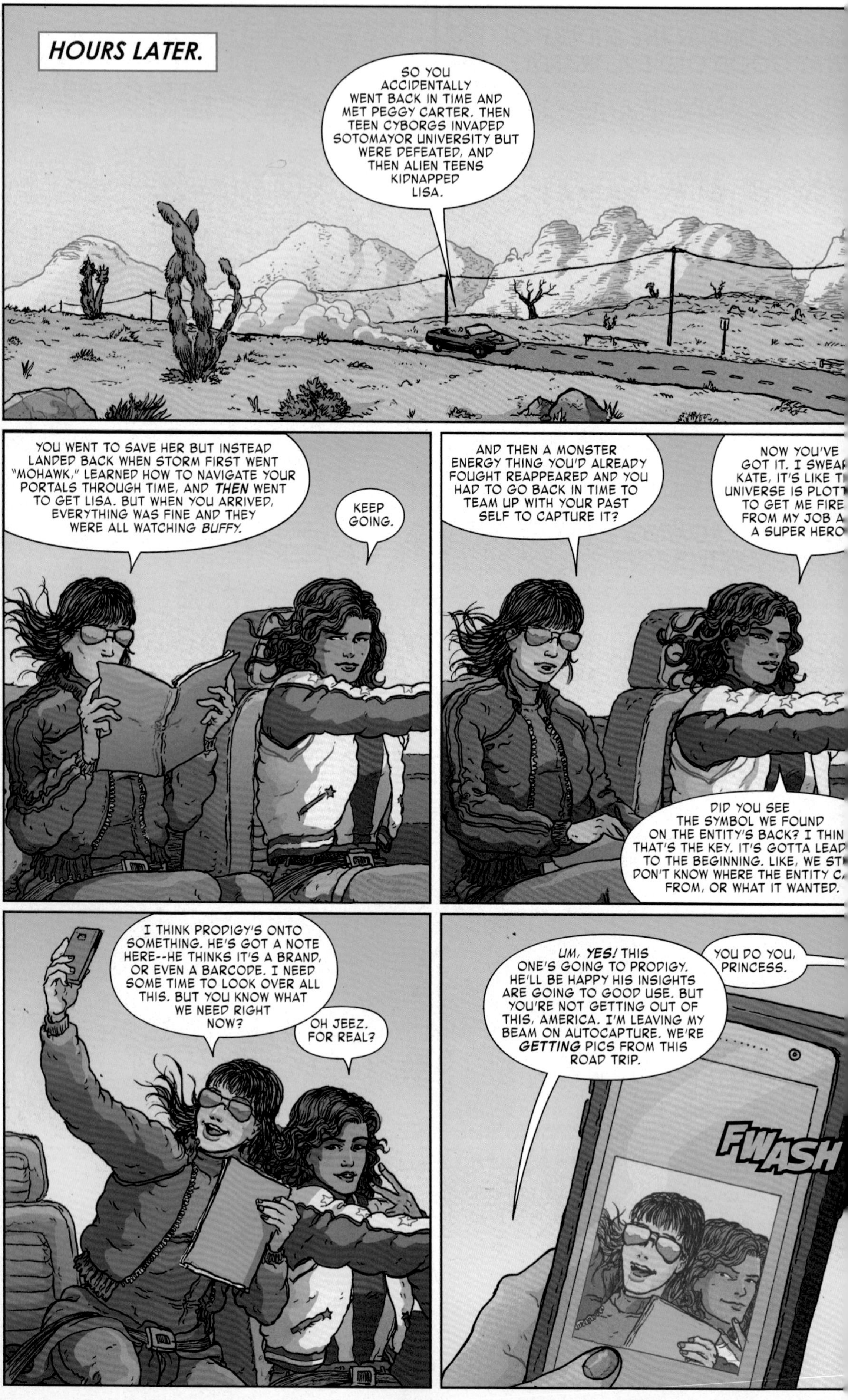
HOURS LATER.
SO YOU ACCIDENTALLY WENT BACK IN TIME AND MET PEGGY CARTER. THEN TEEN CYBORGS INVADED SOTOMAYOR UNIVERSITY BUT WERE DEFEATED, AND THEN ALIEN TEENS KIDNAPPED LISA.
YOU WENT TO SAVE HER BUT INSTEAD LANDED BACK WHEN STORM FIRST WENT "MOHAWK," LEARNED HOW TO NAVIGATE YOUR PORTALS THROUGH TIME, AND THEN WENT TO GET LISA. BUT WHEN YOU ARRIVED, EVERYTHING WAS FINE AND THEY WERE ALL WATCHING BUFFY.
KEEP GOING.
AND THEN A MONSTER ENERGY THING YOU'D ALREADY FOUGHT REAPPEARED AND YOU HAD TO GO BACK IN TIME TO TEAM UP WITH YOUR PAST SELF TO CAPTURE IT?
NOW YOU'VE GOT IT. I SWEAR KATE, IT'S LIKE T UNIVERSE IS PLOTT TO GET ME FIRE FROM MY JOB A A SUPER HERO
DID YOU SEE THE SYMBOL WE FOUND ON THE ENTITY'S BACK? I THIN THAT'S THE KEY. IT'S GOTTA LEAD TO THE BEGINNING. LIKE, WE ST DON'T KNOW WHERE THE ENTITY C FROM, OR WHAT IT WANTED.
I THINK PRODIGY'S ONTO SOMETHING. HE'S GOT A NOTE HERE--HE THINKS IT'S A BRAND, OR EVEN A BARCODE. I NEED SOME TIME TO LOOK OVER ALL THIS. BUT YOU KNOW WHAT WE NEED RIGHT NOW?
OH JEEZ. FOR REAL?
UM, YES! THIS ONE'S GOING TO PRODIGY. HE'LL BE HAPPY HIS INSIGHTS ARE GOING TO GOOD USE. BUT YOU'RE NOT GETTING OUT OF THIS, AMERICA. I'M LEAVING MY BEAM ON AUTOCAPTURE. WE'RE GETTING PICS FROM THIS ROAD TRIP.
YOU DO YOU, PRINCESS.
FWASH

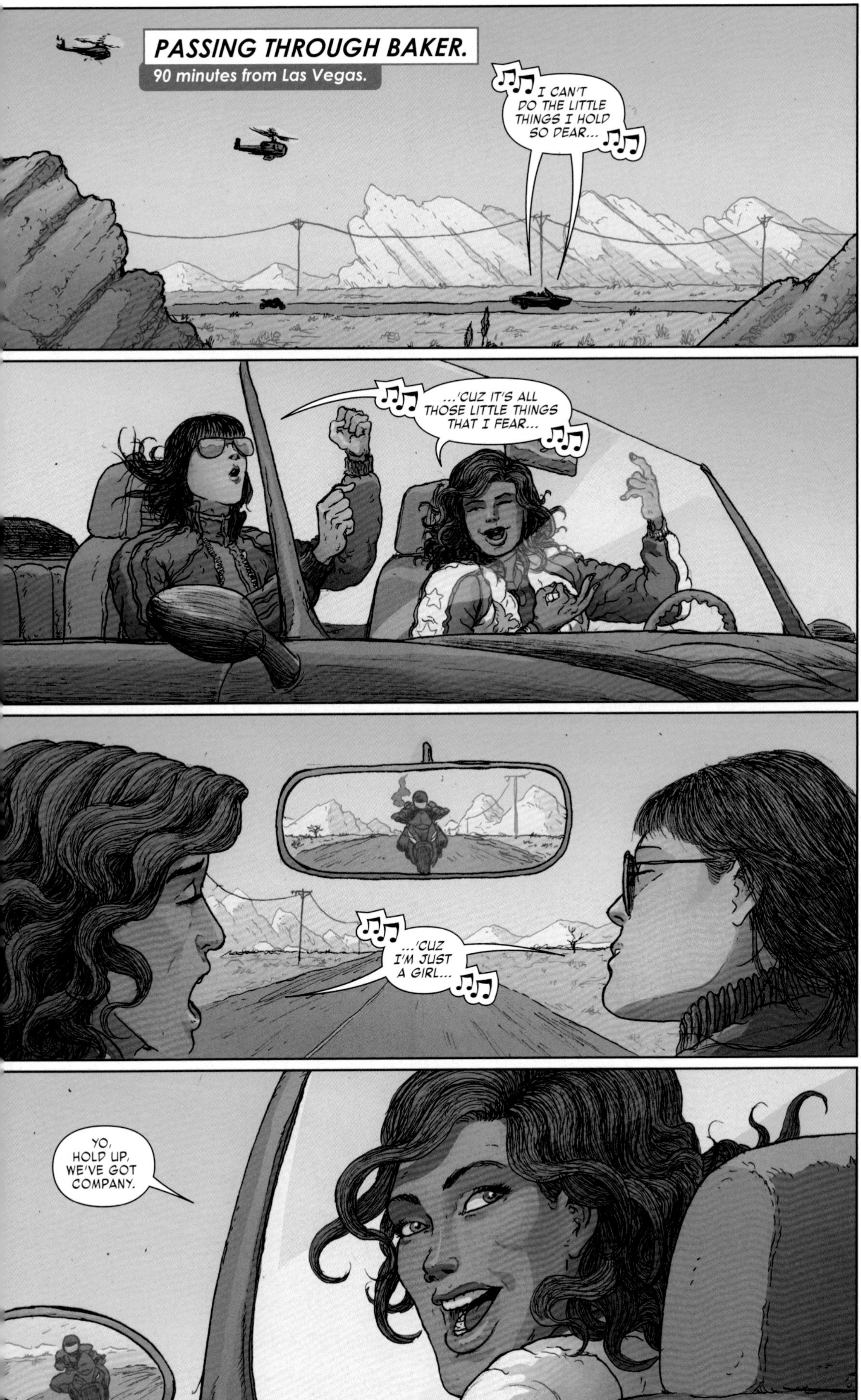
PASSING THROUGH BAKER.
90 minutes from Las Vegas.
I CAN'T DO THE LITTLE THINGS I HOLD SO DEAR...
...'CUZ IT'S ALL THOSE LITTLE THINGS THAT I FEAR...
...'CUZ I'M JUST A GIRL...
YO, HOLD UP, WE'VE GOT COMPANY.

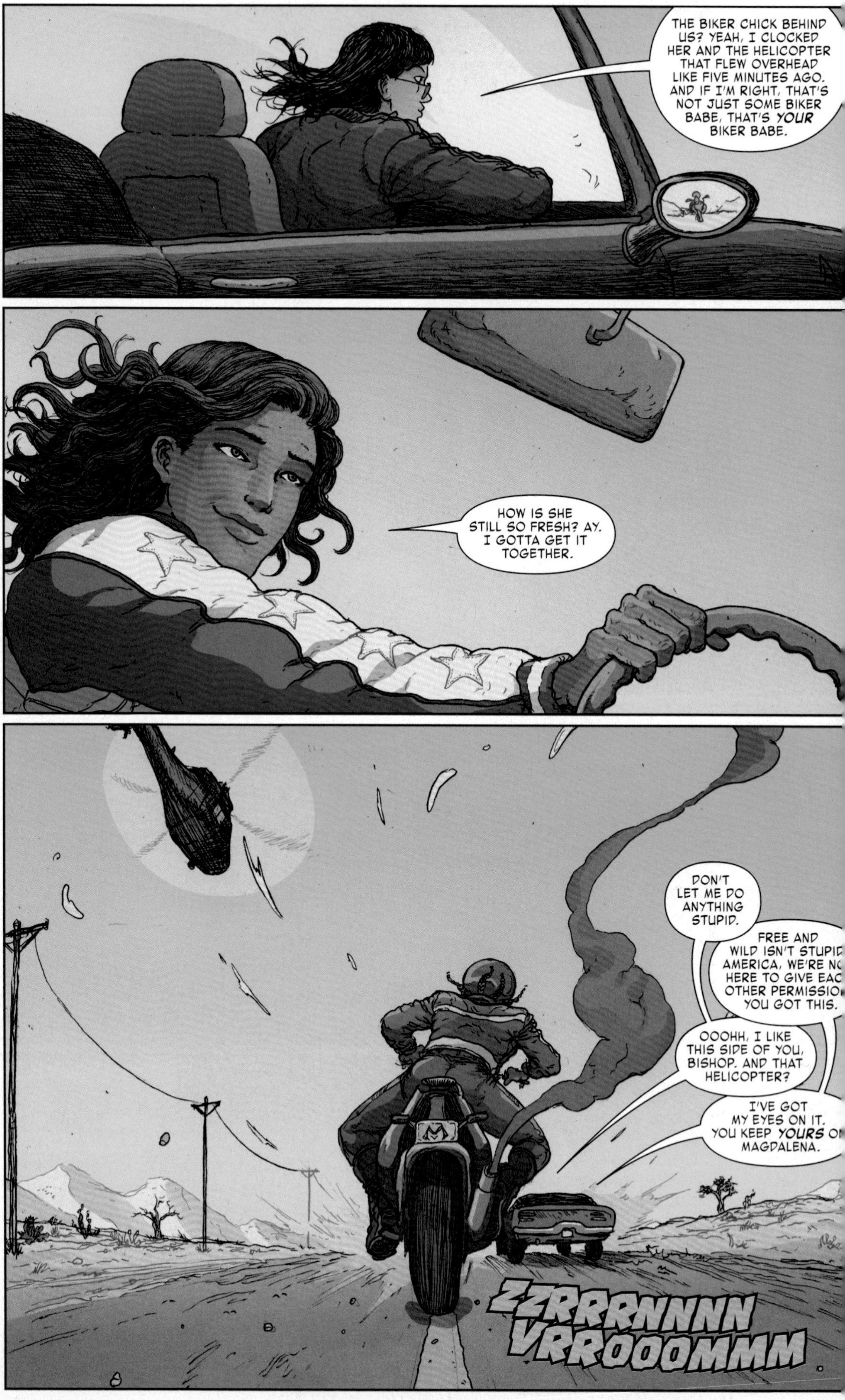
THE BIKER CHICK BEHIND US? YEAH, I CLOCKED HER AND THE HELICOPTER THAT FLEW OVERHEAD LIKE FIVE MINUTES AGO. AND IF I'M RIGHT, THAT'S NOT JUST SOME BIKER BABE, THAT'S *YOUR* BIKER BABE.
HOW IS SHE STILL SO FRESH? AY. I GOTTA GET IT TOGETHER.
DON'T LET ME DO ANYTHING STUPID.
FREE AND WILD ISN'T STUPI AMERICA, WE'RE N HERE TO GIVE EAC OTHER PERMISSIO YOU GOT THIS.
OOOHH, I LIKE THIS SIDE OF YOU, BISHOP. AND THAT HELICOPTER?
I'VE GOT MY EYES ON IT. YOU KEEP *YOURS* O MAGDALENA.
ZZRRRNNNNN VRROOOMMMM

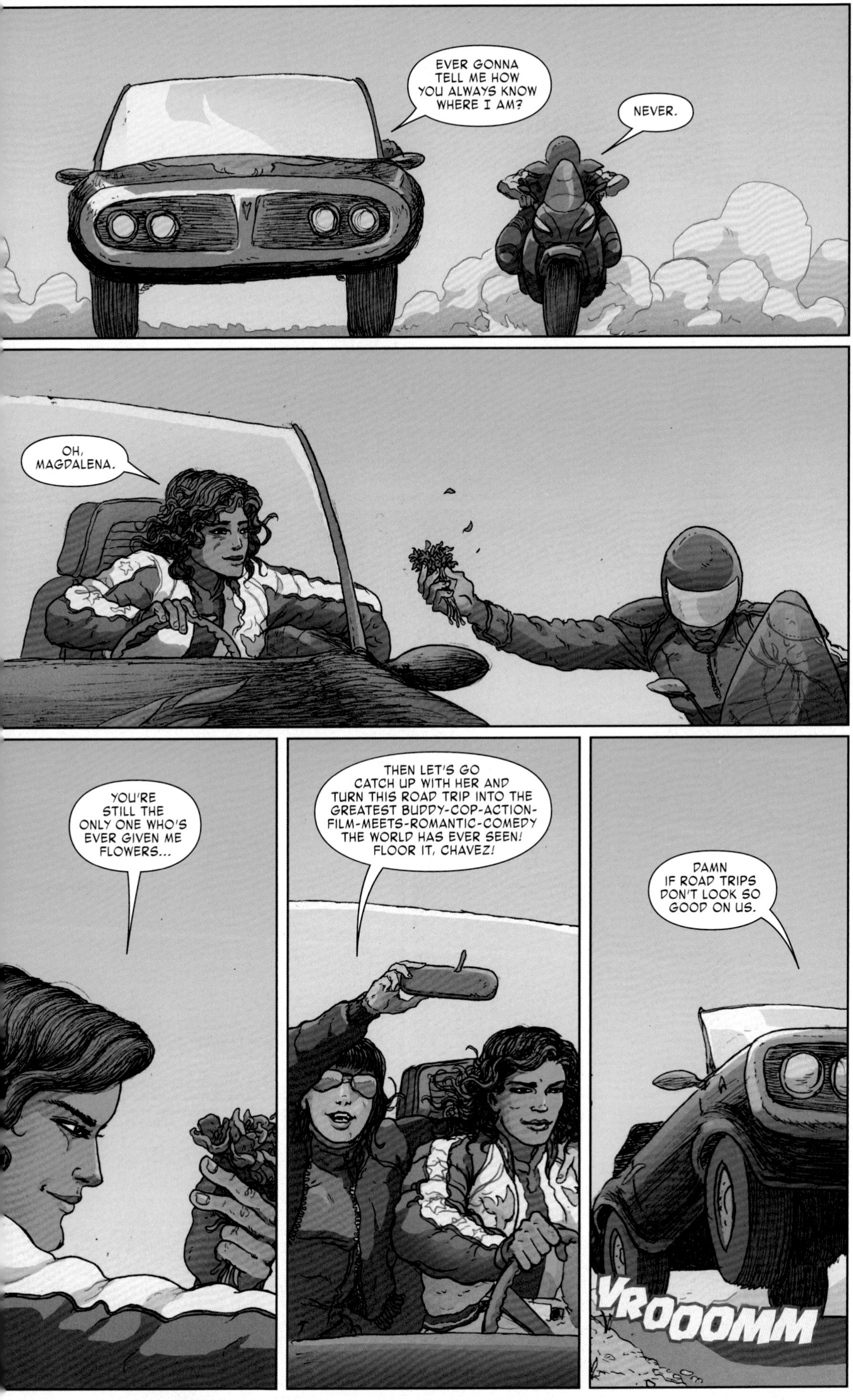

EVER GONNA TELL ME HOW YOU ALWAYS KNOW WHERE I AM?
NEVER.
OH, MAGDALENA.
YOU'RE STILL THE ONLY ONE WHO'S EVER GIVEN ME FLOWERS...
THEN LET'S GO CATCH UP WITH HER AND TURN THIS ROAD TRIP INTO THE GREATEST BUDDY-COP-ACTION-FILM-MEETS-ROMANTIC-COMEDY THE WORLD HAS EVER SEEN! FLOOR IT, CHAVEZ!
DAMN IF ROAD TRIPS DON'T LOOK SO GOOD ON US.
VROOOMM

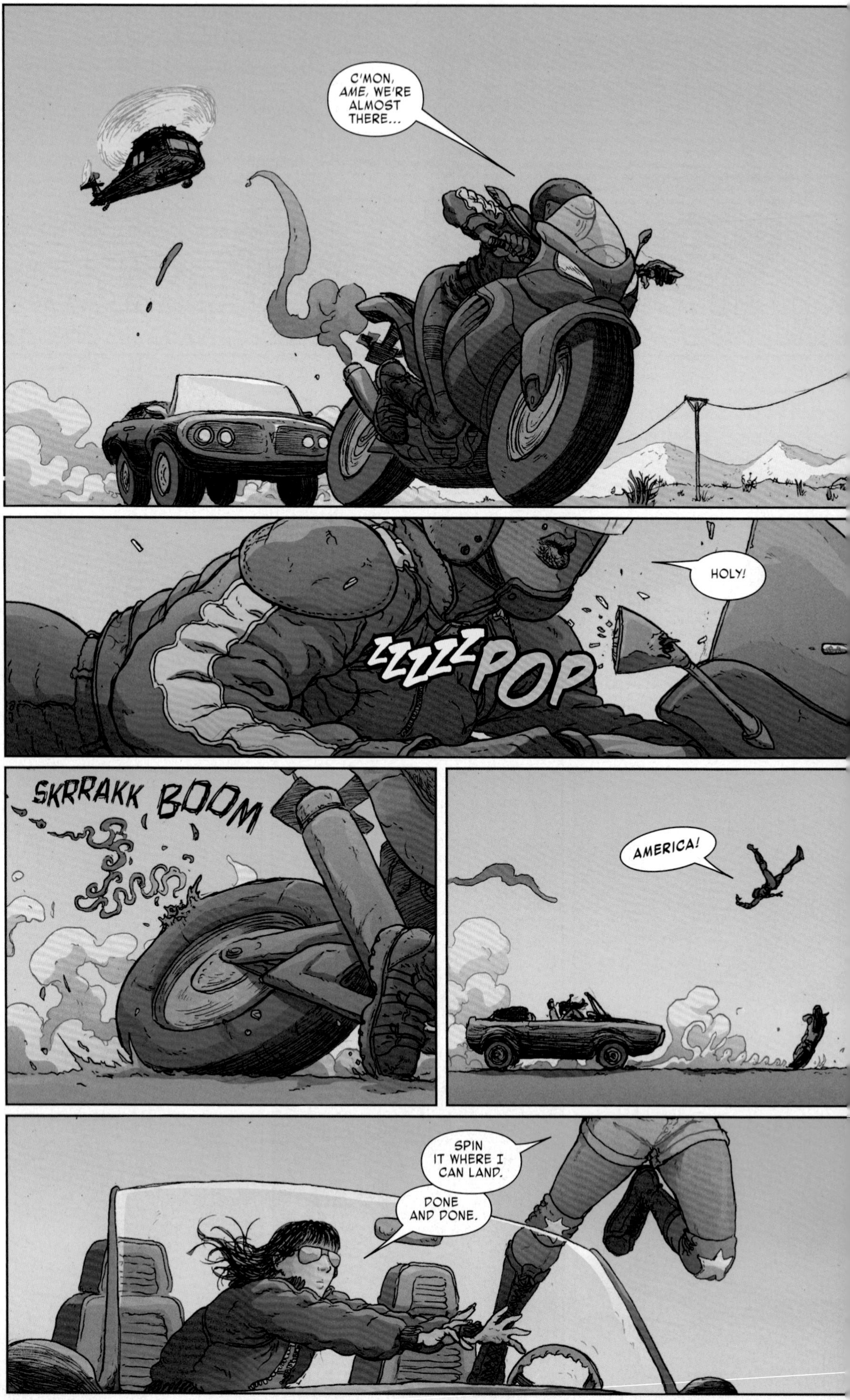
C'MON, AME, WE'RE ALMOST THERE...
HOLY!
ZZZZZPOP
SKRRAKK BOOM
AMERICA!
SPIN IT WHERE I CAN LAND.
DONE AND DONE.

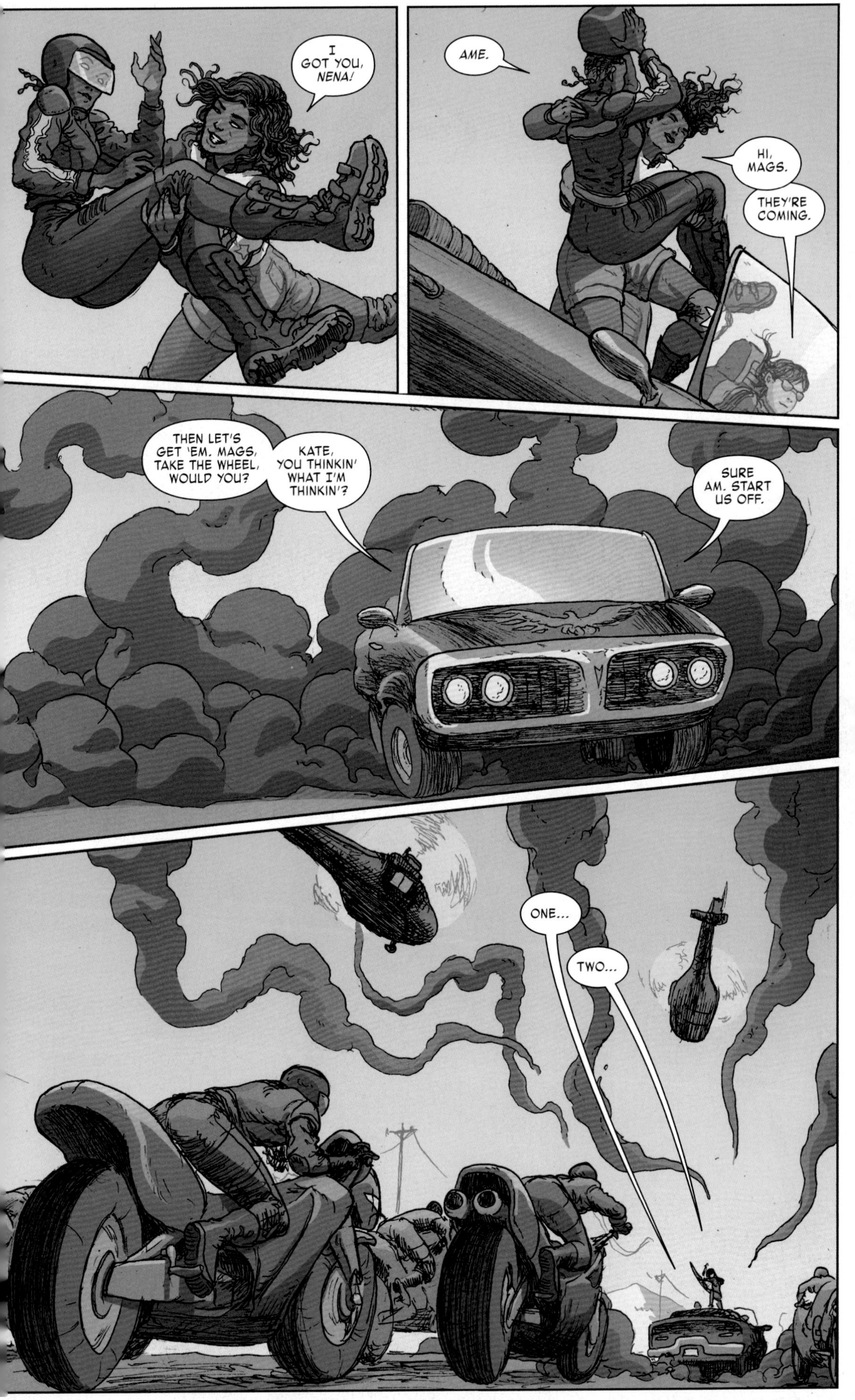
I GOT YOU, NENA!
AME.
HI, MAGS.
THEY'RE COMING.
THEN LET'S GET 'EM. MAGS, TAKE THE WHEEL, WOULD YOU?
KATE, YOU THINKIN' WHAT I'M THINKIN'?
SURE AM. START US OFF.
ONE...
TWO...

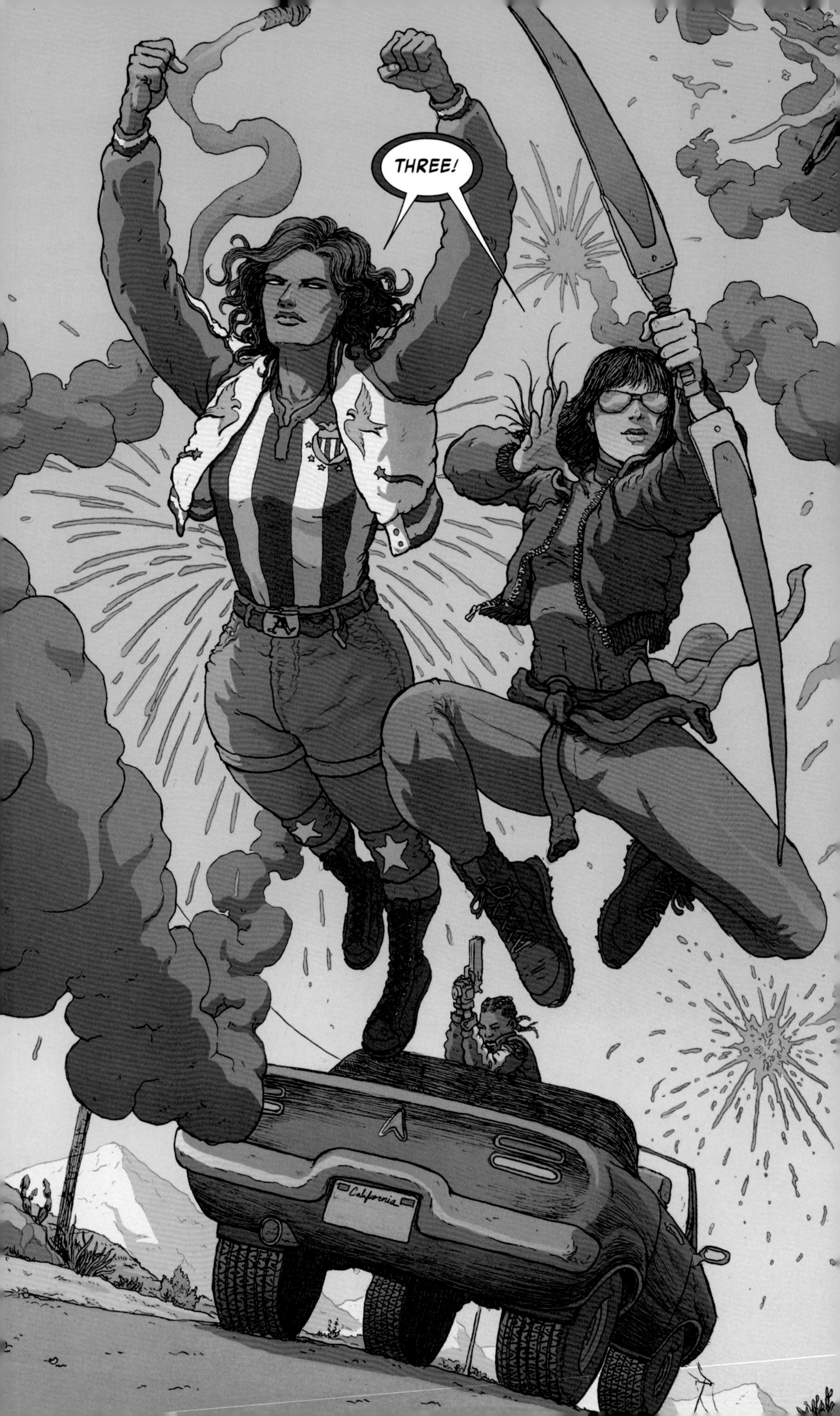
THREE!
California

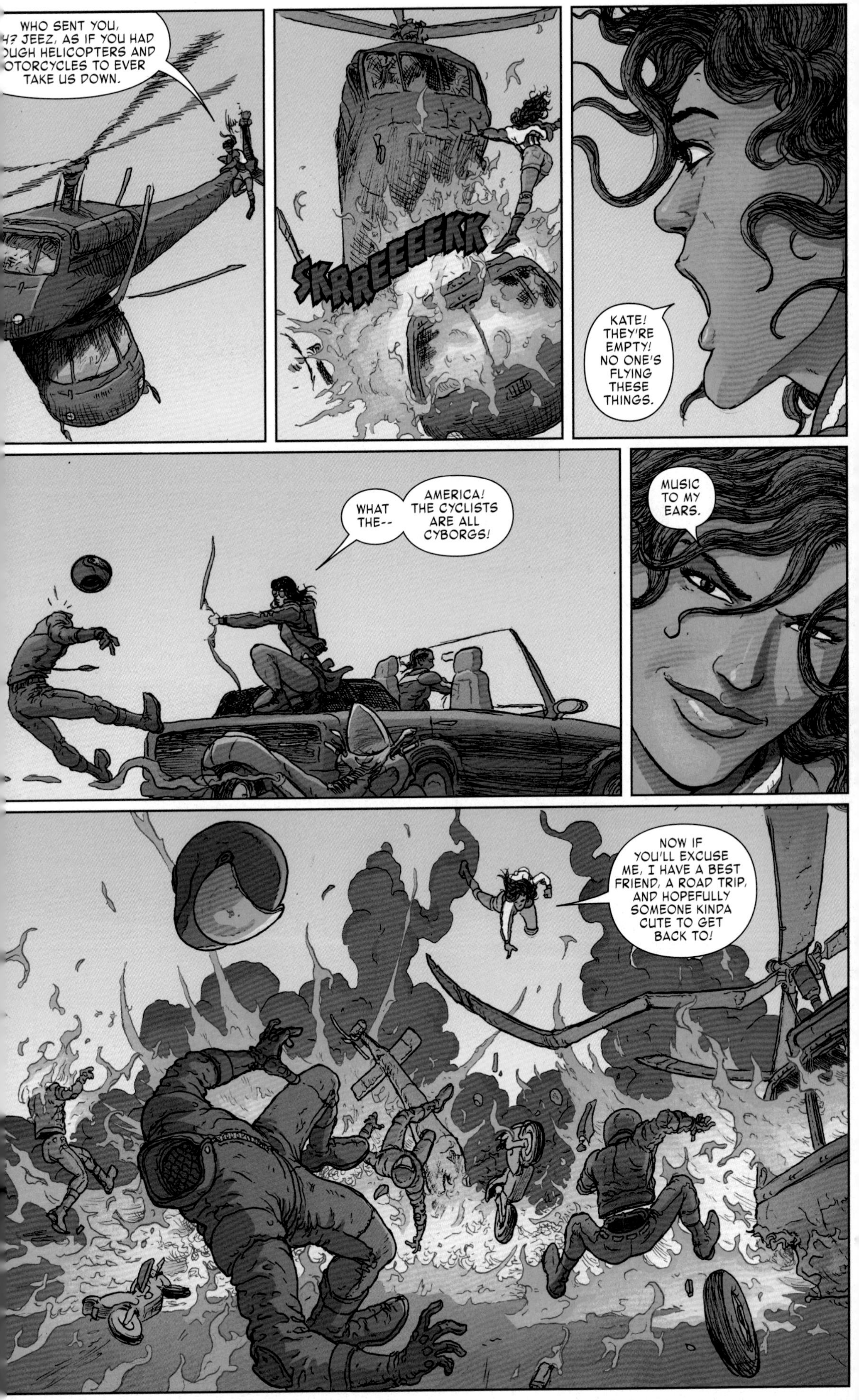

WHO SENT YOU, H? JEEZ, AS IF YOU HAD UGH HELICOPTERS AND OTORCYCLES TO EVER TAKE US DOWN.
SKRREEEEEKK
KATE! THEY'RE EMPTY! NO ONE'S FLYING THESE THINGS.
WHAT THE--
AMERICA! THE CYCLISTS ARE ALL CYBORGS!
MUSIC TO MY EARS.
NOW IF YOU'LL EXCUSE ME, I HAVE A BEST FRIEND, A ROAD TRIP, AND HOPEFULLY SOMEONE KINDA CUTE TO GET BACK TO!

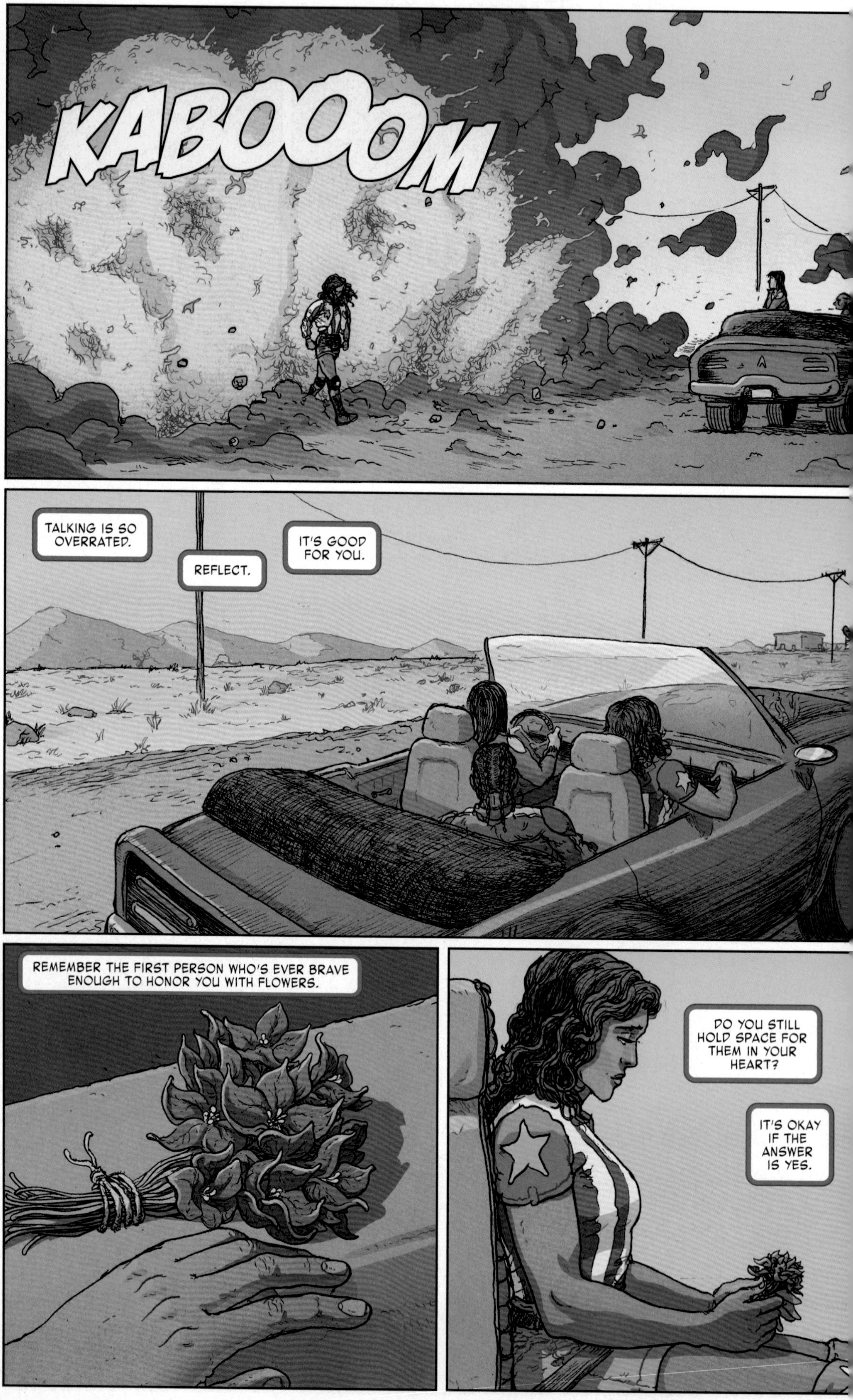
KABOOOM
TALKING IS SO OVERRATED.
REFLECT.
IT'S GOOD FOR YOU.
REMEMBER THE FIRST PERSON WHO'S EVER BRAVE ENOUGH TO HONOR YOU WITH FLOWERS.
DO YOU STILL HOLD SPACE FOR THEM IN YOUR HEART?
IT'S OKAY IF THE ANSWER IS YES.

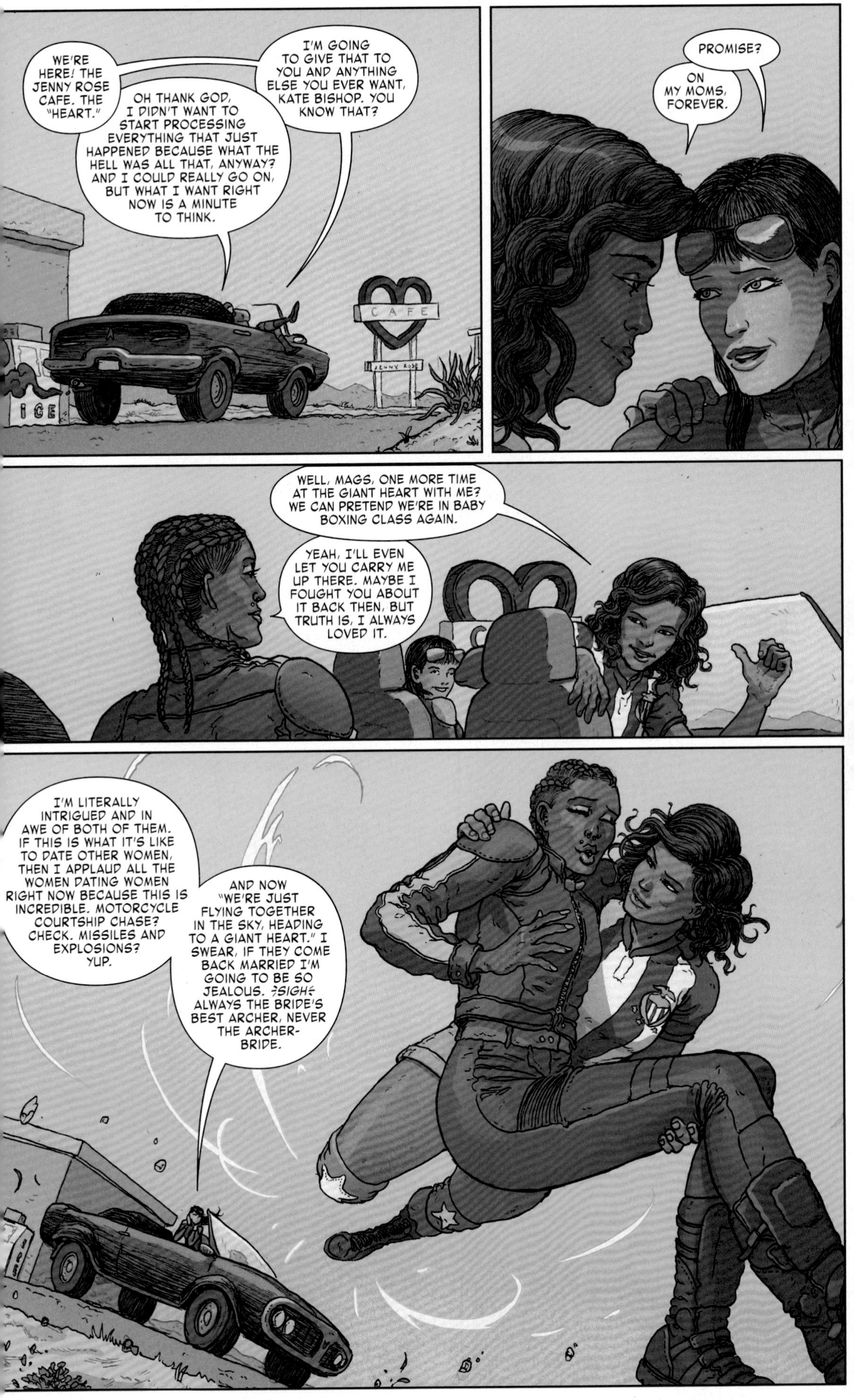
WE'RE HERE! THE JENNY ROSE CAFE. THE "HEART."
OH THANK GOD, I DIDN'T WANT TO START PROCESSING EVERYTHING THAT JUST HAPPENED BECAUSE WHAT THE HELL WAS ALL THAT, ANYWAY? AND I COULD REALLY GO ON, BUT WHAT I WANT RIGHT NOW IS A MINUTE TO THINK.
I'M GOING TO GIVE THAT TO YOU AND ANYTHING ELSE YOU EVER WANT, KATE BISHOP. YOU KNOW THAT?
CAFE
JENNY ROSE
ICE
PROMISE?
ON MY MOMS, FOREVER.
WELL, MAGS, ONE MORE TIME AT THE GIANT HEART WITH ME? WE CAN PRETEND WE'RE IN BABY BOXING CLASS AGAIN.
YEAH, I'LL EVEN LET YOU CARRY ME UP THERE. MAYBE I FOUGHT YOU ABOUT IT BACK THEN, BUT TRUTH IS, I ALWAYS LOVED IT.
I'M LITERALLY INTRIGUED AND IN AWE OF BOTH OF THEM. IF THIS IS WHAT IT'S LIKE TO DATE OTHER WOMEN, THEN I APPLAUD ALL THE WOMEN DATING WOMEN RIGHT NOW BECAUSE THIS IS INCREDIBLE. MOTORCYCLE COURTSHIP CHASE? CHECK. MISSILES AND EXPLOSIONS? YUP.
AND NOW "WE'RE JUST FLYING TOGETHER IN THE SKY, HEADING TO A GIANT HEART." I SWEAR, IF THEY COME BACK MARRIED I'M GOING TO BE SO JEALOUS. ⁼SIGH⁼ ALWAYS THE BRIDE'S BEST ARCHER, NEVER THE ARCHER-BRIDE.

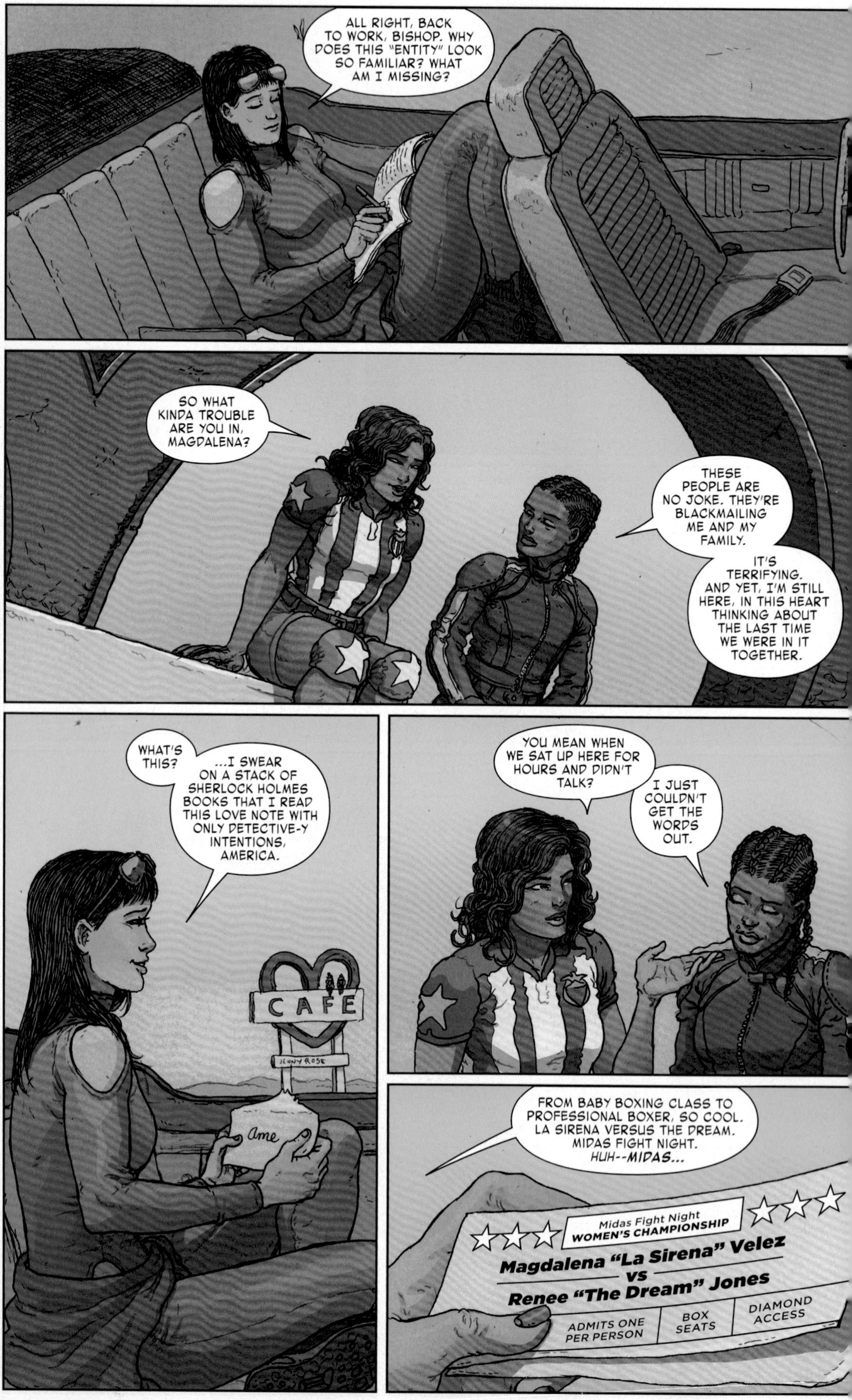
ALL RIGHT, BACK TO WORK, BISHOP. WHY DOES THIS "ENTITY" LOOK SO FAMILIAR? WHAT AM I MISSING?
SO WHAT KINDA TROUBLE ARE YOU IN, MAGDALENA?
THESE PEOPLE ARE NO JOKE. THEY'RE BLACKMAILING ME AND MY FAMILY.
IT'S TERRIFYING. AND YET, I'M STILL HERE, IN THIS HEART THINKING ABOUT THE LAST TIME WE WERE IN IT TOGETHER.
WHAT'S THIS?
...I SWEAR ON A STACK OF SHERLOCK HOLMES BOOKS THAT I READ THIS LOVE NOTE WITH ONLY DETECTIVE-Y INTENTIONS, AMERICA.
CAFE
ame
YOU MEAN WHEN WE SAT UP HERE FOR HOURS AND DIDN'T TALK?
I JUST COULDN'T GET THE WORDS OUT.
FROM BABY BOXING CLASS TO PROFESSIONAL BOXER, SO COOL. LA SIRENA VERSUS THE DREAM. MIDAS FIGHT NIGHT. HUH--MIDAS...
Midas Fight Night
WOMEN'S CHAMPIONSHIP
Magdalena "La Sirena" Velez
vs
Renee "The Dream" Jones
ADMITS ONE PER PERSON
BOX SEATS
DIAMOND ACCESS

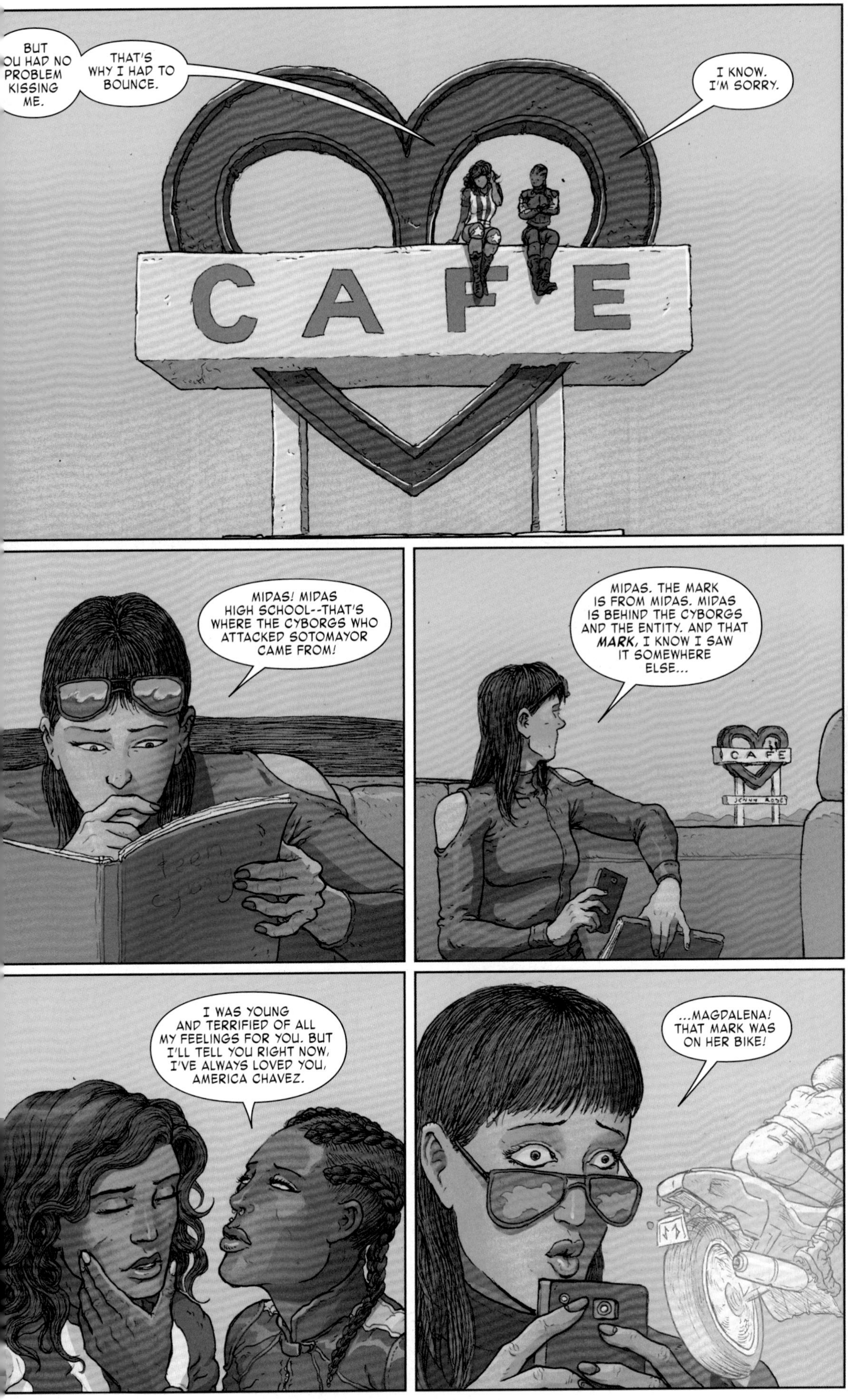
BUT
OU HAD NO PROBLEM KISSING ME.
THAT'S WHY I HAD TO BOUNCE.
I KNOW. I'M SORRY.
CAFE
MIDAS! MIDAS HIGH SCHOOL--THAT'S WHERE THE CYBORGS WHO ATTACKED SOTOMAYOR CAME FROM!
MIDAS. THE MARK IS FROM MIDAS. MIDAS IS BEHIND THE CYBORGS AND THE ENTITY. AND THAT MARK, I KNOW I SAW IT SOMEWHERE ELSE...
CAFE
I WAS YOUNG AND TERRIFIED OF ALL MY FEELINGS FOR YOU. BUT I'LL TELL YOU RIGHT NOW, I'VE ALWAYS LOVED YOU, AMERICA CHAVEZ.
...MAGDALENA! THAT MARK WAS ON HER BIKE!

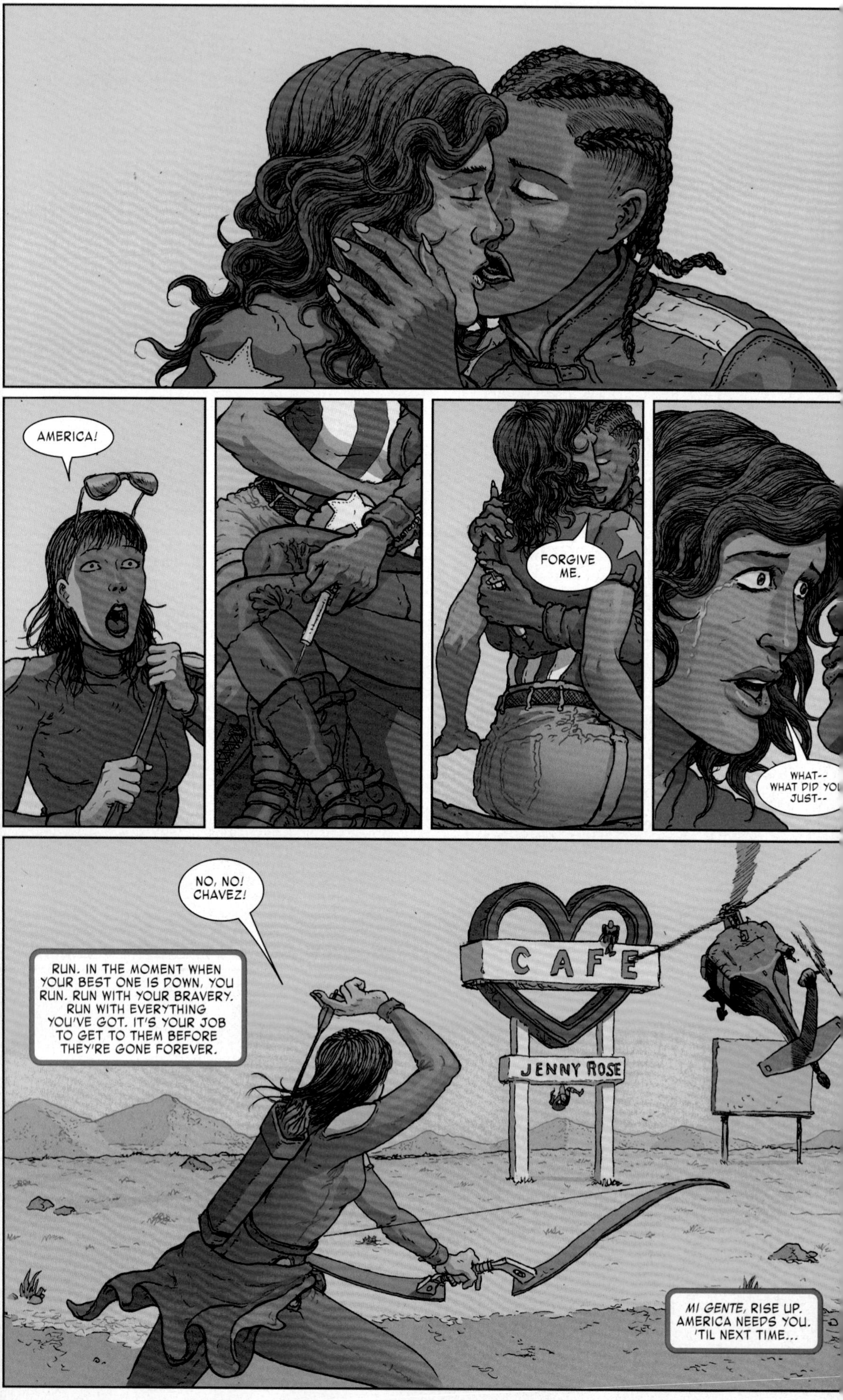
AMERICA!
FORGIVE ME.
WHAT-- WHAT DID YOU JUST--
NO, NO! CHAVEZ!
RUN. IN THE MOMENT WHEN YOUR BEST ONE IS DOWN, YOU RUN. RUN WITH YOUR BRAVERY. RUN WITH EVERYTHING YOU'VE GOT. IT'S YOUR JOB TO GET TO THEM BEFORE THEY'RE GONE FOREVER.
CAFE
JENNY ROSE
MI GENTE, RISE UP. AMERICA NEEDS YOU. 'TIL NEXT TIME...

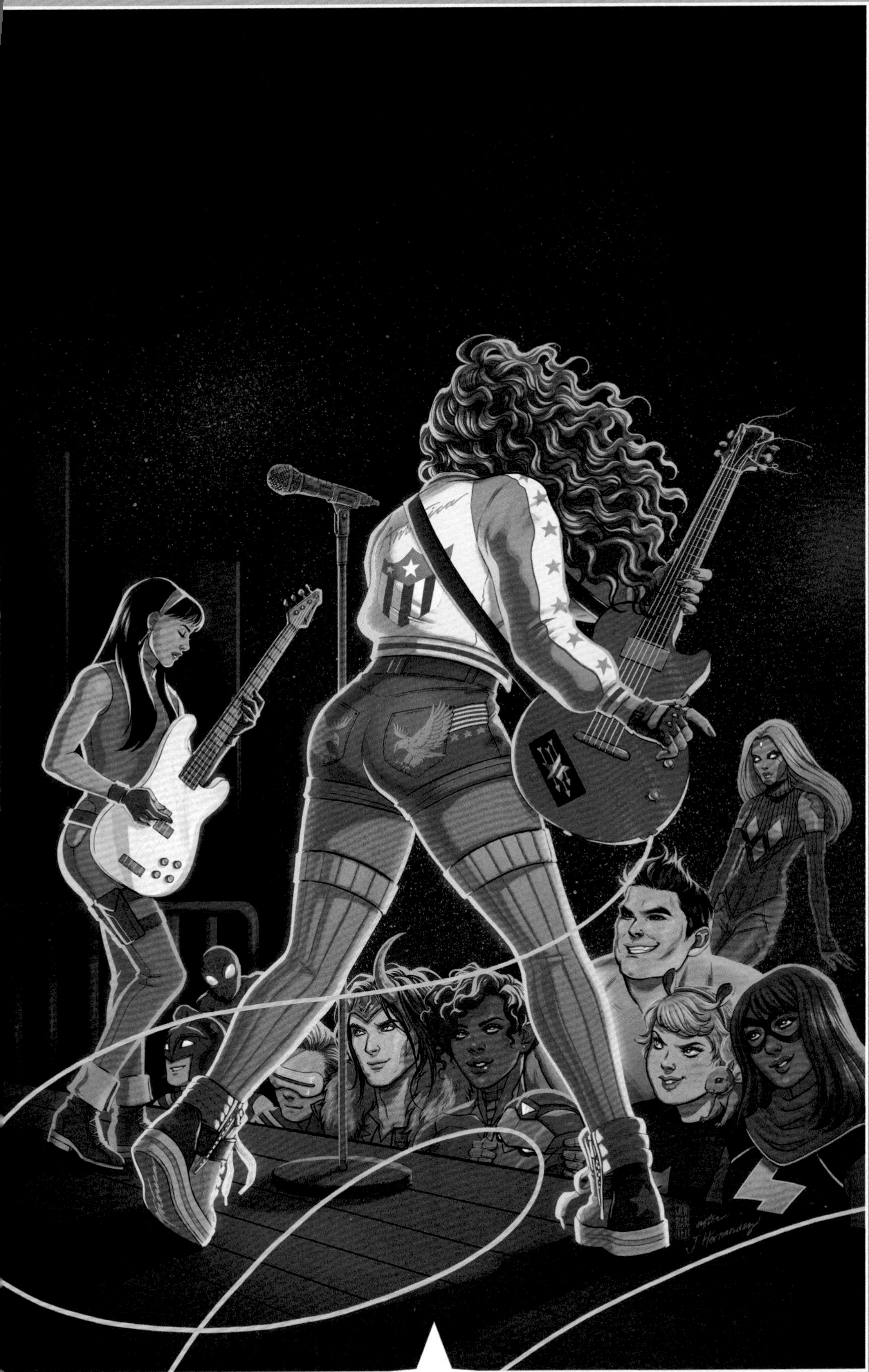

6

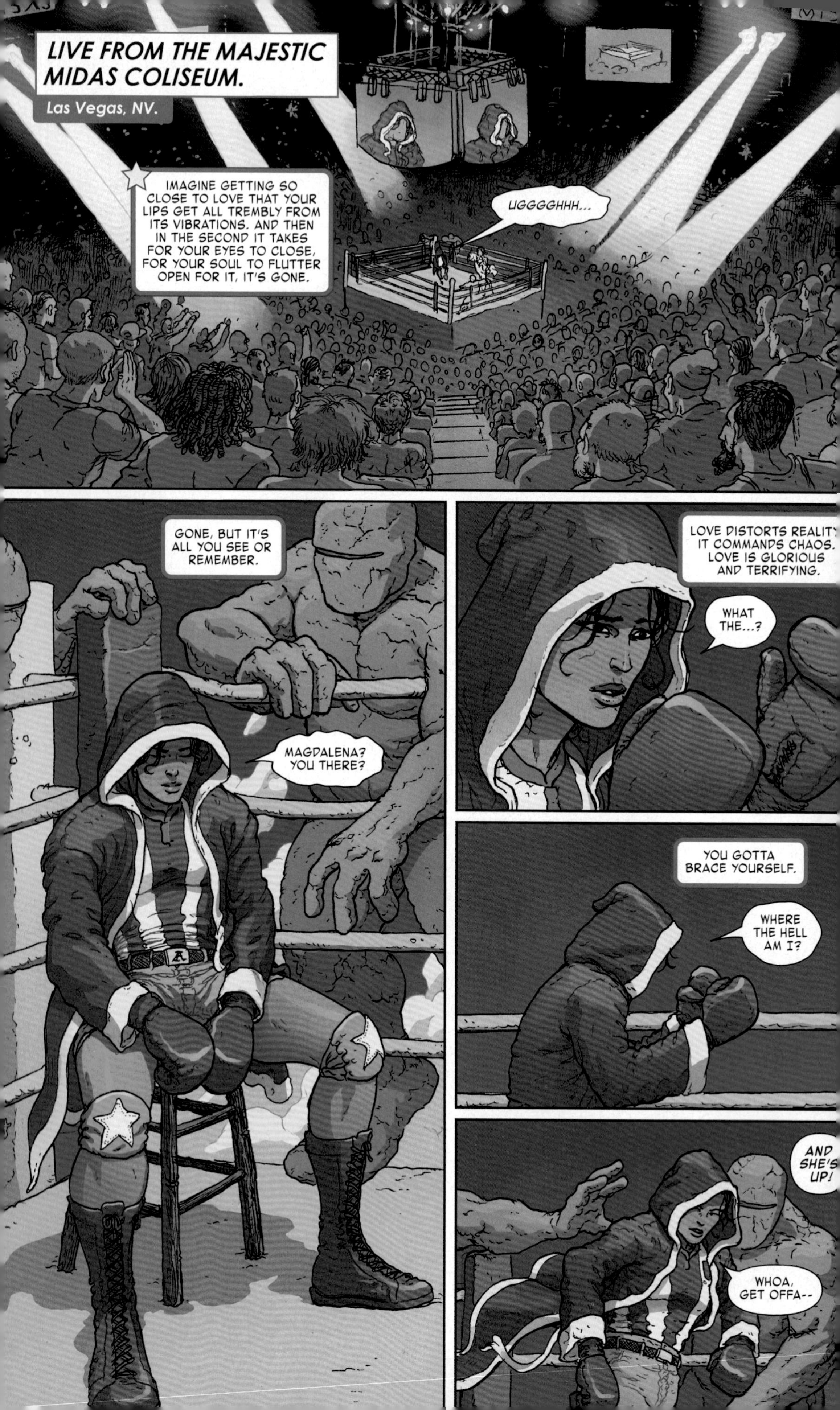
LIVE FROM THE MAJESTIC MIDAS COLISEUM.
Las Vegas, NV.
IMAGINE GETTING SO CLOSE TO LOVE THAT YOUR LIPS GET ALL TREMBLY FROM ITS VIBRATIONS. AND THEN IN THE SECOND IT TAKES FOR YOUR EYES TO CLOSE, FOR YOUR SOUL TO FLUTTER OPEN FOR IT, IT'S GONE.
UGGGGHHH...
GONE, BUT IT'S ALL YOU SEE OR REMEMBER.
MAGDALENA? YOU THERE?
LOVE DISTORTS REALITY. IT COMMANDS CHAOS. LOVE IS GLORIOUS AND TERRIFYING.
WHAT THE...?
YOU GOTTA BRACE YOURSELF.
WHERE THE HELL AM I?
AND SHE'S UP!
WHOA, GET OFFA--

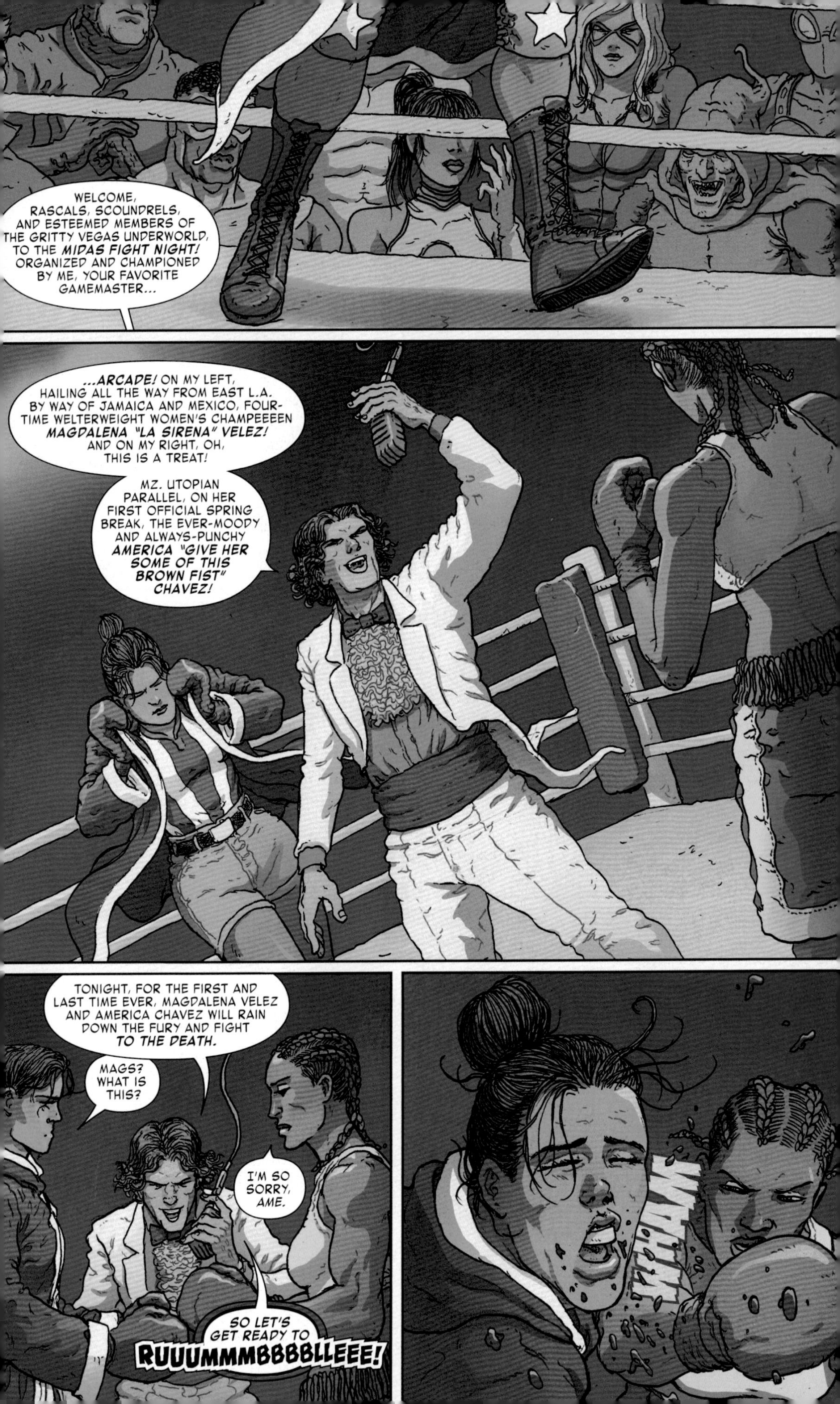
WELCOME, RASCALS, SCOUNDRELS, AND ESTEEMED MEMBERS OF THE GRITTY VEGAS UNDERWORLD, TO THE MIDAS FIGHT NIGHT! ORGANIZED AND CHAMPIONED BY ME, YOUR FAVORITE GAMEMASTER...
...ARCADE! ON MY LEFT, HAILING ALL THE WAY FROM EAST L.A. BY WAY OF JAMAICA AND MEXICO, FOUR-TIME WELTERWEIGHT WOMEN'S CHAMPEEEEEN MAGDALENA "LA SIRENA" VELEZ! AND ON MY RIGHT, OH, THIS IS A TREAT!
MZ. UTOPIAN PARALLEL, ON HER FIRST OFFICIAL SPRING BREAK, THE EVER-MOODY AND ALWAYS-PUNCHY AMERICA "GIVE HER SOME OF THIS BROWN FIST" CHAVEZ!
TONIGHT, FOR THE FIRST AND LAST TIME EVER, MAGDALENA VELEZ AND AMERICA CHAVEZ WILL RAIN DOWN THE FURY AND FIGHT TO THE DEATH.
MAGS? WHAT IS THIS?
I'M SO SORRY, AME.
SO LET'S GET READY TO RUUUMMMBBBBLLEEE!
WHAM

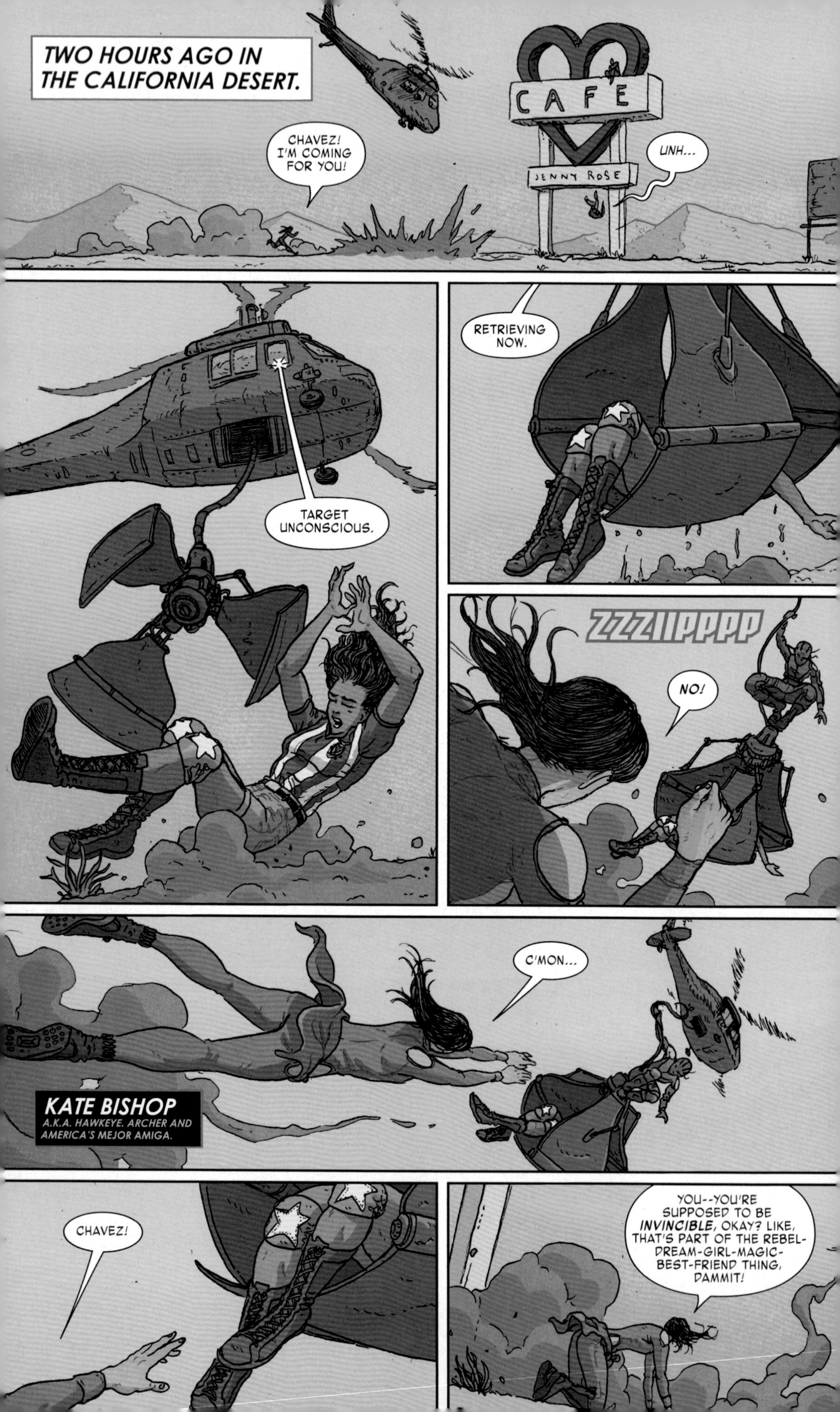

TWO HOURS AGO IN THE CALIFORNIA DESERT.
CAFE
JENNY ROSE
CHAVEZ! I'M COMING FOR YOU!
UNH...
TARGET UNCONSCIOUS.
RETRIEVING NOW.
ZZZIIPPPP
NO!
C'MON...
KATE BISHOP
A.K.A. HAWKEYE. ARCHER AND AMERICA'S MEJOR AMIGA.
CHAVEZ!
YOU--YOU'RE SUPPOSED TO BE *INVINCIBLE*, OKAY? LIKE, THAT'S PART OF THE REBEL-DREAM-GIRL-MAGIC-BEST-FRIEND THING, DAMMIT!

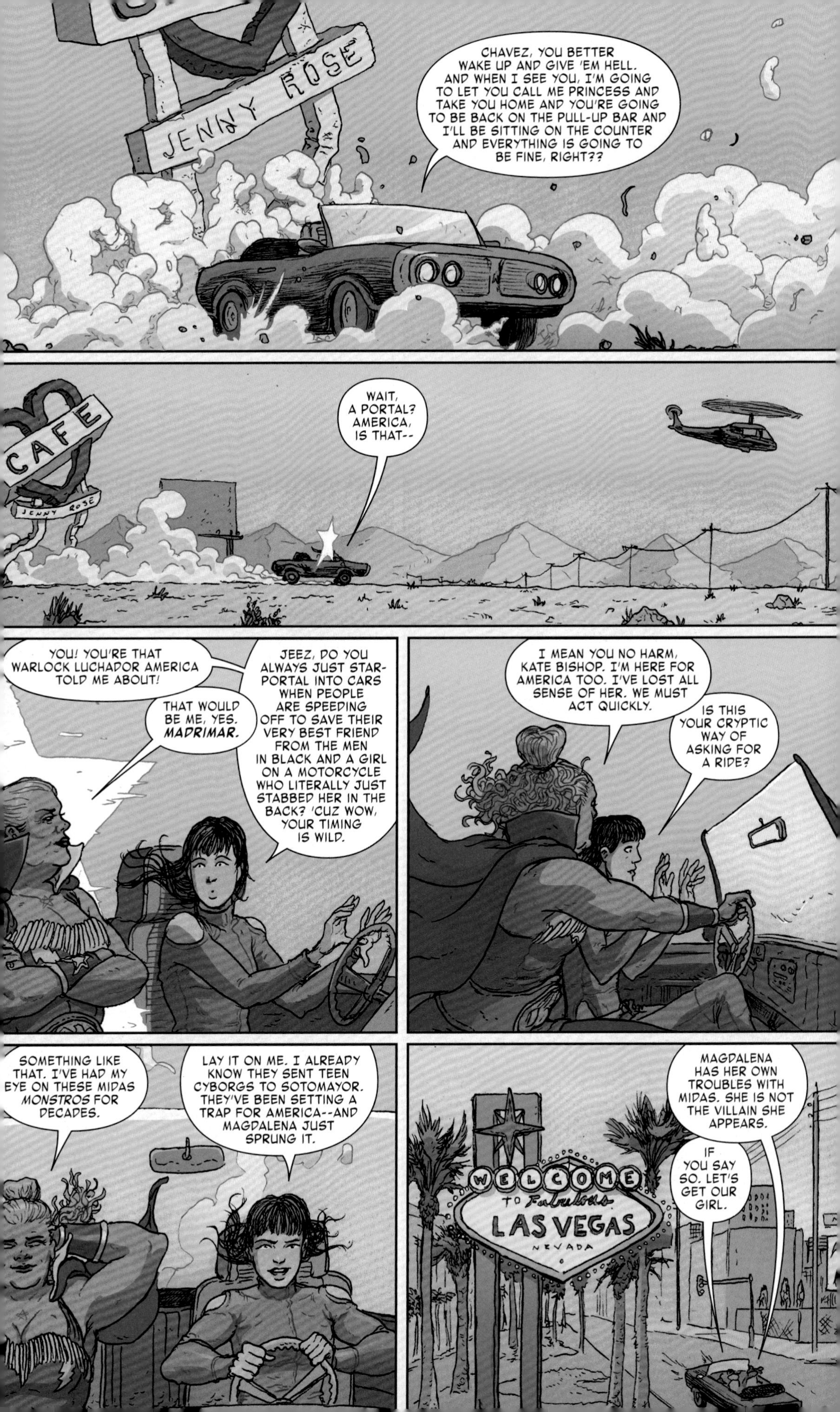
JENNY ROSE
CHAVEZ, YOU BETTER WAKE UP AND GIVE 'EM HELL. AND WHEN I SEE YOU, I'M GOING TO LET YOU CALL ME PRINCESS AND TAKE YOU HOME AND YOU'RE GOING TO BE BACK ON THE PULL-UP BAR AND I'LL BE SITTING ON THE COUNTER AND EVERYTHING IS GOING TO BE FINE, RIGHT??
CAFE
JENNY ROSE
WAIT, A PORTAL? AMERICA, IS THAT--
YOU! YOU'RE THAT WARLOCK LUCHADOR AMERICA TOLD ME ABOUT!
THAT WOULD BE ME, YES. ***MADRIMAR.***
JEEZ, DO YOU ALWAYS JUST STAR-PORTAL INTO CARS WHEN PEOPLE ARE SPEEDING OFF TO SAVE THEIR VERY BEST FRIEND FROM THE MEN IN BLACK AND A GIRL ON A MOTORCYCLE WHO LITERALLY JUST STABBED HER IN THE BACK? 'CUZ WOW, YOUR TIMING IS WILD.
I MEAN YOU NO HARM, KATE BISHOP. I'M HERE FOR AMERICA TOO. I'VE LOST ALL SENSE OF HER. WE MUST ACT QUICKLY.
IS THIS YOUR CRYPTIC WAY OF ASKING FOR A RIDE?
SOMETHING LIKE THAT. I'VE HAD MY EYE ON THESE MIDAS *MONSTROS* FOR DECADES.
LAY IT ON ME. I ALREADY KNOW THEY SENT TEEN CYBORGS TO SOTOMAYOR. THEY'VE BEEN SETTING A TRAP FOR AMERICA--AND MAGDALENA JUST SPRUNG IT.
WELCOME TO Fabulous LAS VEGAS NEVADA
MAGDALENA HAS HER OWN TROUBLES WITH MIDAS. SHE IS NOT THE VILLAIN SHE APPEARS.
IF YOU SAY SO. LET'S GET OUR GIRL.

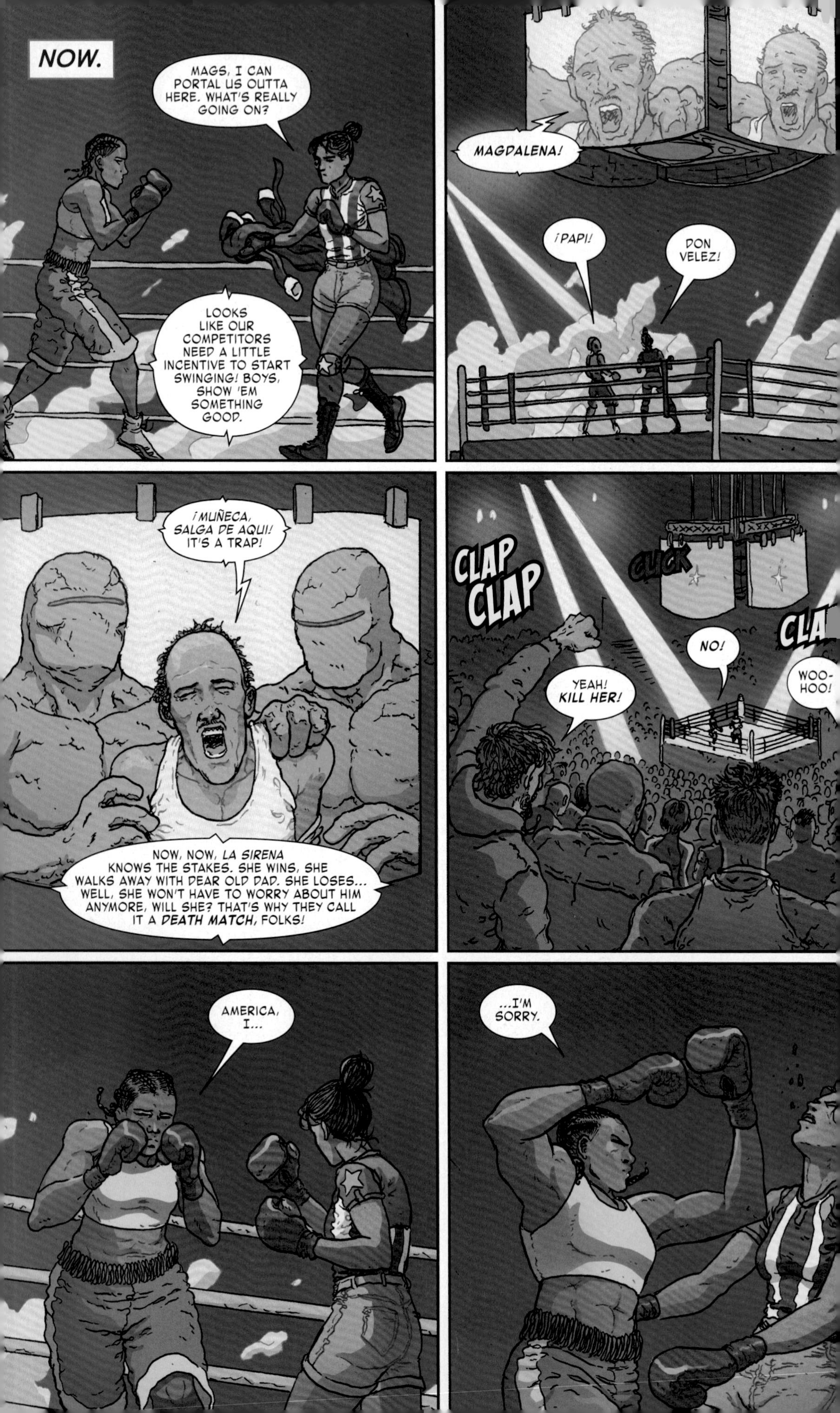
NOW.
MAGS, I CAN PORTAL US OUTTA HERE. WHAT'S REALLY GOING ON?
LOOKS LIKE OUR COMPETITORS NEED A LITTLE INCENTIVE TO START SWINGING! BOYS, SHOW 'EM SOMETHING GOOD.
MAGDALENA!
¡PAPI!
DON VELEZ!
¡MUÑECA, SALGA DE AQUI! IT'S A TRAP!
NOW, NOW, LA SIRENA KNOWS THE STAKES. SHE WINS, SHE WALKS AWAY WITH DEAR OLD DAD. SHE LOSES... WELL, SHE WON'T HAVE TO WORRY ABOUT HIM ANYMORE, WILL SHE? THAT'S WHY THEY CALL IT A DEATH MATCH, FOLKS!
CLAP CLAP
CLICK
NO!
YEAH! KILL HER!
WOO-HOO!
AMERICA, I...
...I'M SORRY.

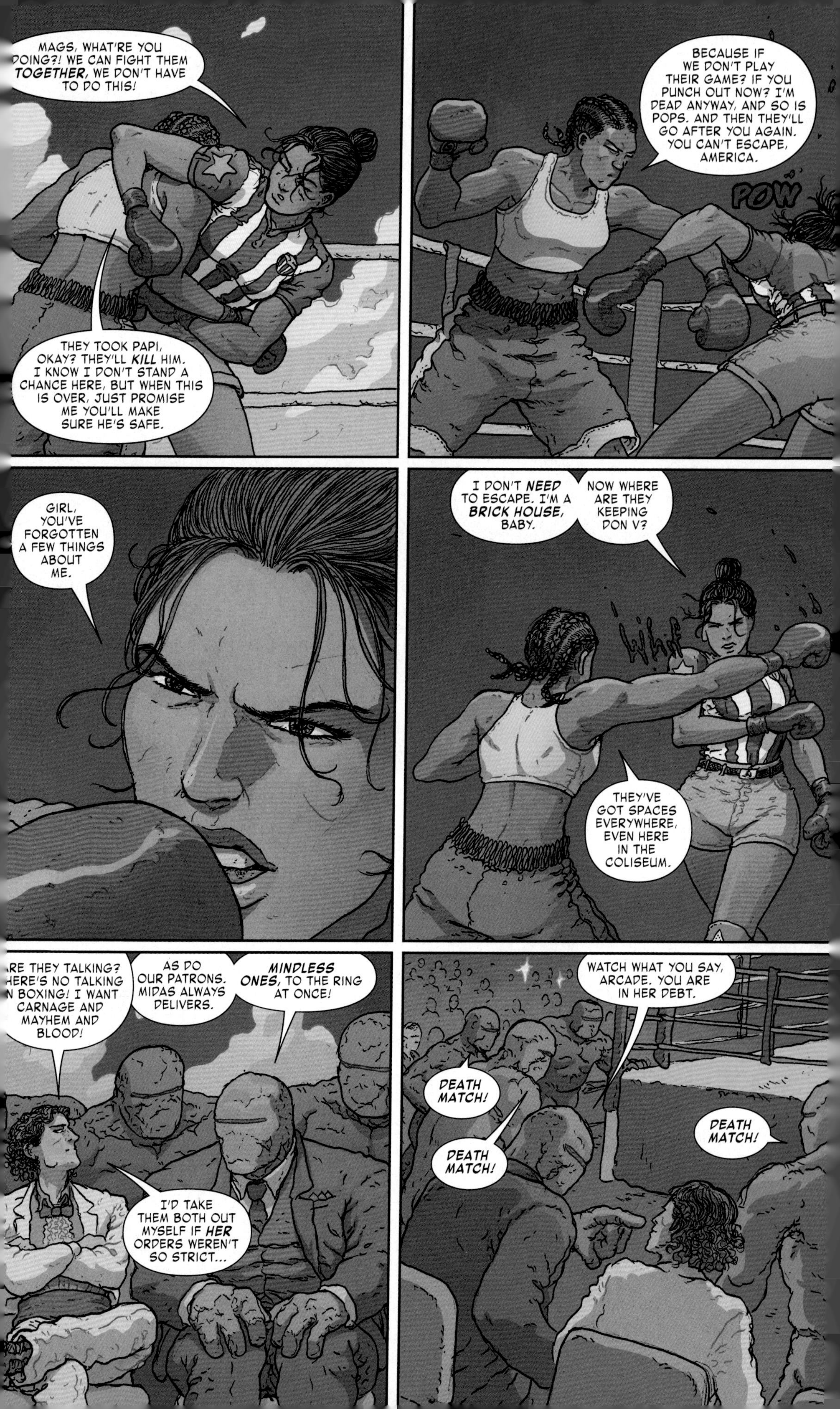

MAGS, WHAT'RE YOU DOING?! WE CAN FIGHT THEM *TOGETHER,* WE DON'T HAVE TO DO THIS!
THEY TOOK PAPI, OKAY? THEY'LL *KILL* HIM. I KNOW I DON'T STAND A CHANCE HERE, BUT WHEN THIS IS OVER, JUST PROMISE ME YOU'LL MAKE SURE HE'S SAFE.
BECAUSE IF WE DON'T PLAY THEIR GAME? IF YOU PUNCH OUT NOW? I'M DEAD ANYWAY, AND SO IS POPS. AND THEN THEY'LL GO AFTER YOU AGAIN. YOU CAN'T ESCAPE, AMERICA.
POW
GIRL, YOU'VE FORGOTTEN A FEW THINGS ABOUT ME.
I DON'T *NEED* TO ESCAPE. I'M A *BRICK HOUSE,* BABY.
NOW WHERE ARE THEY KEEPING DON V?
Whif
THEY'VE GOT SPACES EVERYWHERE, EVEN HERE IN THE COLISEUM.
ARE THEY TALKING? THERE'S NO TALKING IN BOXING! I WANT CARNAGE AND MAYHEM AND BLOOD!
AS DO OUR PATRONS. MIDAS ALWAYS DELIVERS.
MINDLESS ONES, TO THE RING AT ONCE!
I'D TAKE THEM BOTH OUT MYSELF IF *HER* ORDERS WEREN'T SO STRICT...
WATCH WHAT YOU SAY, ARCADE. YOU ARE IN HER DEBT.
DEATH MATCH!
DEATH MATCH!
DEATH MATCH!

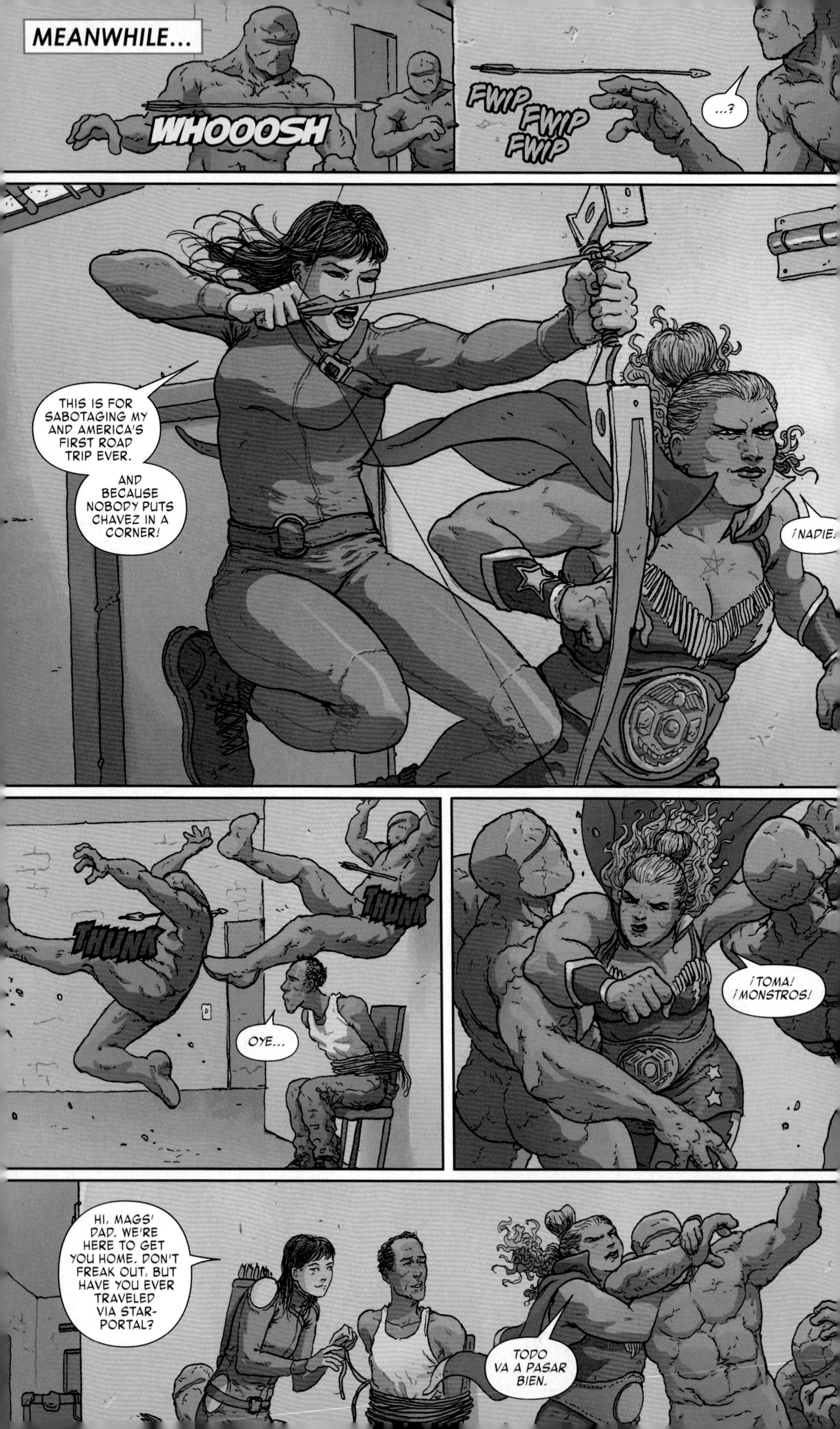
MEANWHILE...
WHOOOSH
FWIP FWIP FWIP
...?
THIS IS FOR SABOTAGING MY AND AMERICA'S FIRST ROAD TRIP EVER.
AND BECAUSE NOBODY PUTS CHAVEZ IN A CORNER!
¡NADIE!
THUNK
THUNK
OYE...
¡TOMA! ¡MONSTROS!
HI, MAGS' DAD. WE'RE HERE TO GET YOU HOME. DON'T FREAK OUT, BUT HAVE YOU EVER TRAVELED VIA STAR-PORTAL?
TODO VA A PASAR BIEN.

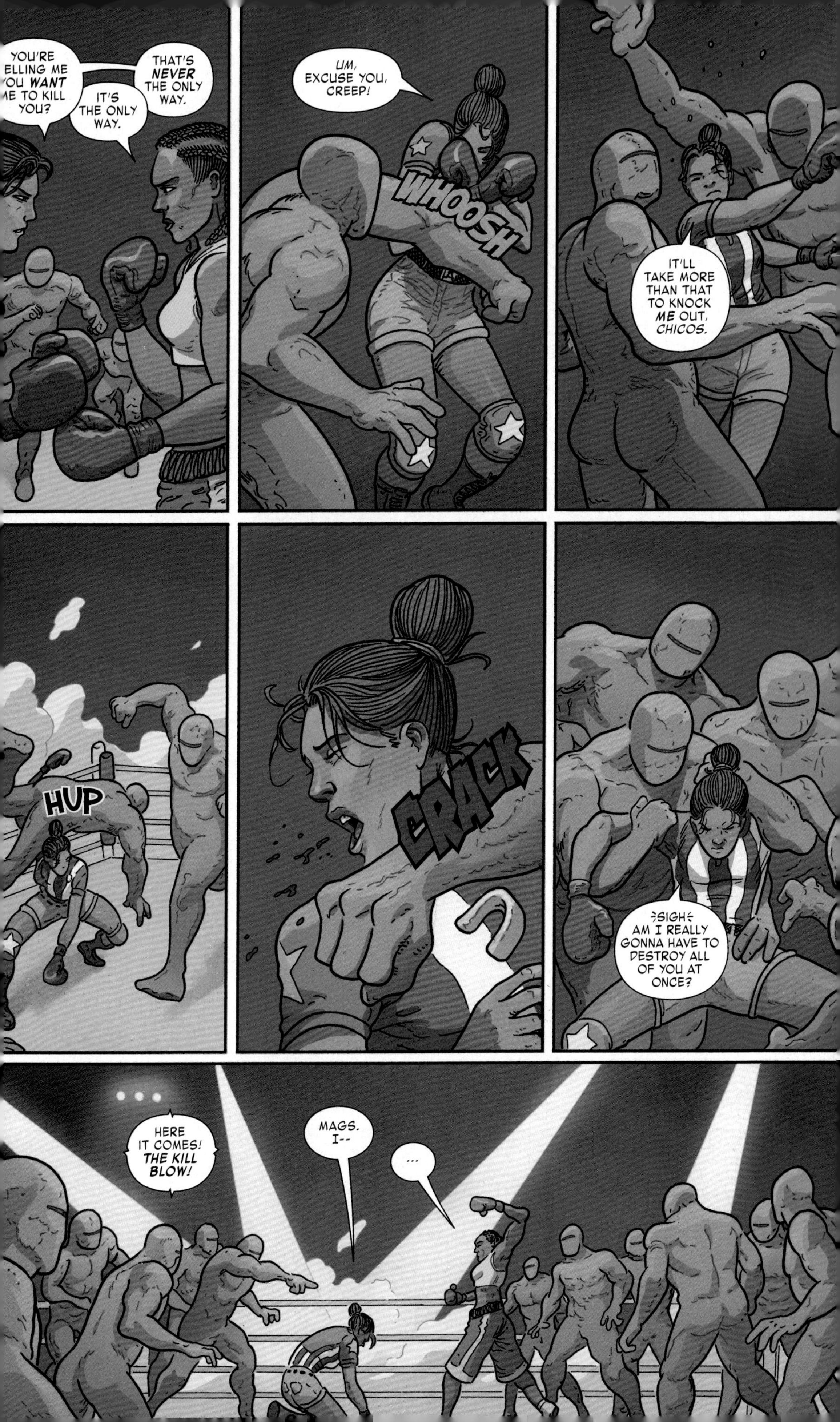
YOU'RE
ELLING ME
OU WANT
E TO KILL
YOU?
IT'S THE ONLY WAY.
THAT'S NEVER THE ONLY WAY.
UM, EXCUSE YOU, CREEP!
WHOOSH
IT'LL TAKE MORE THAN THAT TO KNOCK ME OUT, CHICOS.
HUP
CRACK
SIGH
AM I REALLY GONNA HAVE TO DESTROY ALL OF YOU AT ONCE?
HERE IT COMES! THE KILL BLOW!
MAGS. I--
...

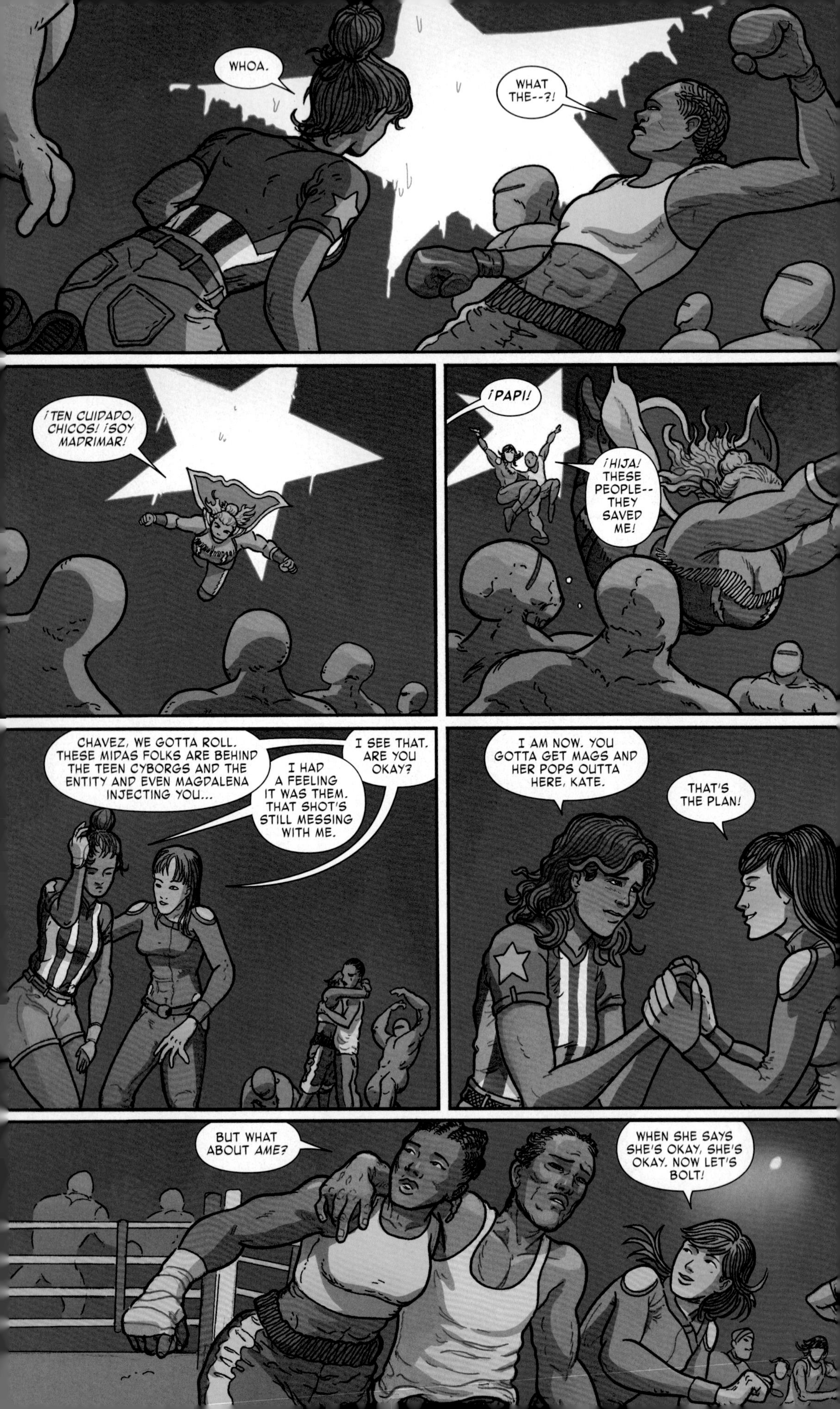
WHOA.
WHAT THE--?!
¡TEN CUIDADO, CHICOS! ¡SOY MADRIMAR!
¡PAPI!
¡HIJA! THESE PEOPLE-- THEY SAVED ME!
CHAVEZ, WE GOTTA ROLL. THESE MIDAS FOLKS ARE BEHIND THE TEEN CYBORGS AND THE ENTITY AND EVEN MAGDALENA INJECTING YOU...
I SEE THAT. ARE YOU OKAY?
I HAD A FEELING IT WAS THEM. THAT SHOT'S STILL MESSING WITH ME.
I AM NOW. YOU GOTTA GET MAGS AND HER POPS OUTTA HERE, KATE.
THAT'S THE PLAN!
BUT WHAT ABOUT AME?
WHEN SHE SAYS SHE'S OKAY, SHE'S OKAY. NOW LET'S BOLT!

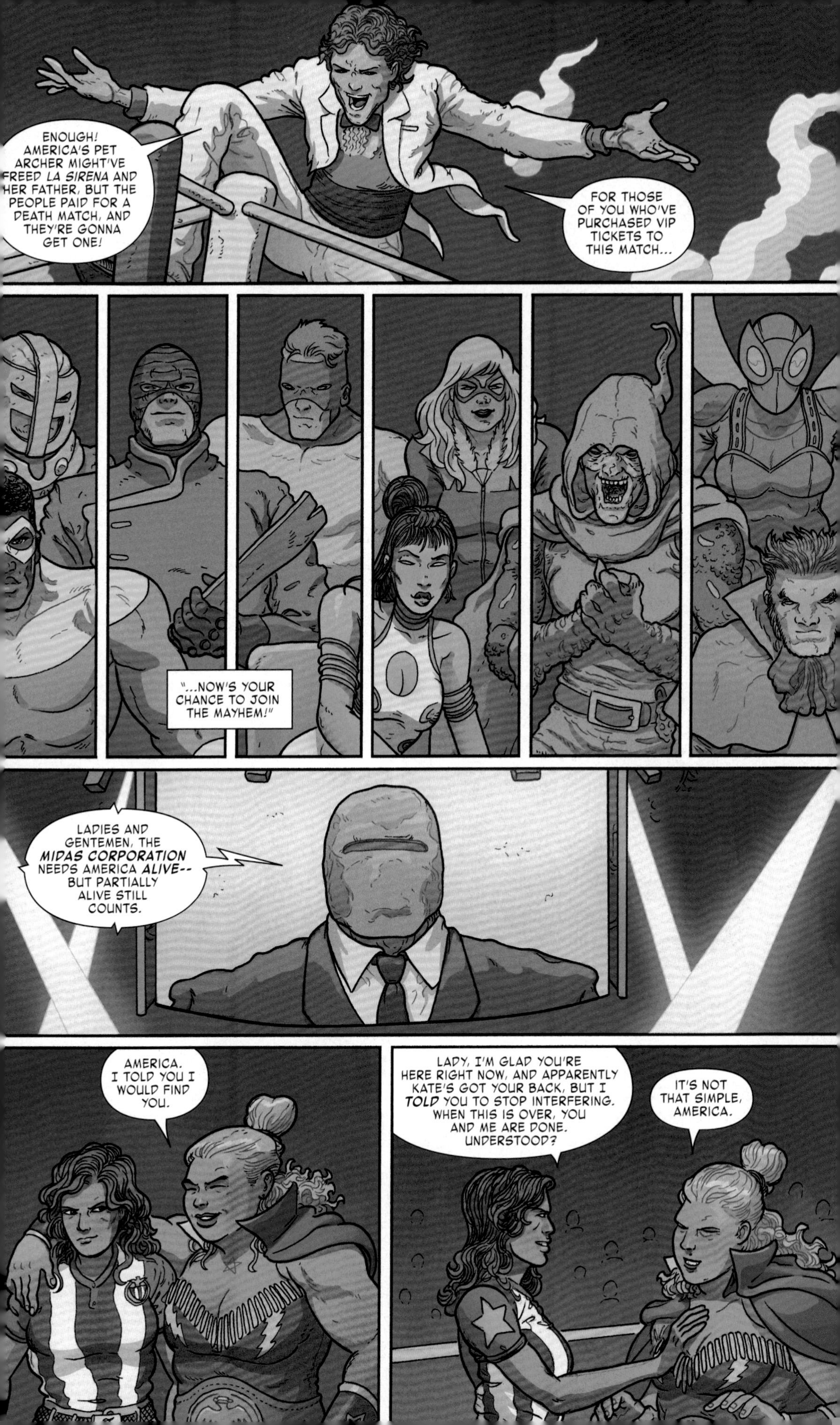
ENOUGH! AMERICA'S PET ARCHER MIGHT'VE FREED LA SIRENA AND HER FATHER, BUT THE PEOPLE PAID FOR A DEATH MATCH, AND THEY'RE GONNA GET ONE!
FOR THOSE OF YOU WHO'VE PURCHASED VIP TICKETS TO THIS MATCH...
"...NOW'S YOUR CHANCE TO JOIN THE MAYHEM!"
LADIES AND GENTEMEN, THE MIDAS CORPORATION NEEDS AMERICA ALIVE-- BUT PARTIALLY ALIVE STILL COUNTS.
AMERICA. I TOLD YOU I WOULD FIND YOU.
LADY, I'M GLAD YOU'RE HERE RIGHT NOW, AND APPARENTLY KATE'S GOT YOUR BACK, BUT I TOLD YOU TO STOP INTERFERING. WHEN THIS IS OVER, YOU AND ME ARE DONE. UNDERSTOOD?
IT'S NOT THAT SIMPLE, AMERICA.

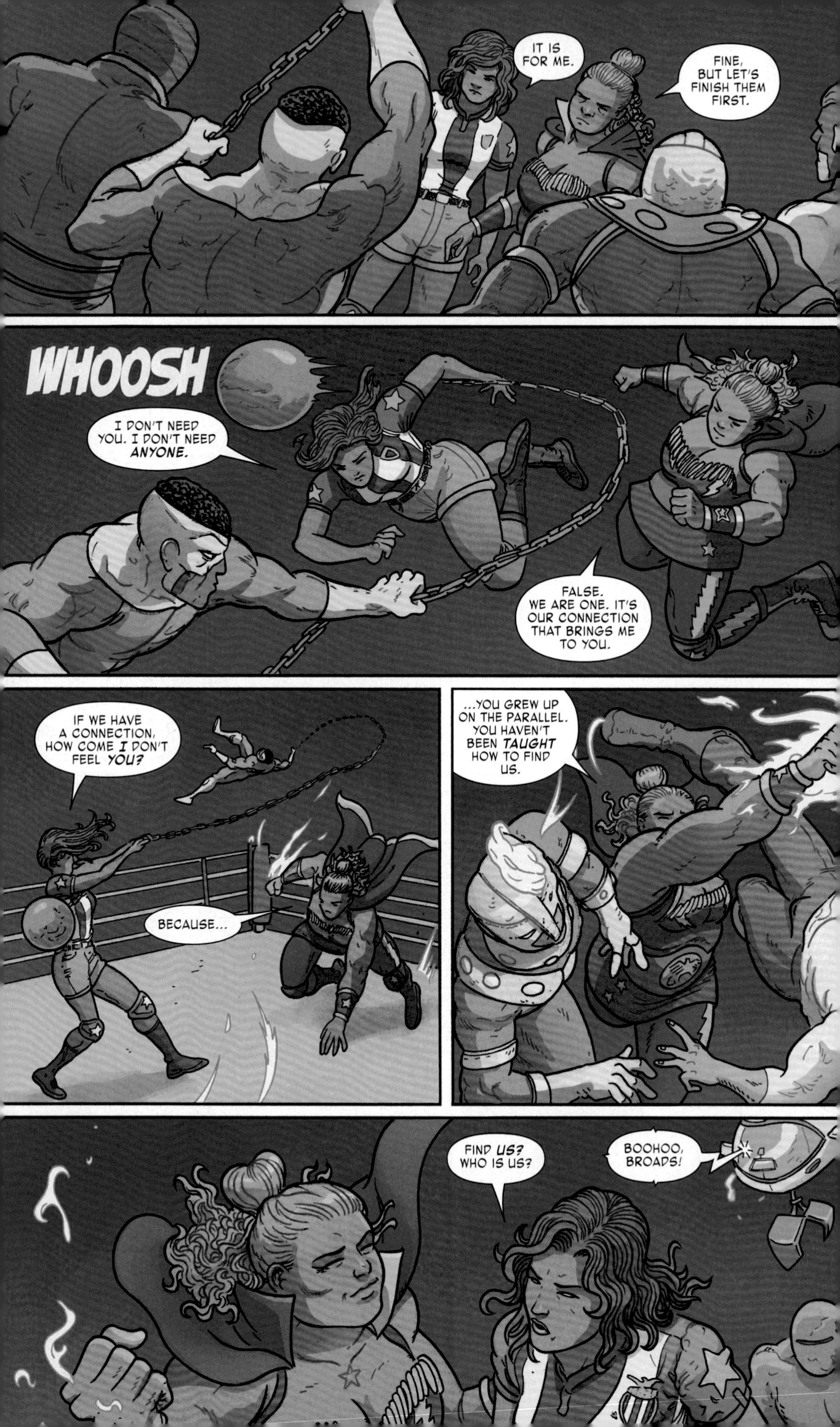
IT IS FOR ME.
FINE, BUT LET'S FINISH THEM FIRST.
WHOOSH
I DON'T NEED YOU. I DON'T NEED ANYONE.
FALSE. WE ARE ONE. IT'S OUR CONNECTION THAT BRINGS ME TO YOU.
IF WE HAVE A CONNECTION, HOW COME I DON'T FEEL YOU?
BECAUSE...
...YOU GREW UP ON THE PARALLEL. YOU HAVEN'T BEEN TAUGHT HOW TO FIND US.
FIND US? WHO IS US?
BOOHOO, BROADS!

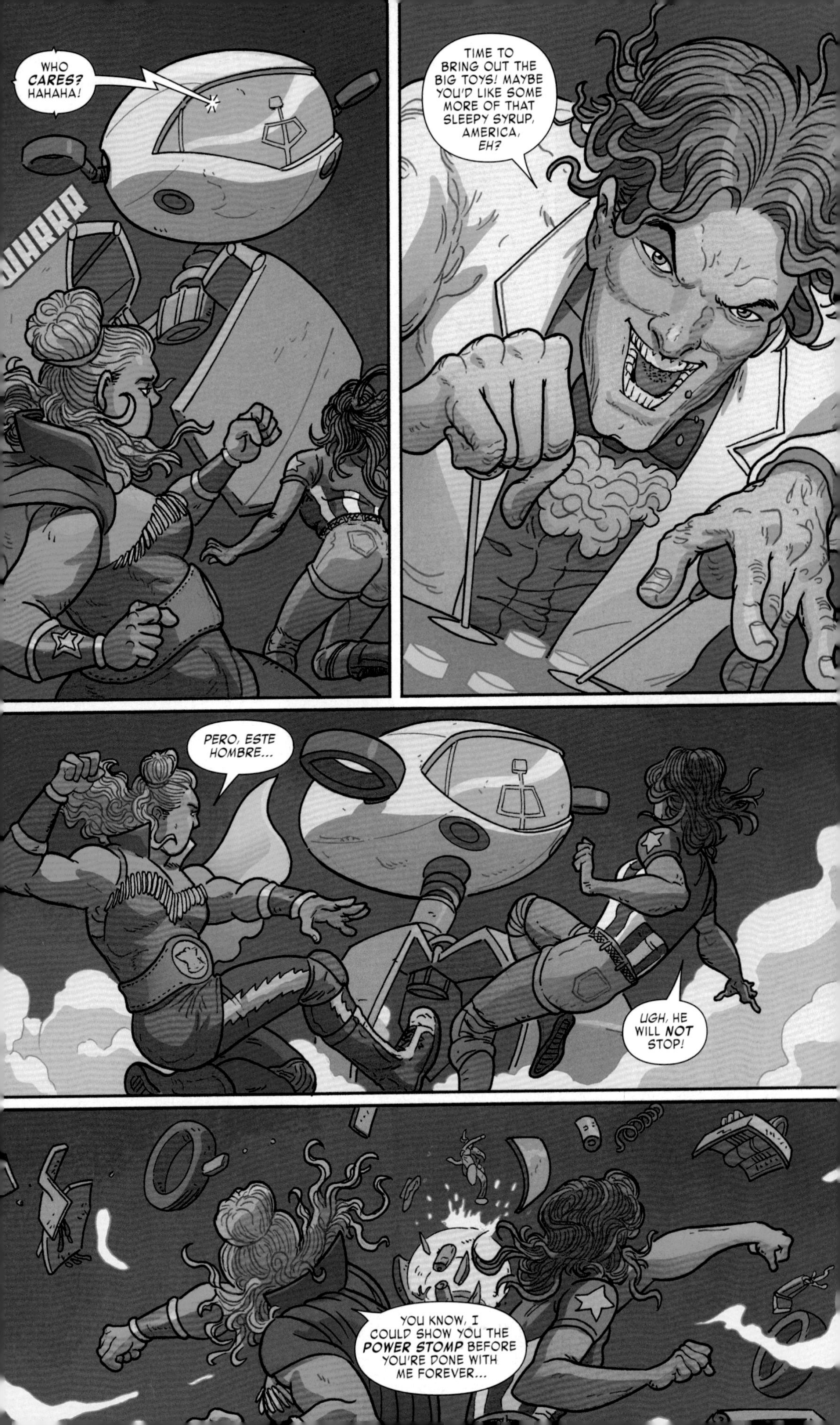
WHO CARES? HAHAHA!
WHRRR
TIME TO BRING OUT THE BIG TOYS! MAYBE YOU'D LIKE SOME MORE OF THAT SLEEPY SYRUP, AMERICA, EH?
PERO, ESTE HOMBRE...
UGH, HE WILL NOT STOP!
YOU KNOW, I COULD SHOW YOU THE POWER STOMP BEFORE YOU'RE DONE WITH ME FOREVER...

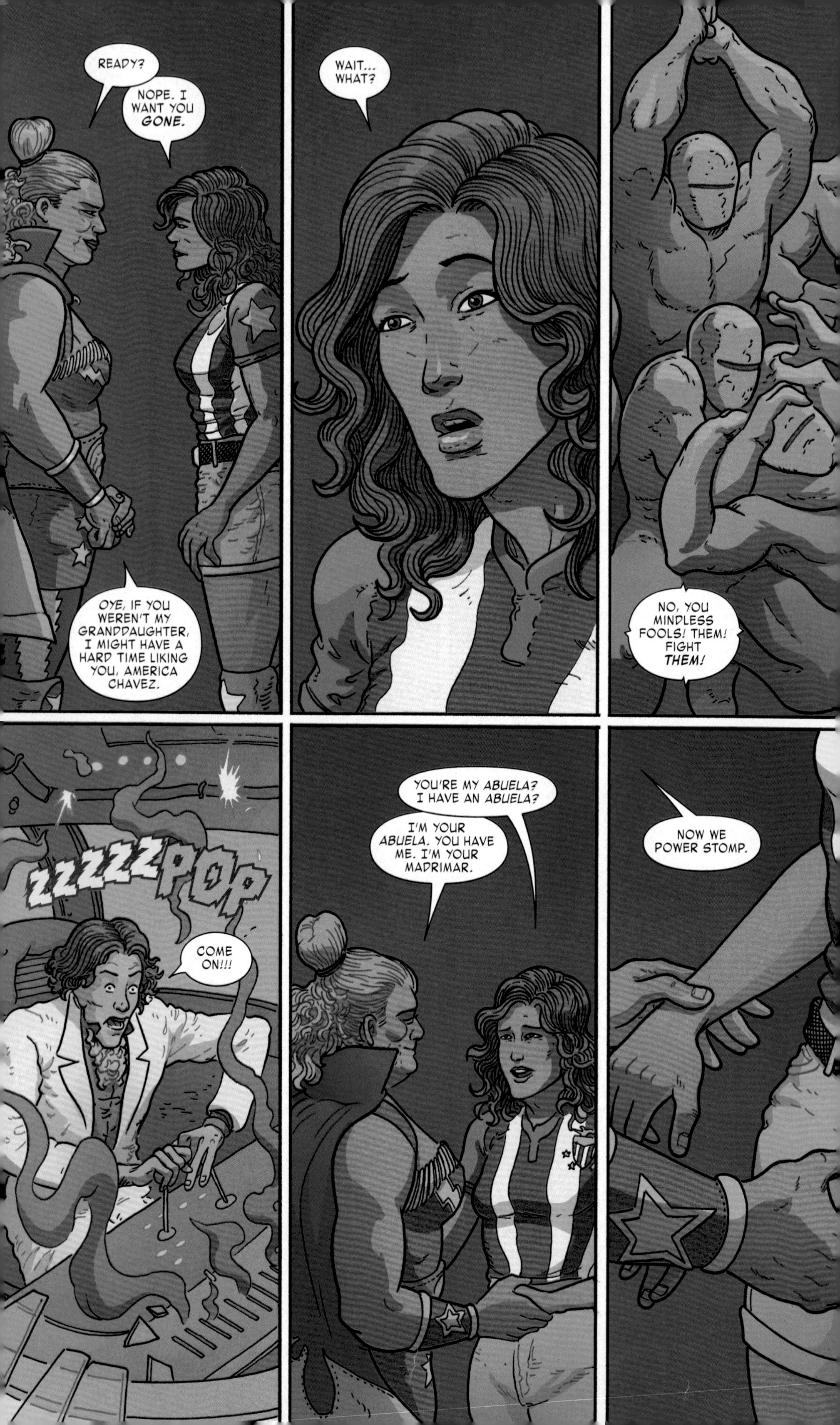
READY?
NOPE. I WANT YOU *GONE.*
OYE, IF YOU WEREN'T MY GRANDDAUGHTER, I MIGHT HAVE A HARD TIME LIKING YOU, AMERICA CHAVEZ.
WAIT... WHAT?
NO, YOU MINDLESS FOOLS! THEM! FIGHT *THEM!*
ZZZZZPOP
COME ON!!!
YOU'RE MY *ABUELA?* I HAVE AN *ABUELA?*
I'M YOUR *ABUELA.* YOU HAVE ME. I'M YOUR MADRIMAR.
NOW WE POWER STOMP.

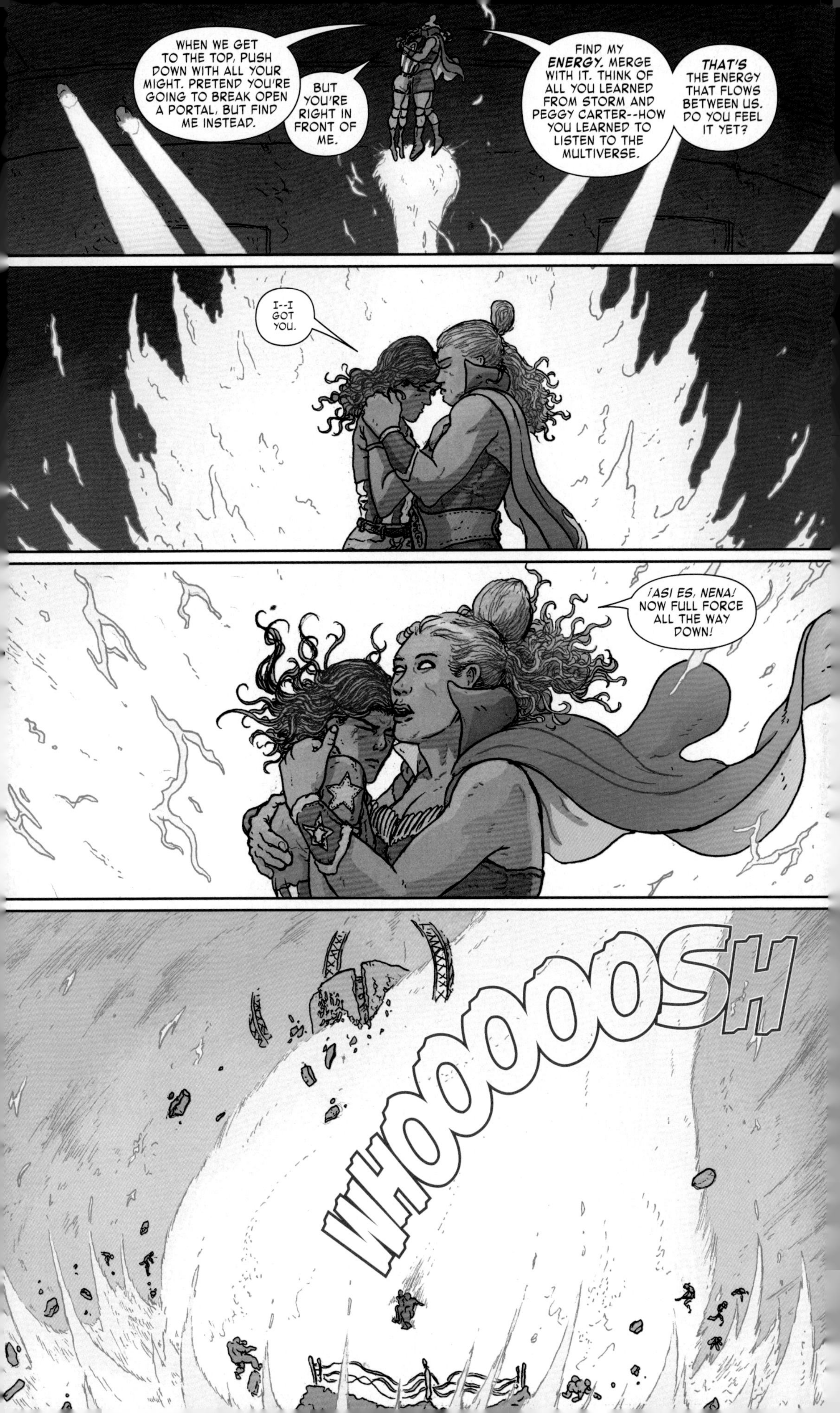
WHEN WE GET TO THE TOP, PUSH DOWN WITH ALL YOUR MIGHT. PRETEND YOU'RE GOING TO BREAK OPEN A PORTAL, BUT FIND ME INSTEAD.
BUT YOU'RE RIGHT IN FRONT OF ME.
FIND MY ENERGY. MERGE WITH IT. THINK OF ALL YOU LEARNED FROM STORM AND PEGGY CARTER--HOW YOU LEARNED TO LISTEN TO THE MULTIVERSE.
THAT'S THE ENERGY THAT FLOWS BETWEEN US. DO YOU FEEL IT YET?
I--I GOT YOU.
¡ASI ES, NENA! NOW FULL FORCE ALL THE WAY DOWN!
WHOOOOOSH

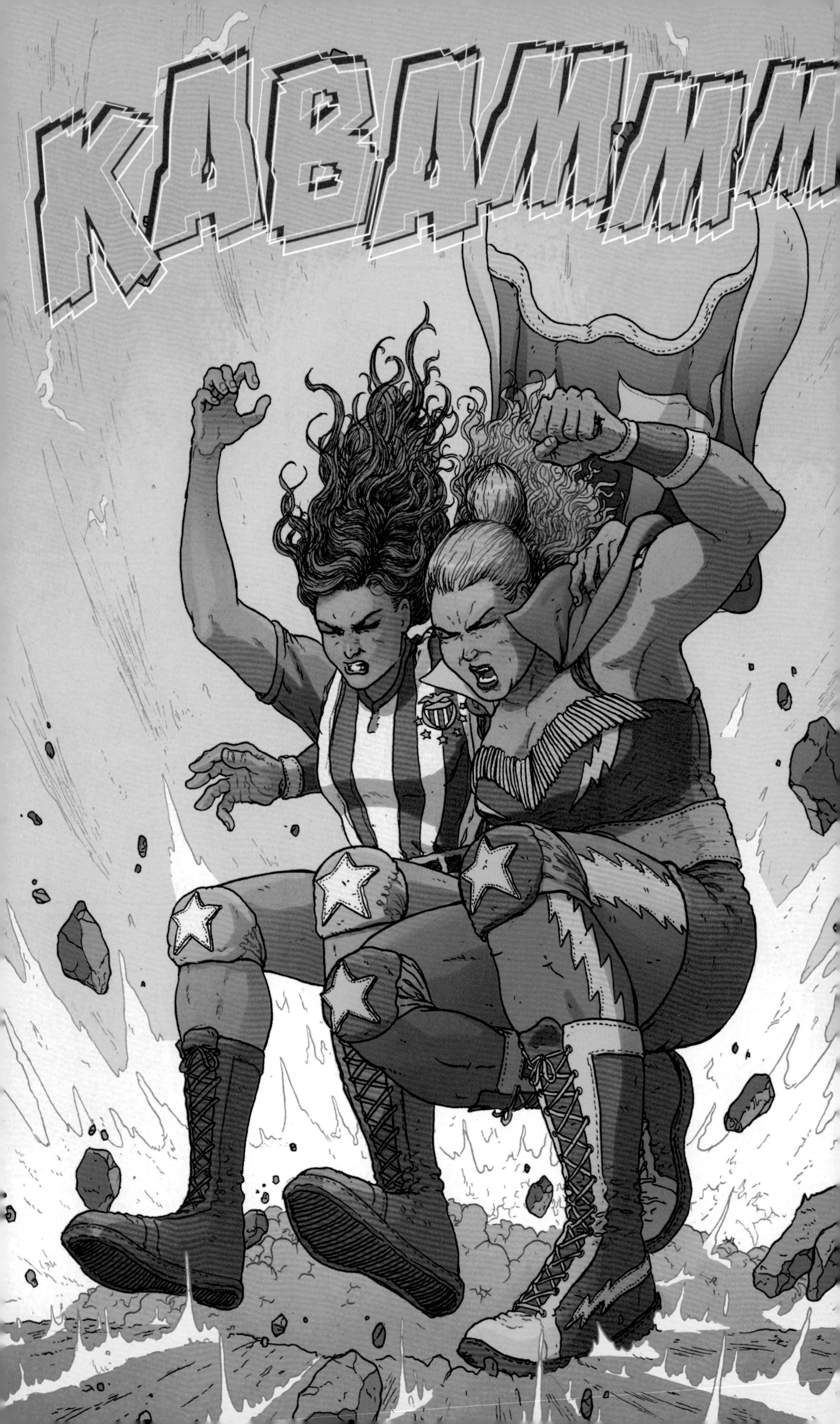
KABAMMM

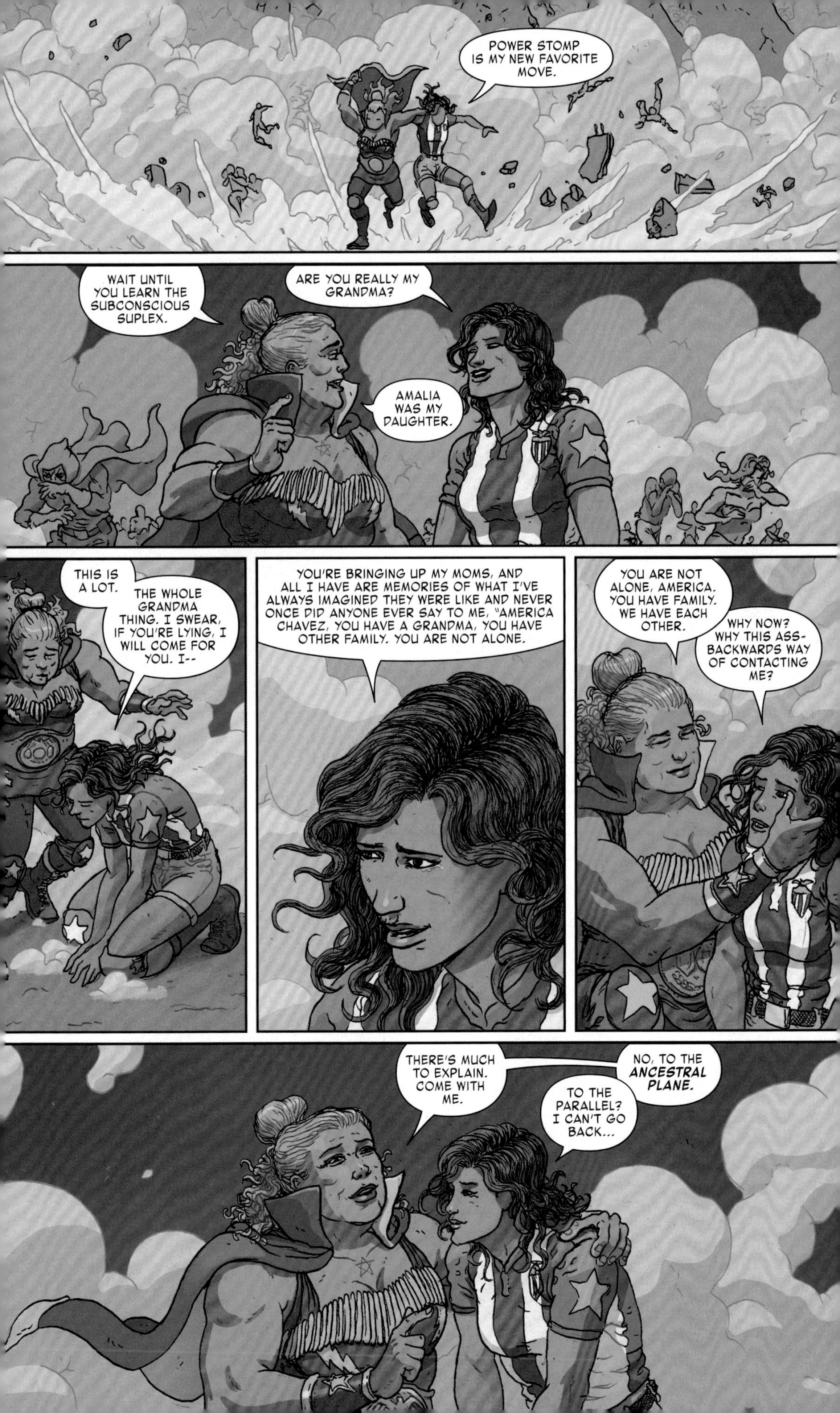
POWER STOMP IS MY NEW FAVORITE MOVE.
WAIT UNTIL YOU LEARN THE SUBCONSCIOUS SUPLEX.
ARE YOU REALLY MY GRANDMA?
AMALIA WAS MY DAUGHTER.
THIS IS A LOT.
THE WHOLE GRANDMA THING. I SWEAR, IF YOU'RE LYING, I WILL COME FOR YOU. I--
YOU'RE BRINGING UP MY MOMS, AND ALL I HAVE ARE MEMORIES OF WHAT I'VE ALWAYS IMAGINED THEY WERE LIKE AND NEVER ONCE DID ANYONE EVER SAY TO ME, "AMERICA CHAVEZ, YOU HAVE A GRANDMA, YOU HAVE OTHER FAMILY. YOU ARE NOT ALONE.
YOU ARE NOT ALONE, AMERICA. YOU HAVE FAMILY. WE HAVE EACH OTHER.
WHY NOW? WHY THIS ASS-BACKWARDS WAY OF CONTACTING ME?
THERE'S MUCH TO EXPLAIN. COME WITH ME.
TO THE PARALLEL? I CAN'T GO BACK...
NO, TO THE *ANCESTRAL PLANE.*

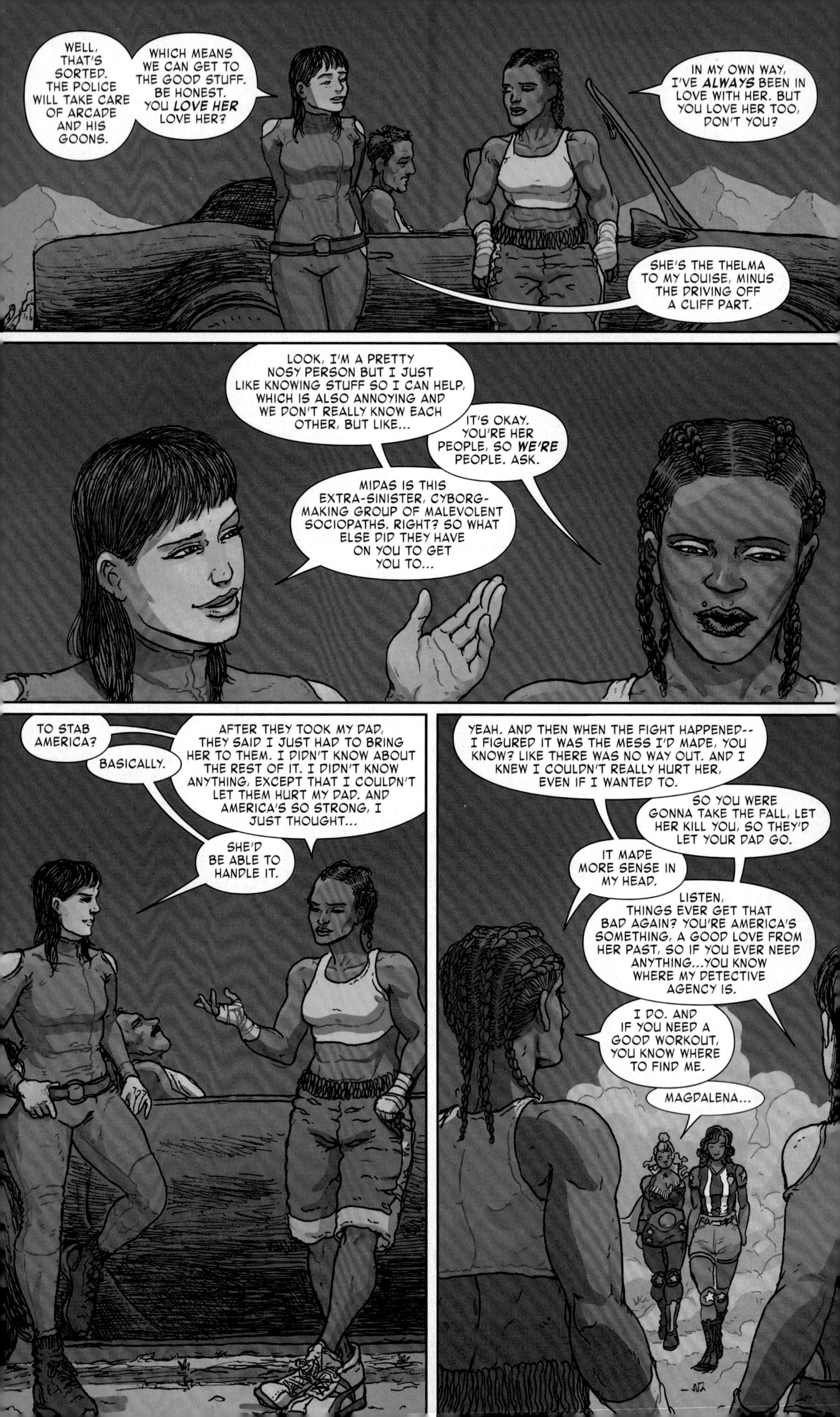
WELL, THAT'S SORTED. THE POLICE WILL TAKE CARE OF ARCADE AND HIS GOONS.
WHICH MEANS WE CAN GET TO THE GOOD STUFF. BE HONEST. YOU *LOVE HER* LOVE HER?
IN MY OWN WAY, I'VE *ALWAYS* BEEN IN LOVE WITH HER. BUT YOU LOVE HER TOO, DON'T YOU?
SHE'S THE THELMA TO MY LOUISE, MINUS THE DRIVING OFF A CLIFF PART.
LOOK, I'M A PRETTY NOSY PERSON BUT I JUST LIKE KNOWING STUFF SO I CAN HELP, WHICH IS ALSO ANNOYING AND WE DON'T REALLY KNOW EACH OTHER, BUT LIKE...
IT'S OKAY. YOU'RE HER PEOPLE, SO *WE'RE* PEOPLE. ASK.
MIDAS IS THIS EXTRA-SINISTER, CYBORG-MAKING GROUP OF MALEVOLENT SOCIOPATHS. RIGHT? SO WHAT ELSE DID THEY HAVE ON YOU TO GET YOU TO...
TO STAB AMERICA?
BASICALLY.
AFTER THEY TOOK MY DAD, THEY SAID I JUST HAD TO BRING HER TO THEM. I DIDN'T KNOW ABOUT THE REST OF IT. I DIDN'T KNOW ANYTHING, EXCEPT THAT I COULDN'T LET THEM HURT MY DAD. AND AMERICA'S SO STRONG, I JUST THOUGHT...
SHE'D BE ABLE TO HANDLE IT.
YEAH. AND THEN WHEN THE FIGHT HAPPENED-- I FIGURED IT WAS THE MESS I'D MADE, YOU KNOW? LIKE THERE WAS NO WAY OUT. AND I KNEW I COULDN'T REALLY HURT HER, EVEN IF I WANTED TO.
SO YOU WERE GONNA TAKE THE FALL, LET HER KILL YOU, SO THEY'D LET YOUR DAD GO.
IT MADE MORE SENSE IN MY HEAD.
LISTEN, THINGS EVER GET THAT BAD AGAIN? YOU'RE AMERICA'S SOMETHING, A GOOD LOVE FROM HER PAST, SO IF YOU EVER NEED ANYTHING...YOU KNOW WHERE MY DETECTIVE AGENCY IS.
I DO. AND IF YOU NEED A GOOD WORKOUT, YOU KNOW WHERE TO FIND ME.
MAGDALENA...

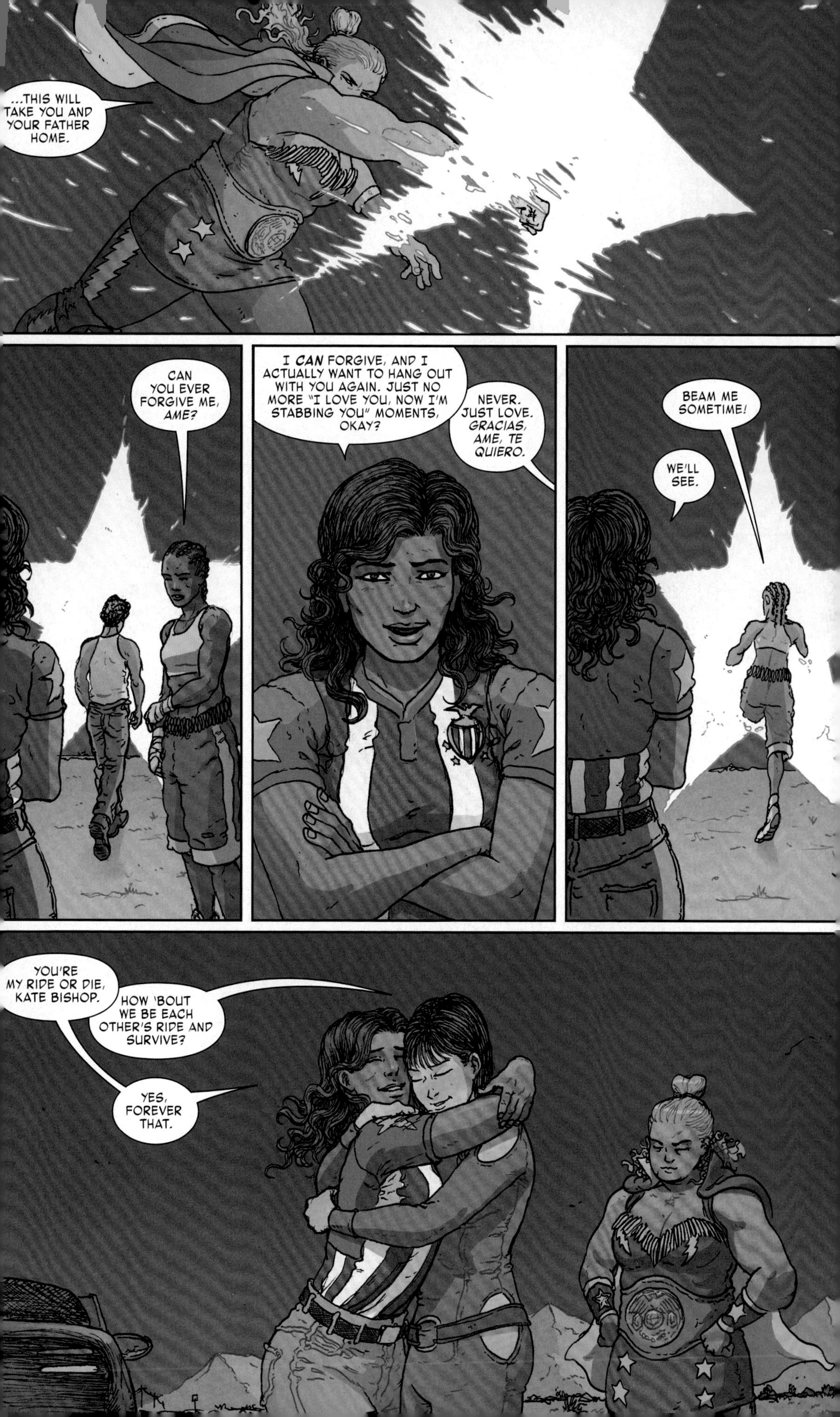
...THIS WILL TAKE YOU AND YOUR FATHER HOME.
CAN YOU EVER FORGIVE ME, AME?
I CAN FORGIVE, AND I ACTUALLY WANT TO HANG OUT WITH YOU AGAIN. JUST NO MORE "I LOVE YOU, NOW I'M STABBING YOU" MOMENTS, OKAY?
NEVER. JUST LOVE. GRACIAS, AME, TE QUIERO.
BEAM ME SOMETIME!
WE'LL SEE.
YOU'RE MY RIDE OR DIE, KATE BISHOP.
HOW 'BOUT WE BE EACH OTHER'S RIDE AND SURVIVE?
YES, FOREVER THAT.

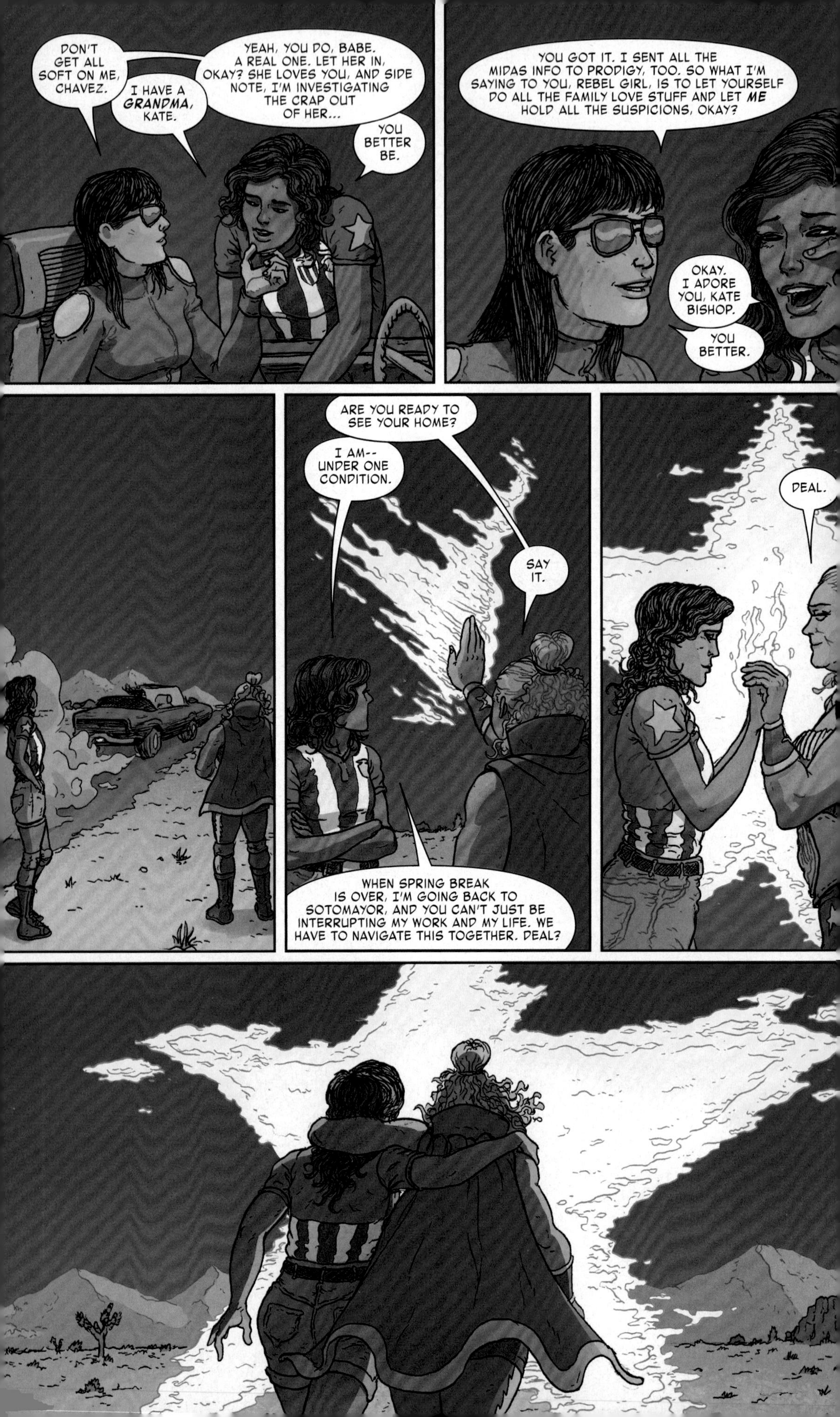
DON'T GET ALL SOFT ON ME, CHAVEZ.
I HAVE A GRANDMA, KATE.
YEAH, YOU DO, BABE. A REAL ONE. LET HER IN, OKAY? SHE LOVES YOU, AND SIDE NOTE, I'M INVESTIGATING THE CRAP OUT OF HER...
YOU BETTER BE.
YOU GOT IT. I SENT ALL THE MIDAS INFO TO PRODIGY, TOO. SO WHAT I'M SAYING TO YOU, REBEL GIRL, IS TO LET YOURSELF DO ALL THE FAMILY LOVE STUFF AND LET ME HOLD ALL THE SUSPICIONS, OKAY?
OKAY. I ADORE YOU, KATE BISHOP.
YOU BETTER.
ARE YOU READY TO SEE YOUR HOME?
I AM-- UNDER ONE CONDITION.
SAY IT.
WHEN SPRING BREAK IS OVER, I'M GOING BACK TO SOTOMAYOR, AND YOU CAN'T JUST BE INTERRUPTING MY WORK AND MY LIFE. WE HAVE TO NAVIGATE THIS TOGETHER. DEAL?
DEAL.

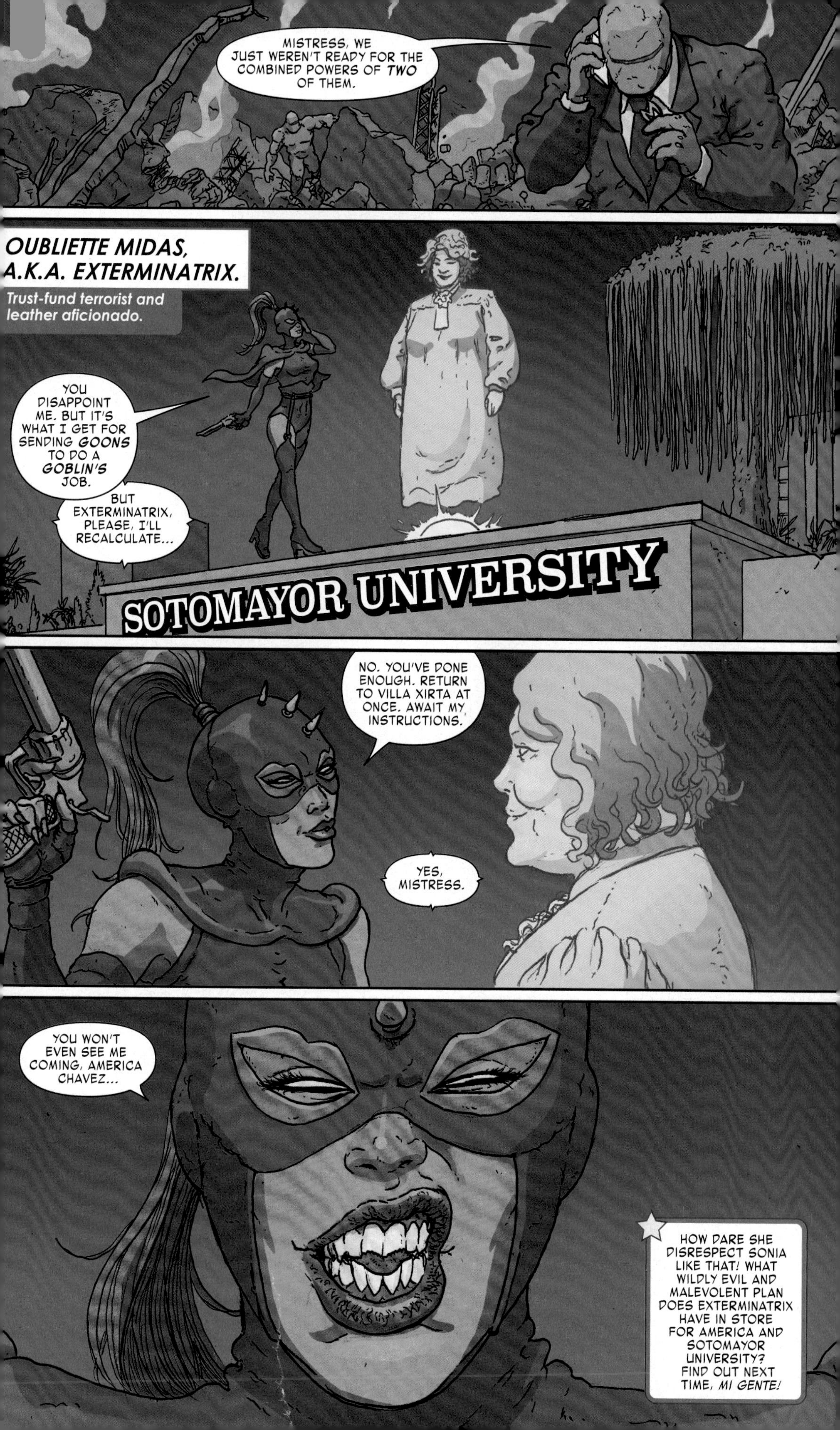
MISTRESS, WE JUST WEREN'T READY FOR THE COMBINED POWERS OF *TWO* OF THEM.
OUBLIETTE MIDAS, A.K.A. EXTERMINATRIX.
Trust-fund terrorist and leather aficionado.
YOU DISAPPOINT ME. BUT IT'S WHAT I GET FOR SENDING *GOONS* TO DO A *GOBLIN'S* JOB.
BUT EXTERMINATRIX, PLEASE, I'LL RECALCULATE...
SOTOMAYOR UNIVERSITY
NO. YOU'VE DONE ENOUGH. RETURN TO VILLA XIRTA AT ONCE. AWAIT MY INSTRUCTIONS.
YES, MISTRESS.
YOU WON'T EVEN SEE ME COMING, AMERICA CHAVEZ...
HOW DARE SHE DISRESPECT SONIA LIKE THAT! WHAT WILDLY EVIL AND MALEVOLENT PLAN DOES EXTERMINATRIX HAVE IN STORE FOR AMERICA AND SOTOMAYOR UNIVERSITY? FIND OUT NEXT TIME, *MI GENTE!*

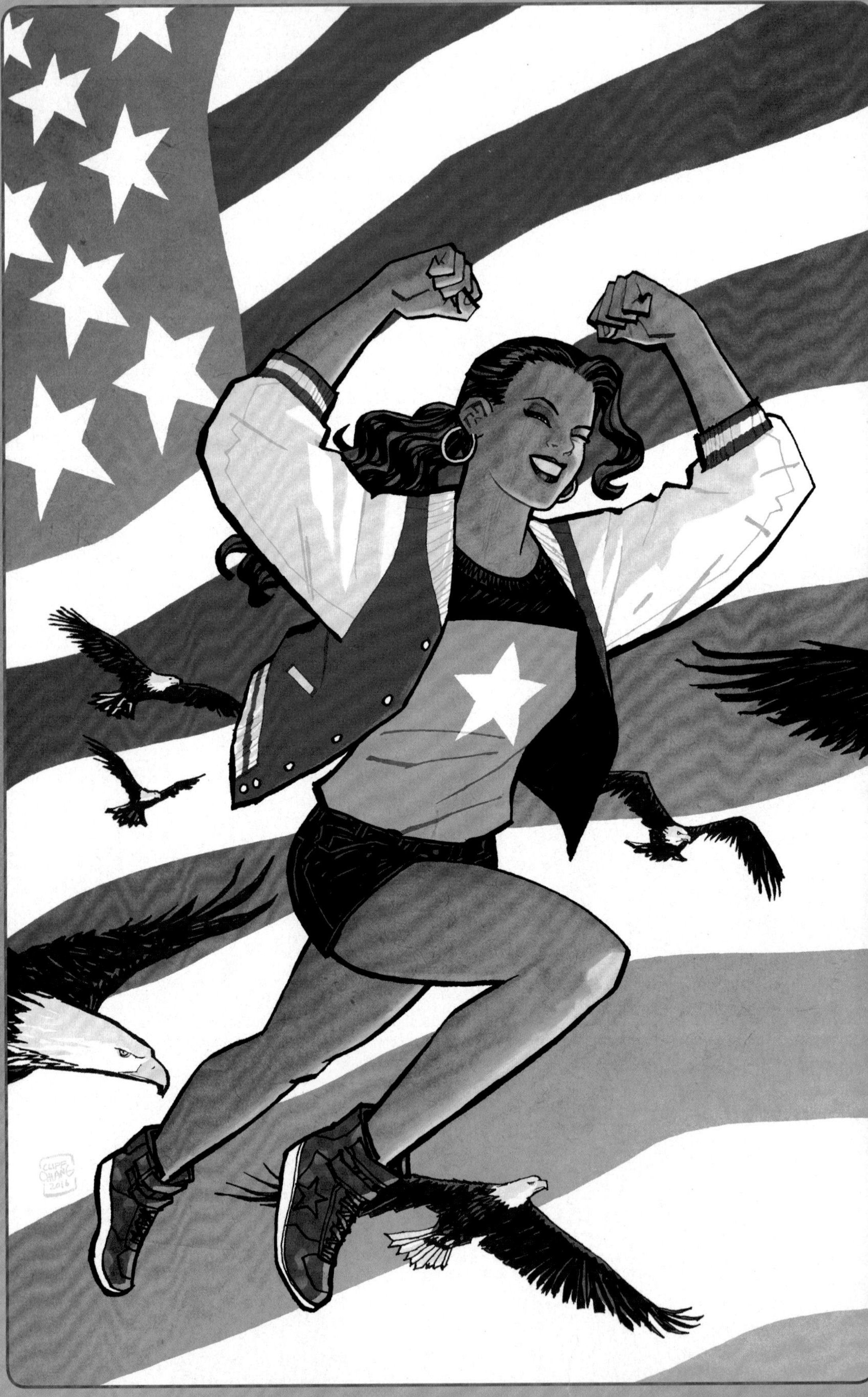
CLIFF CHIANG 2016

CLIFF CHIANG

#1 VARIANT

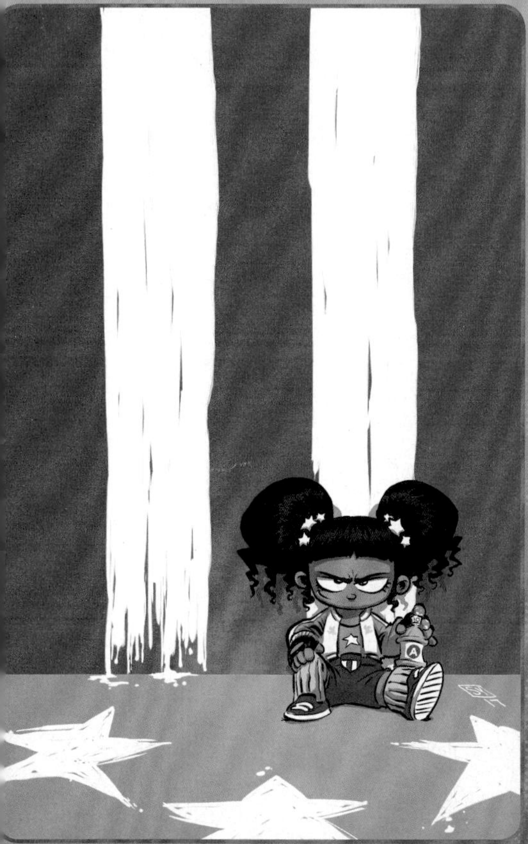

SKOTTIE YOUNG

#1 VARIANT

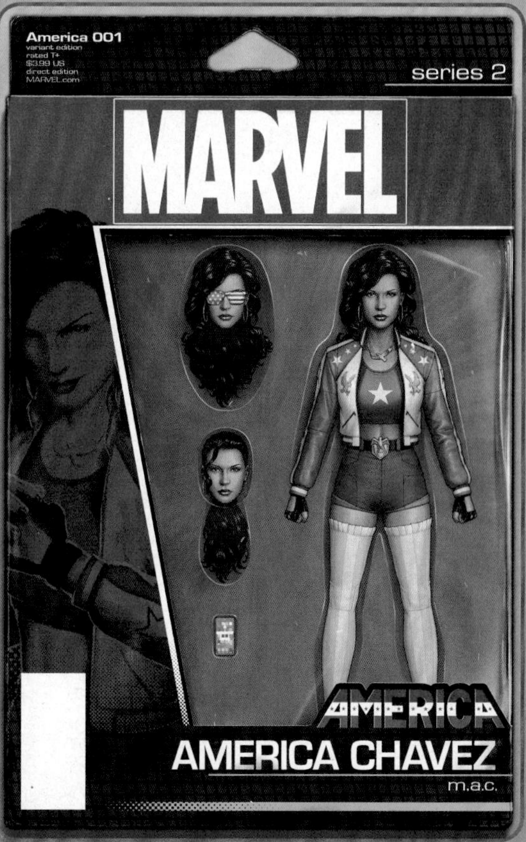
America 001
variant edition
rated T+
$3.99 US
direct edition
MARVEL.com
series 2
MARVEL
AMERICA
AMERICA CHAVEZ
m.a.c.

JOEN TYLER CHRISTOPHER

#1 ACTION FIGURE VARIANT

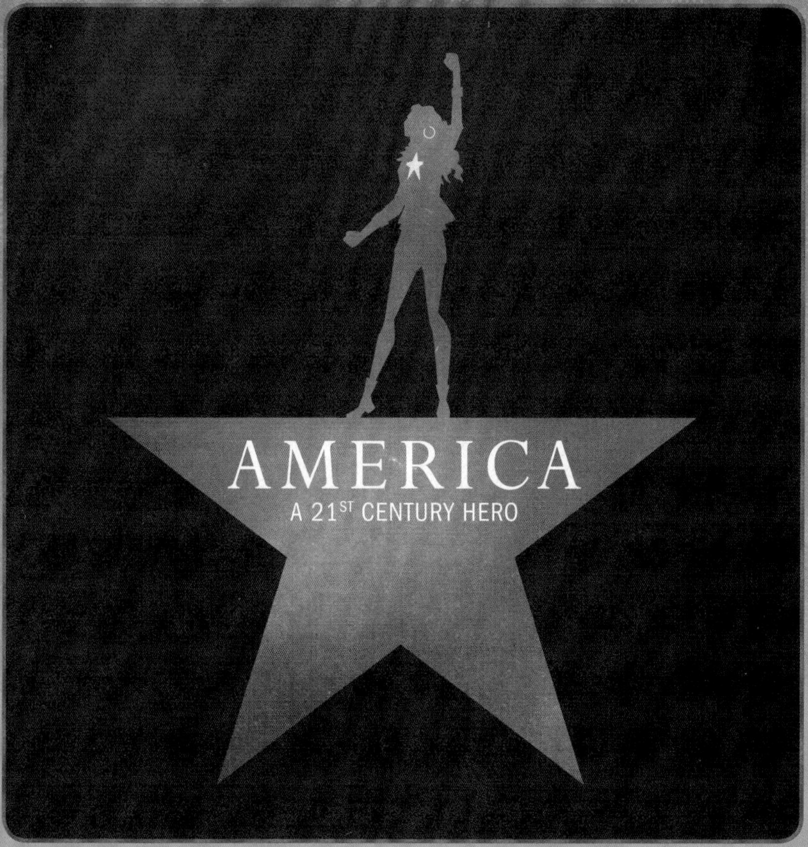
AMERICA
A 21ST CENTURY HERO

JEFFREY VEREGGE

#1 HIP-HOP VARIANT

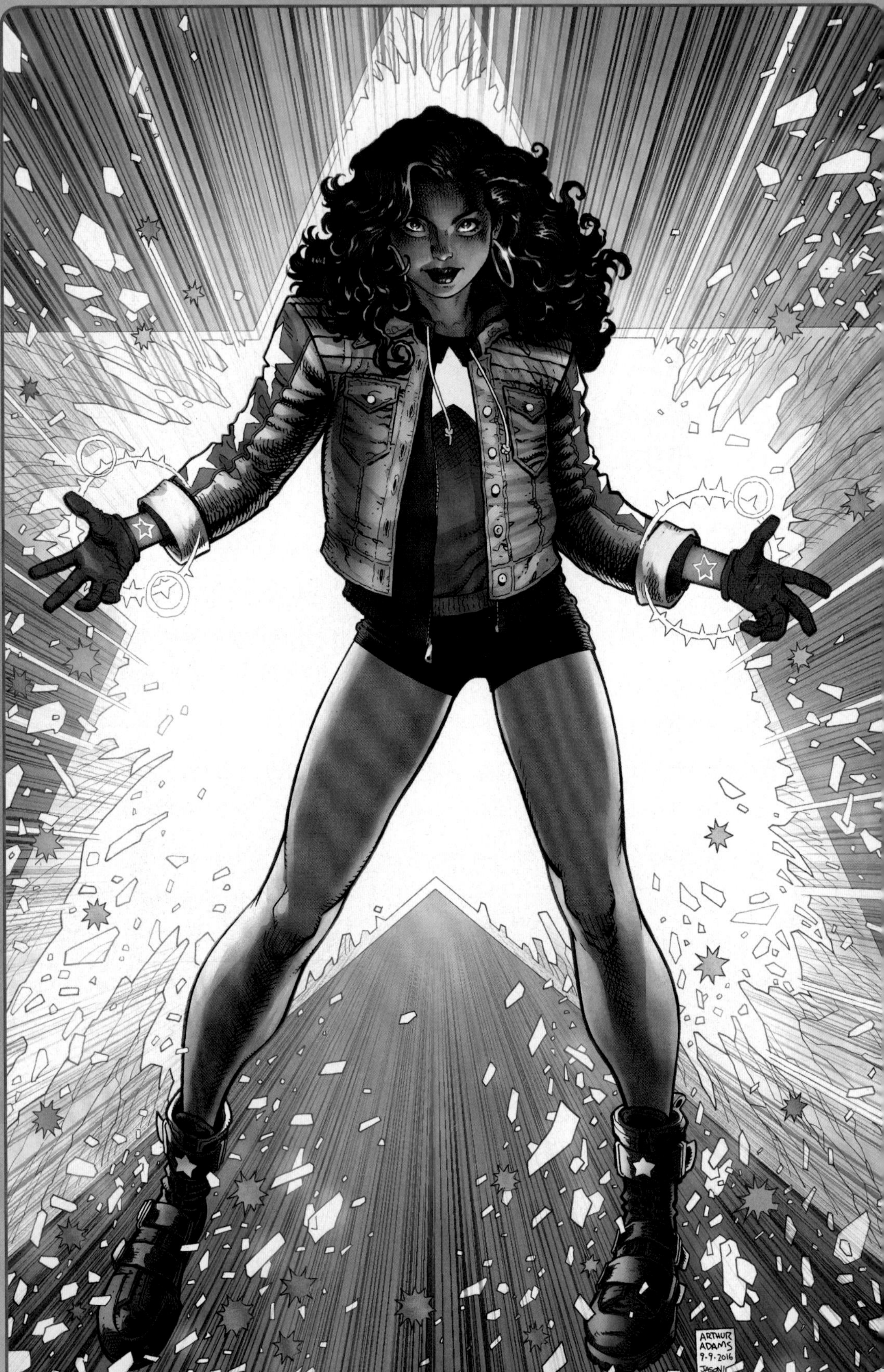
ARTHUR ADAMS 9-9-2016
JASON!C

ARTHUR ADAMS & JASON KEITH
#8 VARIANT

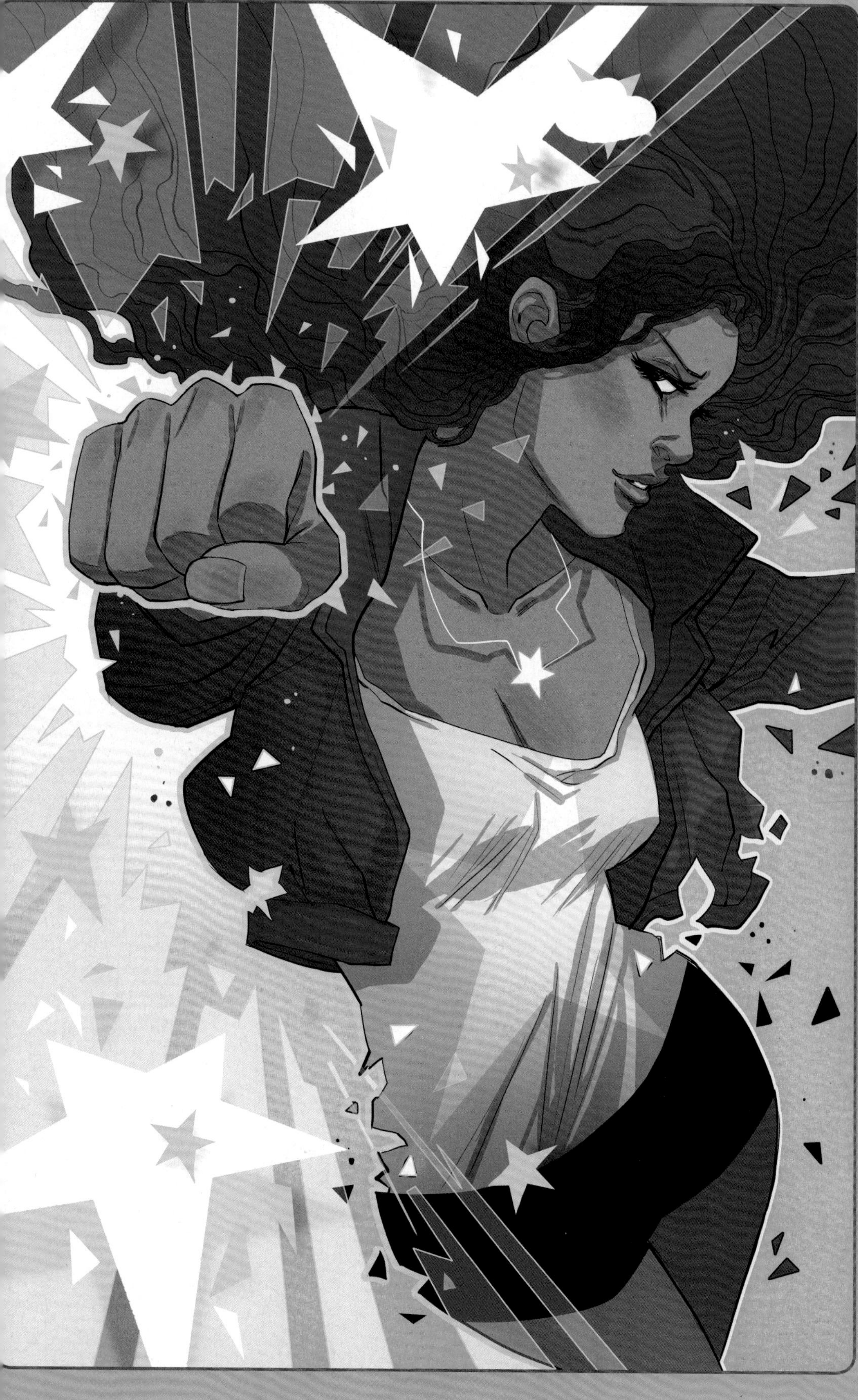

MARGUERITE SAUVAGE

#2 VARIANT

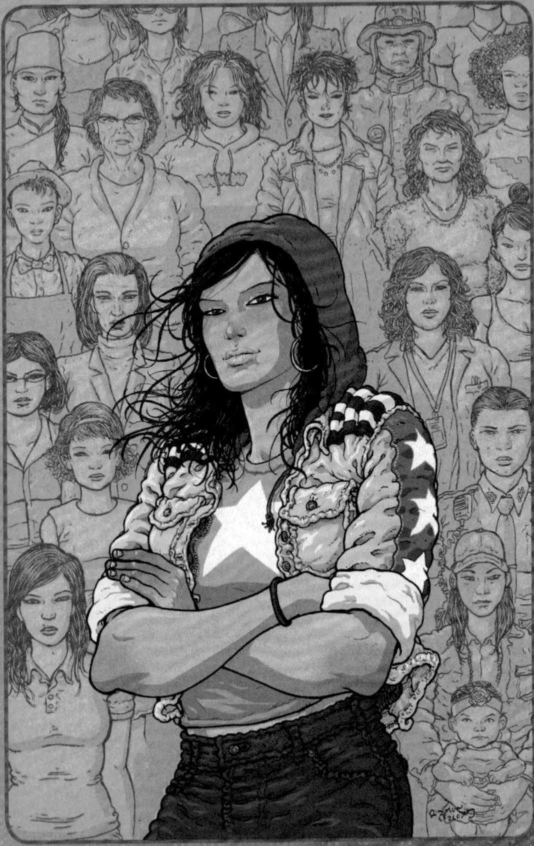

RAMON VILLALOBOS

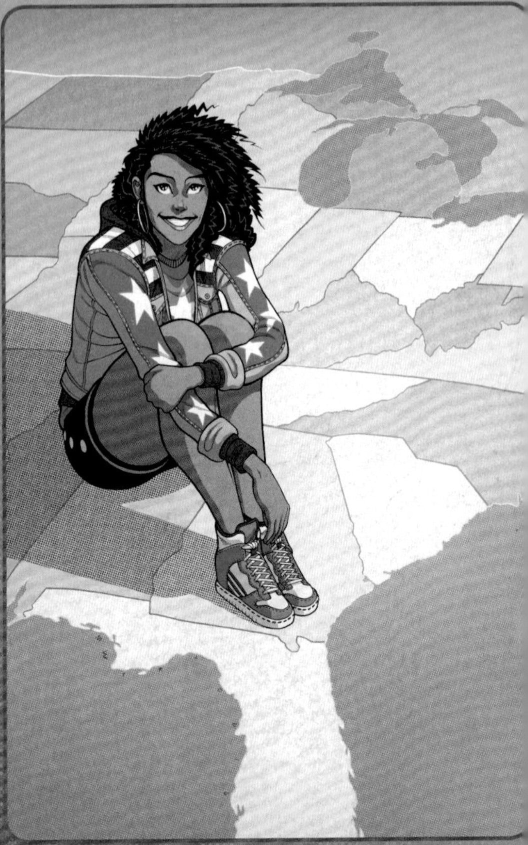

TRADD MOORE & MATTHEW WILSON
#3 VARIANT

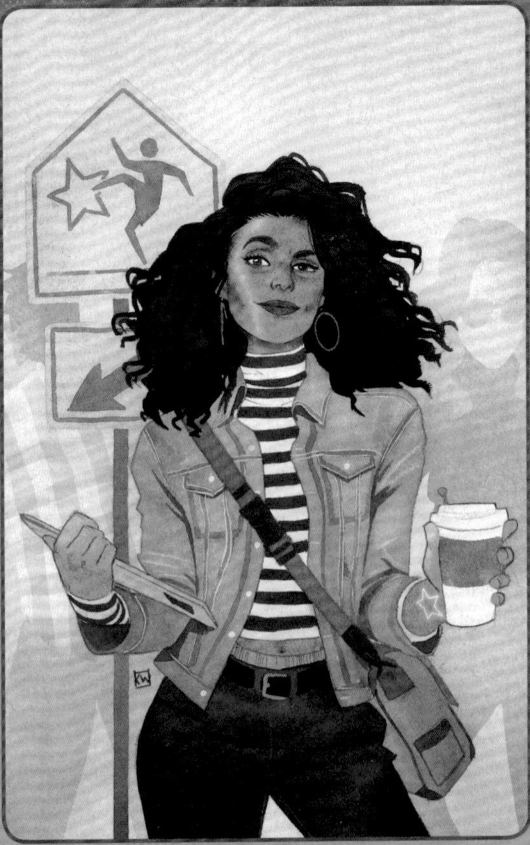

KEVIN WADA
#5 VARIANT